Class Struggle in the Roman Republic

Alan Woods was born in Swansea, South Wales, in 1944 into a working-class family with strong communist traditions. At the age of sixteen, he joined the Labour Party Young Socialists and became a Marxist. He studied Russian at Sussex University and later in Sofia and the Moscow State University.

He has a wide experience of the international labour movement and played an active role in building the Marxist tendency in Spain, where he participated in the struggle against the Franco dictatorship. He was later active in Pakistan, Mexico and other countries, including Venezuela, where he developed a close relationship with the late Hugo Chavez, and founded the international campaign, 'Hands off Venezuela'.

Woods is the author of many works covering a wide spectrum of issues, including politics, economics, history, philosophy, art, music and science. He is also the political editor of the popular website, 'In Defence of Marxism' (marxist.com), and a leading member of the International Marxist Tendency.

He has authored many other books, including: *Lenin and Trotsky: What they Really Stood For* and *Reason in Revolt: Marxist Philosophy and Modern Science*, both in conjunction with the late Ted Grant; *The Ideas of Karl Marx*; *Bolshevism: The Road to Revolution*; *Spain's Revolution Against Franco: The Great Betrayal*; *Ireland: Republicanism and Revolution*; and *The History of Philosophy: A Marxist Perspective.* He also edited and compiled the most authentic edition of Trotsky's last unfinished work, the biography of Stalin, which had remained incomplete for seventy years.

His books have been translated into many languages, including Arabic, Bahasa Indonesian, Chinese, Danish, German, Greek, Italian, Portuguese, Russian, Spanish, Turkish and Urdu.

Class Struggle in the Roman Republic

Alan Woods

Wellred Books
London

Class Struggle in the Roman Republic
Alan Woods

First edition
Wellred Books, July 2023

UK distribution: Wellred Books, wellred-books.com
152-160 Kemp House, City Road
London
EC1V 2NX
books@wellred-books.com

USA distribution: Marxist Books, marxistbooks.com
WR Books
250 44th Street #208
Brooklyn
New York
NY 11232
sales@marxistbooks.com

DK distribution: Forlaget Marx, forlagetmarx.dk
Degnestavnen 19, st. tv.
2400 København NV
forlag@forlagetmarx.dk

Cover design by Jesse Murray-Dean

Cover image: *The Death of Spartacus* by
Hermann Vogel, 1882 (public domain)

Layout by Wellred Books

ISBN: 978 1 913026 86 8

Contents

Acknowledgements

A number of people have been involved in the production of this book at one time or another. I mention here those who have dedicated their time and effort to ensure that it has been done to the highest professional standards.

First and foremost, my thanks go to Josh Holroyd, who has spent a great deal of time in editing, revising and making many valuable suggestions for the numerous additions and clarifications, which have expanded and greatly improved upon the original draft.

I am also deeply indebted to Kevin Ramage, Jayne Pascoe, Laurie O'Connel, Jack Tye Wilson and Kieran Lee for their tireless and painstaking proofreading.

Finally, I wish to express my gratitude to Jesse Murray-Dean for his simple but impactful cover design. We are often told not to judge a book by its cover, which experience has convinced me is very good advice. But in this case, I am sure that it will assist greatly in encouraging people to get acquainted with the subject matter contained within.

London,
2 June 2023

Introduction

This work first saw the light of day as a series of articles some years ago. The articles were well received but have been out of print for some time. Now, in a revised and amplified form, it is published as a book. I am sure it will meet with a receptive audience.

For Marxists the study of history is not an academic exercise but an important way in which we can learn how society develops and how the class struggle unfolds. In saying this, I am conscious of the fact that it flies in the face of the recent fashion for postmodernism, which informs us that it is impossible to draw any conclusions from history, since history follows no laws that can be understood by the human mind. From this point of view, either the study of history is merely a form of entertainment or a complete waste of time.

Despite the pompous way in which this idea is put forward, there is nothing new about it. Shorn of all its pseudo-philosophical pretensions, it merely repeats an idea that was already put forward far more succinctly by Henry Ford who said that "history is bunk", or even more amusingly by the historian Arnold Toynbee, who defined history as "just one damn thing after another."

None other than the great English historian and outstanding scholar of the Enlightenment, Edward Gibbon, wrote in the eighteenth century that history was "little more than the register of the crimes, follies, and misfortunes of mankind".[1]

Anyone who reads the pages of Gibbon's great masterpiece could be excused from drawing similarly pessimistic conclusions. Nevertheless, we must beg to disagree with a method that denies any lawfulness to the history of our species.

If you think of it just for a moment, this really is an extraordinary claim to make. Modern science has firmly established the fact that everything is governed by laws: from the smallest subatomic particle to the galaxies and the universe itself. The idea that, alone in the whole of nature, the history and development of our own species is so special that it stands outside of all laws, is quite preposterous.

Rather than being a scientific theory, it flows directly from the biblical notion that humankind is a special and unique creation of the Almighty – so special and unique that it defies all attempts to understand it. Such supreme arrogance flies in the face of everything we know about nature and the origin of all animal species. And for all our pretensions of superiority, we humans are also animals and subject to the laws of evolution.

It is true that the laws of our social evolution are infinitely more complex than those of other species. But the fact that something is complex does not at all signify that it cannot be analysed, explained and understood. If that were the case, the development of science would have come to a full stop a very long time ago. But science continues to advance, penetrating the most complex mysteries of nature, and is not deterred by all the attempts to place a barrier in its way, upon which is inscribed the words: No admittance!

What is historical materialism?

History presents itself to us as a series of actions and reactions by individuals in the field of politics, economics, wars and revolutions and the whole complex spectrum of social development. To lay bare

---

1 Gibbon, *The History of the Decline and Fall of the Roman Empire*, Vol. 1, p. 84.

the underlying relationship between all these phenomena is the task of historical materialism.

At first sight, the multiplicity of factors that in various ways affect the direction of social change appears to defy any precise analysis. Many historians take refuge behind the mere assertion of this multiplicity, contenting themselves with the idea that history is the result of the constant interaction of different factors. But this is an explanation that explains nothing at all.

Just as the waves of the ocean, which at first sight appear to be unpredictable and arbitrary, are only a surface reflection of invisible currents and changes in the wind, so the actions of individual actors in historical dramas are the unconscious expression of deeper subterranean processes that work their way silently through a complex web of social interrelations, and which ultimately condition the actions of individuals and determine their final outcome.

The great men and women who appear to be the moving force in the historical drama turn out to be merely the unconscious, or semi-conscious agents of profound changes in society that occur unknown to them and which provide a determining framework within which they perform their historical function.

If we seek to define one element that is always present and which ultimately must play the most decisive role, that element is to be found, not in the subjective consciousness of individual players in the historical drama, but in something far more fundamental.

In every interplay of forces, it is always the case that some factors will weigh more heavily than others. Without doubting for a moment the importance of such things as historical accidents, the competence or incompetence, bravery or cowardice, of individuals, the influence of religious fanaticism, or even philosophical and oral ideas, the most fundamental condition for the viability of a given socio-economic system is its ability to satisfy basic human needs.

Karl Marx uncovered the hidden mainsprings that lie behind the development of human society from the earliest tribal societies up to the present day. Before men and women can think great thoughts, produce great works of art and literature, create new religions or schools of philosophy, they must first of all have food to eat, clothes to cover their nakedness and houses to shelter them from the assaults of the elements.

It is here that we will find the ultimate cause of the rise and fall of civilisations, of wars and revolutions and all the great dramas that make up the history of humankind. That was already understood by the great Aristotle who wrote in his *Metaphysics* that philosophy began "when practically all the necessities of life were already supplied."[2]

This statement goes right to the heart of historical materialism – 2,300 years before Karl Marx. The materialist conception of history is a scientific method, which for the first time enables us to understand history, not as a series of unconnected and unforeseen incidents, but rather as part of a clearly understood and interrelated process.

As Marx explains in a celebrated passage from his preface to *A Contribution to the Critique of Political Economy*:

> In the social production of their existence, men inevitably enter into definite relations, which are independent of their will, namely relations of production appropriate to a given stage in the development of their material forces of production. [...] The mode of production of material life conditions the general process of social, political and intellectual life. It is not the consciousness of men that determines their existence, but their social existence that determines their consciousness.[3]

In *Anti-Dühring*, written much later, Engels provides us with a more developed expression of these ideas. Here we have a brilliant and concise exposition of the basic principles of historical materialism:

> The materialist conception of history starts from the proposition that the production of the means to support human life and, next to production, the exchange of things produced, is the basis of all social structure; that in every society that has appeared in history, the manner in which wealth is distributed and society divided into classes or orders is dependent

2 Aristotle, *Metaphysics*, Vol. 1, p. 13.

3 Marx, *A Contribution to the Critique of Political Economy, Marx and Engels Collected Works* (henceforth referred to as *MECW*), Vol. 29, p. 263.

> upon what is produced, how it is produced, and how the products are exchanged. From this point of view, the final causes of all social changes and political revolutions are to be sought, not in men's brains, not in men's better insights into eternal truth and justice, but in changes in the modes of production and exchange.[4]

The Communist Manifesto reminds us, "The history of all hitherto existing society is the history of class struggles."[5] In the ancient world we already have clear proof of this assertion. The first example of a strike in recorded history is to be found in the so-called 'strike papyrus' in the splendid Egyptian museum in Turin, where a very interesting account of a strike of the workers building the tomb of the Pharaoh Ramesses III is explained in detail.

The history of ancient Athens is one of the most violent and continuous class struggle, revolution and counter-revolution. But the clearest and most fully documented history of the class struggle in ancient times is the very rich record that has come down to us of the history of the Roman Republic. Marx was very interested in this phenomenon, as we learn from a letter that he wrote to Engels on 27 February 1861, in which we read the following:

> … for recreation in the evenings I have been reading Appian's *Civil Wars of Rome* in the original Greek. A most valuable book. The fellow comes of Egyptian stock. Schlosser says he is 'soulless', probably because he probes the material basis of the said civil wars. Spartacus emerges as the most capital fellow in the whole history of antiquity. A great general (no Garibaldi he), of noble character, a *real representative* of the proletariat of ancient times. Pompey a real shit; acquired spurious fame only by misappropriating, as Sulla's '*young man*', etc., Lucullus's victories (over Mithridates), then Sertorius's (Spain), etc. As a general, was the Roman Odilon Barrot. As soon as he was brought face to face with Caesar and had to show what stuff he was made of – a mere louse. Caesar perpetrated

---

4 Engels, *Anti-Dühring*, p. 316.

5 Marx and Engels, *The Communist Manifesto*, *The Classics of Marxism: Volume One*, p. 3.

> the most stupendous military blunders, deliberately crazy ones, to discountenance the philistine opposing him. Any ordinary Roman general – Crassus, say – would have annihilated him six times over during the battle in Epirus. But anything could be done with Pompey.[6]

The secret of Rome's greatness

In its heyday, the Roman Empire presented an impressive sight. Its buildings, monuments, roads and aqueducts stand even today as a mute but eloquent reminder of Rome's greatness. But it must never be forgotten that Roman power was based upon violence, mass murder, robbery and deceit. The Roman Empire was, like every subsequent empire, a massive exercise in oppression, slavery and common theft.

The Romans utilised brute force to subjugate other peoples, sold entire cities into slavery and slaughtered thousands of prisoners of war for amusement in the gladiatorial games. Yet the Roman Empire began its existence as a tiny, almost insignificant state that found itself at the mercy not only of its Latin neighbours, but of the far more powerful Etruscans and even, at one point, by the Celtic barbarians that defeated and humiliated the Romans.

In the beginning it did not even possess a standing army. Its armed forces consisted of a militia based upon a free peasantry. Its cultural life was as poor as the peasants themselves. However, within a few centuries, Rome succeeded in dominating not only Italy, but the whole of the Mediterranean and what was then known as the civilised world. How was this remarkable transformation brought about? The answer to this question is still a closed book for some modern historians.

Some time ago, I saw a series about Roman history on British television in which a well-known historian put forward the idea that the secret of Rome's greatness was somehow implanted in the genetic make-up of the Romans themselves. From this point of view, its conquests were a foregone conclusion.

---

6 Marx, 'Letter to Engels', 27 February 1861, *MECW*, Vol. 41, p. 265.

At this point we leave science behind and enter into the realm of fantasy and fairy tales. By what magical process the secret of greatness was implanted into the genes of early Romans is a mystery known only to those who believe it.

Using the Marxist method of historical materialism, I have tried to explain the process whereby Rome was transformed from a humble city state – one might almost say an outsized village – into a powerful and aggressive imperialist power.

I might add that this case is by no means unique in history. History shows the proof of the dialectical law that things can change into their opposite. It is generally forgotten today that the most powerful imperialist nation on earth, the United States of America, started out as an oppressed colony of Great Britain.

Likewise, Rome spent its early life under the dominion of its Etruscan neighbours. Forced by circumstances into an interminable series of wars, Roman society was compelled to develop a powerful military machine, which eventually drove all before it into submission.

But these continuous wars – which were initially wars of defence – turned into wars of offence, aimed at conquering territory and subjugating other peoples. This changed the very character of Roman society and the nature of its army. In turn, it undermined the very existence of the factor that had given early Roman society its coherence, stability and strength – the free Roman peasantry.

Class struggle

From the earliest beginnings there was a violent struggle between rich and poor in Rome. There are detailed accounts in the writings of Livy and others of the struggles between plebeians and patricians, which ended in an uneasy compromise. It is true that Livy's writings, produced at a much later date, have more the flavour of myth than actual history. Yet it is equally possible that these accounts carry the imprint of a distant historical memory of real events, perhaps derived from far older originals, now, alas, lost to us. It is impossible to tell.

The beginnings of a crisis in Rome can already be observed in the latter period of the Republic, a period characterised by acute social and political upheavals and class war. The conquest of foreign states provided the basis for a transformation of productive relationships through the introduction of slavery on a massive scale.

When Rome had already made herself mistress of the Mediterranean by the defeat of her most powerful rival, Carthage, we saw what was, in actual fact, a struggle for the division of the spoils. The free peasants who were forced to spend long periods far from their homeland fighting in foreign wars, returned only to find that their lands had been seized by the big landowners who were making vast fortunes out of the labour of the slaves who were now thrown onto the market at a very low price as the spoils of war.

Here we find the real reason for the ferocious class struggles that characterise Roman history in the last years of the Republic, as Marx points out in *Capital*: "[It] requires but a slight acquaintance with the history of the Roman republic, for example, to be aware that its secret history is the history of its landed property."[7]

In a letter to Engels on 8 March 1855, he wrote:

> A short while ago I took another look at Roman history (ancient) up to the time of Augustus. Internal history resolves itself *plainly* into the struggle between small and large landed property, specifically modified, of course, by slavery relations. Debtor-creditor relations, which play so large a part from the *origines* of Roman history, figure merely as an inherent consequence of small landed property.[8]

It is at this point that the class struggles in Rome reach their greatest intensity. It is a period that is inseparably connected with the names of two brothers: Tiberius and Gaius Gracchus. Tiberius Gracchus demanded that the wealth of Rome be divided up among its free citizens. His central aim was to make Italy a republic of small

7 Marx, *Capital*, Vol. 1, *MECW*, Vol. 35, p. 93, note.

8 Marx, 'Letter to Engels, 8 March 1855', *MECW*, Vol. 39, p. 527, emphasis in original.

farmers and not slaves, but he was defeated and murdered by the nobles and slave-holders. This was the victory of large-scale landed property over small-scale farming, the victory of slavery over free peasant labour.

It was a disaster for Rome in the long run. The ruined peasantry – the backbone of the Republic and its army – drifted to Rome where they constituted a non-productive class, the *proletarii* (proletariat), living off handouts from the state.

Although resentful of the rich, they nevertheless shared a common interest in the exploitation of the slaves – the only really productive class in the period of the Republic and the Empire – and Rome's imperial subjects.

The great slave revolt led by Spartacus was a glorious episode in the history of antiquity. Though, in fact, it was only one of many slave risings that occurred at this time, it stands out as a unique event in the annals of history of revolts of the poor and oppressed.

The spectacle of these most downtrodden people rising up with arms in hand and inflicting defeat after defeat on the armies of the world's greatest power is one of the most incredible events in history. Had they succeeded in overthrowing the Roman state, the course of history would have been significantly altered.

A reading of Roman history, and particularly the moving story of the revolt of the slaves led by that towering revolutionary giant Spartacus, can be a source of great inspiration for the present generation. Although our only record of this great man was written by his enemies, his actions come across sufficiently clearly to shine like a beacon, the light of which has remained undimmed after two millennia.

The basic reason why Spartacus failed in the end was the fact that the slaves were unable to link up with the proletariat in the towns. So long as the latter continued to support the state, the victory of the slaves was impossible. But the Roman proletariat, unlike the modern proletariat, was not a productive but a purely parasitical class, living off the labour of the slaves and dependent on their masters. The failure of the Roman revolution is rooted in this fact.

Caesarism

The defeat of the slaves led straight to the ruin of the Roman Republic. In the absence of a free peasantry, the state was obliged to rely on a mercenary army to fight its wars. Eventually the deadlock in the class struggle produced a situation similar to the modern phenomenon of Bonapartism. The Roman equivalent is what we call Caesarism.

The Roman legionnaire was no longer loyal to the Republic but to his commander – the man who guaranteed his pay, his loot and a plot of land when he retired. The last period of the Republic is characterised by an intensification of the struggle between the classes, in which neither side was able to win a decisive victory. As a result, the state (which Lenin described as "special bodies of armed men"[9]) began to acquire increasing independence, to raise itself above society and to appear as the final arbiter in the continuing power struggles in Rome.

A whole series of military adventurers now step onto the scene: Marius, Sulla, Crassus, Pompey and lastly Julius Caesar – a general of brilliance, a clever politician and a shrewd businessman, who in effect put an end to the Republic whilst paying lip service to it. His prestige boosted by his military triumphs in Gaul, he began to concentrate all power in his hands. Although he was assassinated by a conservative faction who wished to preserve the Republic, the old regime was doomed.

After Brutus and the other conspirators were defeated by the Second Triumvirate, the Republic was formally recognised. This pretence was even kept up by Caesar's adopted son, Octavian, after he defeated his rivals and made himself the first Emperor, Augustus. The very title 'Emperor' (*imperator* in Latin) is a military title, invented to avoid the title of king that was so offensive to republican ears. But a king he was, in all but name.

Contradictions of slavery

By the period of its demise, the political regime of the Republic stood in complete contradiction with the slave system that had become

9 Lenin, *The State and Revolution*, p. 10.

central to the Roman economy. The establishment of the Empire was therefore necessary for the preservation of the property of the great slave-owners, who were forced to submit to the arbitrary rule of a single man, but by this purchased an end to the instability and civil wars of the late Republic.

But like all forms of class oppression, slavery contains an inner contradiction that led to its destruction. Although the labour of the individual slave was not very productive (slaves must be compelled to work), the aggregate of large numbers of slaves, as in the mines and plantations (*latifundia)* in the last period of the Republic and the Empire, produced a considerable surplus.

At the height of the Empire, slaves were plentiful and cheap and the wars of Rome were basically slave hunts on a massive scale. The rich consumed the wealth of society in idle luxury, while the poorest citizens lived in conditions of unimaginable squalor, dependent on state handouts to survive.

But at a certain stage this system reached its limits and then entered into a lengthy period of decline. Since slave labour is only productive when it is employed on a massive scale, the prior condition for its success is an ample supply of slaves at a low cost. But slaves breed very slowly in captivity and so the only way a sufficient supply of slaves can be guaranteed is through continuous warfare, further and further afield.

Once the Empire had reached the limits of its expansion under Hadrian, this became increasingly difficult. The decay of the slave economy, the monstrously oppressive nature of the Empire with its bloated bureaucracy and predatory tax collectors, was already undermining the whole system.

The failure of the oppressed classes of Roman society to unite to overthrow the brutally exploitative slave-state led to an inner exhaustion and a long and painful period of social, economic and cultural decay, which in the end prepared the way for the final collapse of Roman power and a descent into barbarism.

Trade steadily declined, while huge numbers of people flocked from the cities to the countryside in the hope of scratching out a living on one of the estates of the great landowners. The barbarians merely delivered the coup de grâce to a rotten and moribund system. The whole edifice was tottering – they merely gave it a last and violent push.

What are the lessons for today?

It would be a pointless exercise to speculate on what would have been the result of a hypothetical victory of the great slave rebellion led by Spartacus. But whatever that may have been, it could not have put an end to class society. The material basis for a genuine communist society was absent at that time, and would remain absent for a further 2,000 years.

It was necessary to pass through a series of stages of social and economic development – each of them marked by the barbarous oppression and exploitation of the masses, before the productive forces under capitalism had reached a sufficient level for a classless, communist society to exist. For that reason, it is both futile and wholly unscientific to approach the past from the standpoint of the present or the future.

Does this mean that we can learn nothing from a study of the past? Such a conclusion would be radically false. We can draw many valuable lessons from the rich experience of the class struggles of the past, and Roman history provides us with very rich material in this respect.

The rise of modern capitalism and of its gravedigger, the working class, has made much clearer what is at the heart of the materialist conception of history. Just as the rise and fall of Rome was the result of the inherent contradictions of the slave mode of production, so the rise and fall of capitalism is explained by the internal contradictions of the so-called free market economy.

In the period of its ascent, capitalism developed the productive forces to a degree that has no parallel in history. But that period has long since receded into history. The capitalist system has long since exhausted any progressive role that it may once have played.

The capitalist system in its death agony bears a striking resemblance to the monstrous decadence that characterised the Roman Empire in its final stages of degeneration and decrepitude. The symptoms of senile decay are everywhere in evidence.

Our task is not merely to understand the world, but to bring to a successful conclusion the historic struggle of the masses, by means of the victory of the proletariat and the socialist transformation of society. It is to hasten by every means the overthrow of a rotten and oppressive system whose survival threatens the very existence of human civilisation – perhaps of the human race itself.

It is to bring to fulfilment the dreams of countless past generations of the oppressed and exploited majority and to crown with final victory the titanic struggle that was commenced so long ago by that revolutionary giant Spartacus and his never-to-be-forgotten army of slaves.

It was no accident that the leaders of the German Revolution, Karl Liebknecht and Rosa Luxemburg, took the name of Spartacus as the emblem of the revolutionary German proletariat. Like the hero whose example they followed so bravely, they fell victim to the forces of a brutal counter-revolution.

Today, the names of their murderers are forgotten, but the names of Spartacus, Liebknecht and Luxemburg will forever be remembered by every class-conscious worker and revolutionary youth fighting for a better future.

London,
7 March 2023

1. Origins

The origins of Rome are shrouded in mist. We can discount the mythological account that attempts to trace the founders of Rome to the legendary Aeneas, who fled from the burning ruins of Troy. This was originally an invention of Greek historians, which the Romans eagerly took up in an attempt to attribute a noble and illustrious ancestry to what was a far more ignoble affair.

Similarly, the name of the mythical founder of Rome (Romulus) simply means 'man of Rome', and therefore tells us nothing at all. According to the traditional belief, the date of the founding of Rome was 753 BC. But this date is contradicted by the archaeological evidence: too late for the first regular settlements and too early for the time of true urbanisation.

The most celebrated historian of early Rome, Livy, mixes genuine historical material with a mass of legend, speculation and mythology, from which it is difficult to extract the truth. However, even these myths are of tremendous importance because they furnish us with significant clues. By comparing the written record – confused as it is – with the evidence of archaeology, comparative linguistics and other sciences, it is possible to reconstruct, at least in outline, the origins of Rome.

The pastoral economy of the founders of Rome is probably true, since it corresponds to what we know about the way of life of many of the Latin tribes, although by the beginning of the first millennium BC, they were already practising agriculture and cultivating the soil with light ploughs.

According to Livy, one such group of shepherds and farmers migrated from the area of Mount Alban (Monte Cavo), some thirteen miles south-east of Rome in the early years of the first millennium BC, and built their huts on the banks of the Tiber. However, this particular group settled in an area that possessed a key economic importance. Rome's geographical position, controlling the crossing of the Tiber River, which separates the two halves of the Italian peninsula, was of great strategic importance for the nations seeking to control the destiny of Italy. Situated on a ford of the Tiber, Rome was at a crossroads of traffic following the river valley and of traders travelling north and south on the west side of the Italian Peninsula.

To the south of Rome lay the fertile agricultural lands of the Campanian Plain, watered by two rivers and capable of producing as many as three grain crops a year in some districts. Rome also possessed the highly lucrative salt trade, derived from the salt flats at the mouth of the Tiber. The importance of this commodity in the ancient world cannot be overstated.

To this day we say: "a man who is worth his salt". In ancient Rome, this was literally true. The word 'salary' comes from the Latin word, *salarium*, which linked employment, salt and soldiers, although the exact link is unclear. One theory is that the word soldier itself comes from the Latin *sal dare* (to give salt). The Roman historian Pliny the Elder states in his *Natural History* that salt "has a place in magistracies also and on service abroad, from which comes the term 'salary'".[1] More likely, the *salarium* was either an allowance paid to Roman soldiers for the purchase of salt or the price of having soldiers conquer salt supplies and guard the Salt Roads (*Via Salarium*) that led to Rome.

---

1 Pliny, *Natural History*, Vol. 8, Book 31, p. 433.

Whatever version one accepts, there is no question about the vital importance of salt. The salt trade must have played a key role in the establishment of a prosperous settled community in Rome, which will also have attracted the unwelcome attention of less favoured tribes. The picture that emerges of the first Roman community is that of a group of clans fighting to defend their territory against the pressure of other peoples (Latins, Etruscans, Sabines etc.).

Early Roman society

According to Livy, Rome was formed by shepherds, under the leadership of chieftains. He refers to the ancient tribes of Rome, the Ramnenses, Titienses and Luceres, about which we know little. As the story goes, the first settlement was established by a number of Latin clans, or *gentes*, who were soon joined by a "promiscuous crowd of freemen and slaves" from neighbouring states.[2] Concerned by the lack of women in their new community, the Romans staged a mass abduction of women from the neighbouring Sabines, who, although understandably put out at first, eventually joined the growing city, women, men and all.

Whatever the truth of this tale, which is almost certainly more myth than fact, what appears likely is that from very early on the population of Rome itself seems to have been a mixture of different peoples. This was the natural consequence of Rome's geographical situation and long years of war. Over a long period, during which the original inhabitants were mixed with many other elements, they gradually succeeded in uniting the scattered inhabitants under a common state.

No one could belong to the Roman people unless he or she was a member of a *gens*. Ten *gentes* formed a *curia*. Every *curia* had its own religious rites, shrines and priests; the latter, as a body, formed one of the Roman priestly colleges. Ten *curiae* formed a *tribus* or tribe, which probably, like the rest of the Latin tribes, originally had an elected president-military leader and high priest. The three tribes together formed the Roman people, the *Populus Romanus*.

---

2 Livy, *History of Rome*, Vol. 1, Book 1, p. 11.

Friedrich Engels, in his *The Origin of the Family, Private Property and the State*, lists the following characteristics of the Roman *gens*:

1. Mutual right of inheritance among gentile members; the property remained within the gens;
2. Possession of a common burial place;
3. Common religious rites (the *sacra gentilitia*);
4. Obligation not to marry within the *gens*;
5. Common ownership of land;
6. Obligation of mutual protection and help among members of the *gens*;
7. Right to bear the gentile name;
8. Right to adopt strangers into the *gens*; and
9. The right to elect the chief and to depose him.[3]

Initially, it seems that public affairs were managed by the Senate (the council of elders, from the Latin *senex*, an old man). This was composed of the chiefs of the 300 *gentes*. It was for this reason that they were called 'fathers', *patres*, from which we later get the denomination patricians. Here we see how the original patriarchal relations of the old, egalitarian gentile system gradually produced a privileged tribal aristocracy, which crystallised into the Patrician Order – the ruling class in early Roman society. As Engels explains:

> [...] the custom of electing always from the same family in the gens brought into being the first hereditary nobility. These families called themselves 'patricians', and claimed for themselves exclusive right of entry into the senate and tenure of all other offices. The acquiescence of the people in this claim, in course of time, and its transformation into an actual right, appear in legend as the story that Romulus conferred the patriciate and its privileges on the first senators and their descendants. The senate, like the Athenian *boulè*, made final decisions in many matters and held preparatory discussions on those of greater importance, particularly new laws. With regard to these, the decision rested with the assembly of the people called the *comitia curiata* (assembly of the *curiae*). The people

3 See Engels, *The Origin of the Family, Private Property and the State*, pp. 104-5.

> assembled together grouped in *curiae*, each *curia* probably grouped in *gentes*; each of the thirty *curiae* had one vote in the final decision. The assembly of the curiae accepted or rejected all laws, elected all higher officials, including the *rex* (so-called king), declared war (the senate, however, concluded peace), and, as supreme court, decided, on the appeal of the parties concerned, all cases involving death sentence on a Roman citizen. Lastly, besides the senate and the assembly of the people, there was the *rex*, who corresponded exactly to the Greek *basileus* and was not at all the almost absolute king which Mommsen made him out to be. He also was military leader, high priest, and president of certain courts. He had no civil authority whatever, nor any power over the life, liberty, or property of citizens, except such as derived from his disciplinary powers as military leader or his executive powers as president of a court.[4]

As chiefs of the *gentes*, the patricians had an important degree of authority over the use and distribution of the *gentes'* communal lands. Heritable property was limited to livestock, slaves and a small plot of land called a *heredium*. However, the majority of the arable and pastoral land inhabited by each *gens* was the property of the *gens* itself, which was granted to individuals on a revocable basis. Through their domination of the institutions of the *gens*, the patrician chiefs were able to grant lands to their own followers and dependents, known as *clientes*, and began to accrue a degree of wealth over and above the rest of the population. This economic power of the patricians was also expressed militarily, in that only members of this emerging aristocracy could afford to maintain their own horses.

The exact process by which the old gentile society was destroyed is unclear. The increased wealth derived from the salt trade must have played a role, creating a growing gulf between the rich and the poor members of the *gens*. What is clear, however, is that eventually the granting of revocable plots out of the communal lands became fixed into private, heritable property.

The rise of private property created sharp divisions in society from a very early date. The harshness of the property laws in early Roman

4 Ibid., pp. 110-1.

society coincided with the form of the family, which in Rome was the most extreme expression of patriarchy. The (male) head of the family enjoyed absolute power over all other members of the family, who were also regarded as private property, a fact that was already noted by Hegel:

> We thus find family relations among the Romans not as a beautiful, free relation of love and feeling; the place of confidence is usurped by the principle of severity, dependence, and subordination. Marriage, in its strict and formal shape, bore quite the aspect of a mere contract; the wife was part of the husband's property (*in manum conventio*), and the marriage ceremony was based on a *coemtio,* in a form such as might have been adopted on the occasion of any other purchase. The husband acquired a power over his wife, such as he had over his daughter; nor less over her property; so that everything which she gained, she gained for her husband. [...]
>
> The relation of sons was perfectly similar: they were, on the one hand, about as dependent on the paternal power as the wife on the matrimonial; they could not possess property – it made no difference whether they filled a high office in the State or not (though the *peculia castrensia,* and *adventitia* were differently regarded); but on the other hand, when they were emancipated, they had no connection with their father and their family. An evidence of the degree in which the position of children was regarded as analogous to that of slaves, is presented in the *imaginaria servitus* (*mancipium*), through which emancipated children had to pass. In reference to inheritance, morality would seem to demand that children should share equally. Among the Romans, on the contrary, testamentary caprice manifests itself in its harshest form.
>
> Thus perverted and demoralised, do we here see the fundamental relations of ethics.[5]

The new form of the patriarchal family, based upon the tyrannical rule of the *pater familias*, was at the same time a reflection of the changed social and property relations and a firm base upon which the latter

5 Hegel, *Lectures on the Philosophy of History*, pp. 286-7.

rested. And gradually, the state as an organ of class domination raised itself above society. The history of the Roman Republic is merely the continuation, extension and deepening of these tendencies, which in the end destroyed the Republic itself.

The Etruscans

In his masterpiece, *History of the Russian Revolution*, Leon Trotsky explains one of the most important laws of history, the law of combined and uneven development:

> Unevenness, the most general law of the historic process, reveals itself most sharply and complexly in the destiny of the backward countries. Under the whip of external necessity their backward culture is compelled to make leaps. From the universal law of unevenness thus derives another law which, for the lack of a better name, we may call the law of *combined development* – by which we mean a drawing together of the different stages of the journey, a combining of the separate steps, an amalgam of archaic with more contemporary forms. Without this law, to be taken of course in its whole material content, it is impossible to understand the history of Russia, and indeed of any country of the second, third or tenth cultural class.[6]

The historical development of Russia was shaped by its more advanced neighbours. It was not helped by its early contacts with the more backward Tartars and other nomadic steppe dwellers from the East who contributed nothing to its culture and barely left an imprint on its language. It was held back for centuries by its subjugation by the Mongols, although the latter left its imprint on Russian society and particularly the state, which had certain semi-Asiatic characteristics. But it received a strong impulse from its wars with the more developed Poles and Swedes.

The case of Rome is analogous. What determined its course of cultural and economic development was not the long wars with the barbarian Latin tribes, but rather their contact with other peoples

6 Trotsky, *History of the Russian Revolution*, Vol. 1, pp. 27-8.

that had reached a higher level of socio-economic development: the Etruscans, the Greeks of southern Italy, and the Carthaginians.

As a general rule, backward nations tend to assimilate the material and intellectual conquests of more advanced countries, although this process can often take the most complicated and contradictory forms, combining elements of extreme backwardness with the most modern innovations imported from external sources. This was true of ancient Rome. Like the Japanese in more modern times, the Romans showed a tremendous ability to learn from and assimilate the experiences of other nations, although these borrowings from other peoples were always coloured by a peculiar Roman outlook.

Roman art began by copying Greek originals and never freed itself from Greek influences. But the flexibility and the free and cheerful spirit of Greek art was alien to the psychology of the Romans, who, originating as a race of hill-dwelling shepherds and small farmers never completely freed themselves from a certain narrowness of mind – an unsmiling provincial 'practicality' that expressed itself in art and religion by a stern and implacable austerity.

In the early days their gods were the simple deities of an agricultural people, though infused with a strong warrior spirit. Their most important god was originally Mars. But they were pragmatic about religion as about everything else, and regularly imported any foreign deity that seemed useful to them.

When they conquered an enemy, they not only took his wealth and his women, but also his main gods, who were immediately installed in a new temple in Rome. This was a way of emphasising the completeness of their domination and also provided them with allies in Heaven, which they hoped would provide them with some assistance for the next war in this world. In this way, over a period, Rome acquired, alongside a wealth of loot, a superabundance of gods, which must have been quite bewildering at times.

The Romans succeeded in fighting off the neighbouring Latin tribes, whose level of socio-economic development was not so very different from their own. But to the North they were faced with pressure from a more advanced people: the Etruscans. The exact origin of the Etruscans is still a matter of controversy, since very little Etruscan literature remains and the language of inscriptions on their monuments has been only partially deciphered. We have gained most of our knowledge of the Etruscans from studying the remains of their city walls, houses, monuments and tombs.

Some scholars, both ancient and modern, considered them a seafaring people from Asia Minor. But the fact that their language did not belong to the Indo-European family, like Latin and Greek, has led others to suggest that they may have been an original Italian population, a theory which has been supported by recent genetic studies.

At any rate, as early as 1000 BC they were living in Italy in an area that was roughly equivalent to modern Tuscany, from the Tiber River north almost to the Arno River. After 650 BC, the Etruscans became dominant in north-central Italy. According to tradition, Rome had been under the control of seven kings, beginning with the mythical Romulus who along with his brother Remus were said to have founded the city of Rome.

The last three 'kings' of Rome were said to have been Etruscan: Tarquinius Priscus, Servius Tullius and Tarquinius Superbus. Although the list of kings is of dubious historical value, it is believed that the last-named kings may have been historical figures. This suggests that Rome was under the influence of the Etruscans for about a century. The early histories state that Rome was at one time under the rule of Etruscan 'kings', and the archaeological record shows that Rome was indeed at one stage an Etruscan city.

Actually, the use of the word 'king' is incorrect. Engels points out that the Latin word for king (*rex*) is the same as the Celtic-Irish *righ* (tribal chief) and the Gothic *reiks*, which signified the head of the *gens* or tribe:

> The office of *rex* was not hereditary; on the contrary, he was first elected by the assembly of the *curiae* probably on the nomination of his predecessor, and then at a second meeting solemnly installed in office. That he could also be deposed is shown by the fate of Tarquinius Superbus.

> Like the Greeks of the heroic age, the Romans in the age of the so-called kings lived in a military democracy founded on gentes, phratries, and tribes and developed out of them. Even if the *curiae* and tribes were to a certain extent artificial groups, they were formed after the genuine, primitive models of the society out of which they had arisen and by which they were still surrounded on all sides. Even if the primitive patrician nobility had already gained ground, even if the *reges* were endeavouring gradually to extend their power, it does not change the original, fundamental character of the constitution, and that alone matters.[7]

The Etruscans were interested in Rome for both economic and strategic reasons. South of Rome, Italy was dominated by powerful and prosperous Greek colonies. Indeed, the ancients referred to southern Italy and Sicily as Magna Graecia (Greater Greece). Etruscan expansion brought them into contact with the Latins, and eventually they reached the very frontier of Magna Graecia, where they began to establish colonies.

This opened up a new period of conflict between the Etruscans and Greeks for the domination of Latium, the homeland of the Latin tribes. It was impossible for the Etruscans to hold Latium unless they took Rome, which lay between Latium and themselves. In addition to its strategic importance, the salt from the mouth of the Tiber was essential to Etruscan cities, which had no other source of this important commodity.

Rome was surrounded by prosperous Etruscan city states like Tarquinii, Cere and Veii, and it was under their influence that Rome was transformed. They were on a higher plane of economic and cultural development than the Romans, with whom they traded, and whom they eventually dominated. The fact that the Etruscans were on a higher level explains why they succeeded in establishing this superiority. They were organised, like the Greeks, in city-states, and their art and culture showed strong Greek influences. Weapons and other implements, exquisite jewellery, coins, statues of stone, bronze, and terracotta, and black pottery (called *bucchero*) have been found.

7 Engels, *The Origin of the Family, Private Property and the State*, p. 111.

Roman historians never actually state that the Etruscans conquered Rome, but that may be for reasons of national pride. But it is clear that, in one way or another, they took control of the city. Before the arrival of the Etruscans, Rome was a small conglomeration of villages approaching what Engels would have called the higher stage of barbarism.

From an economic, cultural and technical point of view, the Etruscans must have had a profound effect on the economic life of Rome, its development, culture and social structure. Only the later influence of the Greeks of southern Italy was greater. Contact with a more advanced civilisation would have finally put an end to whatever was left of the old gentile constitution, strengthening the position of the old tribal aristocracy, undermining the old clan solidarity and preparing the ground for a transition to new legal and class relations.

The Etruscans are said to have been great engineers and were probably responsible for the transformation of Rome from a relatively primitive tribal centre to a thriving city in the late seventh and early sixth centuries BC. It was under these new masters that, according to tradition, the first public works such as the walls of the Capitoline Hill were constructed.

Until then the Tiber was crossed by ford and Rome itself was not more than a collection of poor huts. It was during this period that a bridge called the Pons Sublicius was built. It was also at this time that we can date the construction of the impressive sewerage and drainage system, the Cloaca Maxima.

Political and military reform

Rome's military organisation also underwent an important change in this period. Hitherto, the Romans had essentially fought on the basis of clan warfare, with the patrician horsemen leading a number of warrior bands made up of their clients. At some point however, likely during the period of Etruscan rule, Rome adopted the Greek phalanx: densely packed infantry fighting with shields and spears.

The phalanx was potentially a very effective way of fighting by the standards of the times, but its adoption was not simply a tactical or technical question. The formation of infantry into a phalanx required not only bronze shields and spears but men with the means to maintain them, the strength to carry them, and the training and discipline to fight in close formation.

All of these things required a class of robust peasants, epitomised by the famous Athenian *hoplites* of the Persian war. Such men could be found in the Roman countryside, but not entirely within the old *populus romanus*, which was limited to the original patrician *gentes*.

The rural tribes that had been incorporated into Roman territory, either by conquest or immigration, formed the bulk of what was known as the plebs. These plebeians were free and a section of them could even rival the patricians in wealth, but under the original tribal constitution they remained totally excluded from political power, which was originally monopolised by the clan aristocracy.

The question of Rome's military organisation therefore became a pressing social and class question. Sooner or later, the economic and social weight of the plebs, and in particular its wealthier layer, would be reflected in the political organisation of the state. This was understood by the ancients themselves, not least Aristotle, who explains:

> And indeed the earliest form of constitution among the Greeks after the kingships consisted of those who were actually soldiers, the original form consisting of the cavalry (for war had its strength and its pre-eminence in cavalry, since without orderly formation heavy-armed infantry is useless, and the sciences and systems dealing with tactics did not exist among the men of old times, so that their strength lay in their cavalry); but as the states grew and the wearers of heavy armour had become stronger, more persons came to have a part in the government.[8]

The old gentile order of society based on personal ties of blood was in open contradiction to the new economic and social relations. It was already irremediably decayed and in its place was set up a new state constitution based on territorial division and difference of property and wealth. This constitution excluded not only the slaves, but also

8 Aristotle, *Politics*, p. 343.

those without property who were barred from service in the army and from possession of arms, the so-called proletarians.

The new Centuriate Assembly (*comitia centuriata*) popular assembly, while democratic in appearance, was in reality a fraud that served to disguise the real domination of the patrician aristocracy. The whole male population liable to bear arms was divided into six classes on a property basis. The cavalry was drawn from the wealthiest men, who could afford to provide their own horses. And the cavalry and the first class alone had ninety-eight votes, an inbuilt majority; if they were agreed, they did not even need to ask the others; they made their decision, and that was the end of it. On this point Livy writes:

> The rest of the population whose property fell below this were formed into one century and were exempt from military service.
>
> After thus regulating the equipment and distribution of the infantry, he [Servius Tullius] re-arranged the cavalry. He enrolled from amongst the principal men of the State twelve centuries. In the same way he made six other centuries (though only three had been formed by Romulus) under the same names under which the first had been inaugurated. For the purchase of the horse, 10,000 lbs were assigned them from the public treasury; whilst for its keep certain widows were assessed to pay 2000 lbs each, annually. The burden of all these expenses was shifted from the poor onto the rich.
>
> Then additional privileges were conferred. The former kings had maintained the constitution as handed down by Romulus, viz., manhood suffrage in which all alike possessed the same weight and enjoyed the same rights. Servius introduced a graduation; so that whilst no one was ostensibly deprived of his vote, all the voting power was in the hands of the principal men of the State. The knights were first summoned to record their vote, then the eighty centuries of the infantry of the First Class; if their votes were divided, which seldom happened, it was arranged for the Second Class to be summoned; very seldom did the voting extend to the lowest Class.[9]

---

9 Livy, *History of Rome*, Vol. 1, Book 1, pp. 50-1.

According to Livy this constitution was instituted under the second of the Etruscan kings, Servius Tullius. Whether or not this is the case, the reforms accredited to Tullius were likely instituted by the time the Roman Republic first came into being, and this uneasy compromise between patricians and plebeians would set the stage for almighty future struggles.

2. The Birth of the Republic

According to tradition, the last Etruscan 'king' of Rome, Tarquinius Superbus, also known as Tarquin the Proud, was expelled by the Roman people in 509 BC. It may be that he tried to change the status of a tribal chief (*rex*), to which the Romans were accustomed, into something resembling an actual king and thus came into collision with the Roman aristocracy.

In any case, it is clear that the revolt against Etruscan rule coincided with a sharp decline in Etruscan power. As we have seen, the southerly expansion of the Etruscans brought them into direct conflict with the wealthy and powerful Greek city-states. This encounter proved fatal.

After some initial successes Etruria suffered defeat and its fortunes were eclipsed. It was this weakening of Etruscan power that enabled the Romans, around 500 BC, to carry out a successful rebellion against the Etruscans and gain their independence. This prepared the way for their future development.

It is at this point that Rome abandoned monarchy in favour of a republican system. The banishment of the last *rex* led to the replacement of the office of *rex* by two military leaders (consuls) with equal powers. The new republican constitution was based on a Senate, composed of the patricians of the city, along with popular assemblies which involved political participation for most of the freeborn men and elected magistrates annually. The public power consisted of the body of citizens liable for military service.

The two consuls were elected and possessed almost absolute powers (*imperium*). They controlled the army and interpreted and executed the laws. But the consuls' powers were limited by two things: firstly, they were elected for only one year; secondly, each could veto the decisions of the other.

In theory, the Senate possessed no executive powers. It merely advised the consuls on domestic and foreign policy, as well as finance and religious matters. But since the senators and consuls all came from the same class, they almost always acted in the same spirit and followed the same class interests. In fact, Rome was ruled by an exclusive and aristocratic club.

Ultimate power supposedly resided in the popular assembly of the *comitia centuriata*, which elected the consuls on a yearly basis. But just as in our modern bourgeois democracy the power of the electorate remains in practice a legal fiction to a large extent, so in Rome, the power of the assembly of Roman citizens was effectively annulled, as Michael Grant points out:

> However, this Assembly had been weighted from the beginning so that the centuries of the well-to-do possessed far greater voting power than the poor. Moreover, candidates for the consulship were proposed in the Assembly *by the senators*, from their own ranks. The Assembly, it was true, enacted laws and declared war and peace, and conducted trials (*iudicia populi*). Yet the senators, with their superior prestige and wealth, controlled its votes on all such occasions. In many respects, therefore, the legal appearance of democracy was sharply corrected by what in fact happened.[1]

Patronage

There was yet another factor that undermined the power of the Assembly. In the fifth century BC there were around fifty-three patrician clans (*gentes*) that are known to us, although the actual

1 Grant, *History of Rome*, p. 59, emphasis in original.

number may have been greater. This would mean that a closed body of not more than a thousand families ruled Rome.

In turn, a smaller body of especially powerful clans exercised supreme control: the Aemilii, the Cornelii, the Fabii, and later on, the Claudii. This means that the patricians comprised less than one-tenth of the total citizen population, and possibly not more than one-fourteenth. The question is: how was it possible for such a small number of people to dominate Rome?

The answer is really quite simple. In any society the ruling class is too small to exercise its class domination without the aid of a larger class of dependents. There is always a large number of sub-exploiters, sub-sub-exploiters and parasites who are at the service of the rulers of society. The relationship between patrons and clients had its roots in the primitive gentile organisation of the city in its earliest days, but was transformed by the division of Roman society into distinct and unequal classes.

The Senate was composed of the heads of families (*patres familias*) and other prominent citizens. The power of the patricians was partly based on tradition (the age-old memory of clan loyalties), partly on their monopoly of religious rites (which were inherited) and the right to consult the auguries, and the calendar (also a religious practice), but also through their inherited clients.

In ancient Rome, in addition to ties of blood and marriage, there existed an extensive system of patronage. The rich and powerful *patroni* were surrounded by a large number of dependent clients (*clientes*), who looked to them for protection and help. The client was a free man who entrusted himself to the patronage of another and received favours and protection in return.

It was similar to the kind of relation found in societies dominated by the Mafia, and it is not impossible that it is the distant historical ancestor of the latter. But in ancient Rome, *clientela* was all-pervasive. It was also hereditary. The obligation of the patrons to their clients was regarded as absolute. A law of the mid-fifth century BC condemns any patron who fails to meet his obligation to his clients.

The system of *clientela* succeeded to some extent in blunting the sharp differences between the patricians and the plebs. As long as the latter was kept happy by the concessions and favours provided by their patrons, they were willing to accept the leading status of the patricians. But although all clients were plebeians, not all plebeians were clients. For example, immigrant traders were left out in the cold. Moreover, the total exclusion of the plebs from political power constituted a constant source of discontent. The lower orders were excluded from the consulship and, initially, from the Senate.

To the poor majority of plebeians, this was an academic question, since they could not afford to take up public office anyway. But to the minority of the plebs who had acquired a certain level of wealth, this exclusion from public office and what is known as 'the fruits of office' was a very sore point. This was the layer that put itself at the head of social protest, either for genuine reasons or to further its own advance.

Their position was comparable to that of the reformist labour leaders of today, who use the labour movement as a means of personal advancement. As one British Labour leader put it: "I am in favour of the emancipation of the working class, one by one, commencing with myself." Such a mentality has been present throughout the history of class struggle, beginning with the Roman Republic, although not all the popular leaders were cynical careerists, then or now.

Debt slavery

This was a time when famine was a permanent threat. Grain shortages occurred at regular intervals. In order to prevent such disasters (and distract the attention of the plebeians) the Roman ruling class established the cult of Ceres, the goddess of grain, about 496 BC. This, for obvious reasons, was a cult of the plebeians, who knew all about the lack of bread.

The number of plebeians who were falling into debt rose inexorably. And if a man did not have the means of settling his debts, his only solution was to offer his own body to his creditors. He became a 'man in fetters' (*nexus*). He was not formally a slave, but in practice the difference was academic. It was similar to the bonded labour in the West Indies in the eighteenth century or on the South-Asian Subcontinent today.

The phenomenon of debt slavery became increasingly common. "If a debtor to the state did not fulfil his obligations, he was without further ceremony sold with all that he had; the simple demand on the part of the state was sufficient to establish the debt."[2] Once a man had sunk into debt slavery, there was little or no possibility of ever regaining freedom.

This problem was at the heart of the bitter class antagonism that emerged in the first century of the Republic, and the blind hatred of the plebeians towards the patrician governing class. Livy's *History* is full of examples of the class struggle in the early period of the Republic:

> But a war with the Volscians was imminent, and the State was torn with internal dissensions; the patricians and the plebeians were bitterly hostile to one another, owing mainly to the desperate condition of the debtors. They loudly complained that whilst fighting in the field for liberty and empire they were oppressed and enslaved by their fellow-citizens at home; their freedom was more secure in war than in peace, safer amongst the enemy than amongst their own people.[3]

He cites the example of a veteran, a former centurion, who emerged in the forum pale and emaciated from hunger and destitution:

> To persons repeatedly inquiring, whence that garb, whence that ghastly appearance of body, (the multitude having now assembled around him almost like a popular assembly), he says "that whilst serving in the Sabine war, because he had not only been deprived of the produce of his land in consequence of the depredations of the enemy, but also his residence had been burned down, all his effects pillaged, his cattle driven off, a tax imposed on him at a time very distressing to him, he had incurred debt; that this debt, aggravated by usury, had stripped him first of his father's and grandfather's farm, then of his other property; lastly that a pestilence,

2 Mommsen, *History of Rome*, Vol. 1, Book 1, p. 209.

3 Livy, *History of Rome*, Vol. 1, Book 2, p. 92.

> as it were, had reached his person. That he was taken by his creditor, not into servitude, but into a house of correction and a place of execution." He then showed his back disfigured with the marks of stripes still recent. At the hearing and seeing of this a great uproar takes place.[4]

The angry mood of the populace is described here in vivid terms. This incident provoked a riot, which spread through the entire city.

These popular tumults continued unabated for a long time. The ruling class responded to the threat from below with the usual methods – a combination of trickery, deceit and bloody repression. The leaders of the plebs were invariably drawn from the wealthiest, who were always willing to betray the interests of the poor in return for political concessions from the patricians. The latter gave concessions to the wealthy plebeian leaders. They first allowed selected representatives of this layer to enter the Senate.

The American Marxist, Daniel de Leon, gives a good description of the position of the latter, which he compares to that of modern labour leaders in bourgeois parliaments:

> But there, among the august and haughty patrician Senators, the Plebs Leaders were not expected to emit a sound. The patricians argued, the patricians voted, the patricians decided. When they were through, the tellers turned to the Plebs Leaders. But they were not even then allowed to give a sign with their mouths. Their mouths had to remain shut: their opinion was expressed with their feet. If they gave a tap, it meant they approved; if they gave no tap, it meant they disapproved; and it didn't much matter either way.[5]

Revolt of the plebs

Every military victory purchased with the blood of the plebeian soldier, merely served to strengthen the position of the patricians and the wealthy plebeians, who were increasingly bound together by economic interests and fear of the poor plebeians.

---

4 Livy, *History of Rome: The First Eight Books*, pp. 105-6.

5 de Leon, *Two Pages from Roman History*, p. 19.

At the other extreme, the problems of the poor continued to worsen, in particular debts and debt slavery, which led to renewed calls for relief. The resulting tensions between the classes flared up in a series of rebellions.

The first recorded strike in history was that of the Egyptian workers engaged on the construction of the mortuary temple of the Pharaoh Ramesses III in 1159 BC. But the first record of what amounted to a general strike was in the early period of the Roman Republic.

The Roman plebs of this period were that nameless majority who from time immemorial have ploughed the fields, planted the grain, baked the bread, fought in the wars. And this fact was brought to the attention of the noble patricians in a very novel way. On at least five occasions, in fact, the plebs threatened to 'secede' by withdrawing from Rome altogether. The problem was that, whereas the plebs could do very well without the patricians, the latter could not do without the plebs at all.

Things came to a head in 494 BC. Livy gives a detailed account, which is possibly more of fiction than history, but offers a captivating illustration of the process of popular rebellion, and in the absence of more reliable sources, it would be a shame not to repeat his account here.

The handing over of plebeian veterans and their families into debt slavery so enraged the masses that they refused to enlist for the army and held "secret conferences" and "nightly gatherings". The response of the senators was to order the consuls to double down on the levy as "it was idleness that made the plebeians lawless". In response, the crowd declared:

> [...] it was impossible to deceive the commons any longer; the consuls would never have a single soldier unless a public guarantee were given: liberty must first be restored to every man before arms were given him, that he might fight for his country and his fellow-citizens, not for a master.[6]

6 Livy, *Livy in Fourteen Volumes*, Vol. 1, Book 2, p. 309.

Again, the consuls turned to the senators for guidance and proposed reforms to allay the discontent of the plebs. The senators, with the hardened reactionary Appius Claudius at their head, instead chose to appoint a 'dictator', a magistrate who was appointed by the Senate to exercise full powers, including over the life and death of citizens, for a limited period in order to tackle a specific problem. However, fearing revolution if they appointed a vicious enemy of the plebs such as Claudius as dictator, the Senate opted for a 'moderate', Manius Valerius, who reassured the plebeians that no oppressive acts would be taken against them.

At this time Rome was threatened by a formidable invasion from the surrounding mountain tribes and Valerius levied an army to fight it off. Following the victory of the Romans, Valerius came to the Senate appealing for measures to alleviate the suffering of the plebs. When the Senate refused, he ominously announced: "For my own part I will not be the means of further disappointing my fellow citizens [...] I will play my part as a private citizen rather than as a dictator, when the mutiny breaks out."[7]

The city rested on a knife edge. At last the tipping point came when the Senate tried to draft the plebs into the army once more, on the pretext of another foreign invasion. The masses immediately left the city and set up camp at the Mons Sacer, or 'Sacred Mount'. "There", Livy writes, "without any leader, they fortified their camp with stockade and trench, and continued quietly, taking nothing but what they required for their subsistence, for several days, neither receiving provocation nor giving any."[8]

In panic, the Senate sent an ambassador to appeal to the plebeians, who offered a fable so characteristic of the psychology of the ruling classes of all times that it deserves repeating in full:

> In the days when man's members did not all agree amongst themselves, as is now the case, but had each its own ideas and a voice of its own, the other parts thought it unfair that they should have the worry and the trouble

7 Ibid., p. 321.

8 Ibid., p. 323.

> and the labour of providing everything for the belly, while the belly remained quietly in their midst with nothing to do but to enjoy the good things which they bestowed upon it; they therefore conspired together that the hands should carry no food to the mouth, nor the mouth accept anything that was given it, nor the teeth grind up what they received. While they sought in this angry spirit to starve the belly into submission, the members themselves and the whole body were reduced to the utmost weakness. Hence it had become clear that even the belly had no idle task to perform, and was no more nourished than it nourished the rest, by giving out to all parts of the body that by which we live and thrive, when it has been divided equally amongst the veins and is enriched with digested food – that is, the blood.[9]

A class that enriches the rest by its consumption, or to put it another way: the trickle-down economics of the fifth century BC.

In addition to these honeyed words a compromise was agreed, in which the plebs were allowed to elect two Tribunes of the Plebs (*tribuni plebis*) who represented their interests and existed side by side with the two patrician consuls. This was the first victory of the plebs.

The tribune had extensive powers, and could veto the consuls, while he was supposed to be inviolate. He could also seal the Public Treasury, and thus bring the whole business of the State to a grinding halt. However, as usual, the Senate found ways and means of getting round this. In the first place, a tribune had no salary, and therefore the office could (yet again) only be held by a citizen of independent means.

The patricians, as we have seen, were descended from the original Roman tribal aristocracy and constituted a privileged class that exploited and oppressed the rest of the population, the plebeians. The influx of immigrants from other tribes may be part of the explanation for the sharp line of differentiation between the patricians and plebs in early Roman history. This has even led some to speculate as to whether the plebeians were a different people to the patricians, who regarded them as racially inferior.

---

9 Quoted ibid., p. 325.

Whether or not one accepts the hypothesis that the original difference between patricians and plebeians can be explained by different ethnic origins, one thing is certain: that throughout the history of class society, the ruling class has always looked upon the poor and labouring classes with contempt, and in fact regards them as something like a different species, an inferior class of people, unfit to rule society or run industry – a class of inferior beings whose sole purpose is to work to keep their 'betters' in luxury, and to breed new generations of slaves for the same purpose.

The very word 'aristocracy' signifies 'rule of the best' in the Greek language, and the Latin word *proletarii*, from which the word 'proletarian' originates, means precisely a class that is only fit for the task of reproduction, like any farmyard animal. Hegel, who was well aware of these class contradictions in Roman society, explained:

> The weaker, the poorer, the later additions of population are naturally underrated by, and in a condition of dependence upon those who originally founded the state, and those who were distinguished by valour, and also by wealth. It is not necessary, therefore, to take refuge in a hypothesis which has recently been a favourite one – that the Patricians formed a particular race.[10]

The Decemvirate

The plebeian agitation led to a series of reforms. In 471 BC the Senate was forced to accept the establishment of a special assembly, composed exclusively of plebeians, the *concilium plebis*. This was to be convened by the tribunes and had the right to adopt certain measures (*plebiscita*). But this was yet another trick, since these decisions did not have the status of law.

At this time the laws were not written down but were interpreted by a Council of Priests *(pontifices)*, who were all still patricians. The background to this unrest was war, famine and pestilence, in which the brunt of the fighting and suffering was borne by the poor plebeian small farmers. None of the economic problems of the poor plebeians

10 Hegel, *Lectures on the Philosophy of History*, p. 285.

were addressed. The central issue was land owned by the State (*ager publicus*), which the patricians wished to monopolise, while the plebs wanted to have it distributed among themselves.

The internal commotions and civil strife caused by the quarrels of patricians and plebeians were followed by a temporary truce. But this broke down again when the college of tribunes attempted to check the power of the consuls by restricting their right to punish plebeians. The patricians were alarmed at what they regarded as an attempt to undermine their hereditary rights, and a long and bitter struggle began.

In the year 452 BC a compromise was reached when a commission of ten men, called *decemviri*, constituting the 'decemvirate', was chosen to write up a code of law defining the principles of Roman administration. During the decemvirate's term in office, all other magistracies would be suspended, and their decisions were not subject to appeal. Originally, all the decemvirs were patricians.

The result was the famous Twelve Tables, where the laws were written down for the first time and set up in stone in the forum. This is traditionally seen as a decisive turning point in the history of Rome and a great advance for democracy. But as a matter of fact, it left the fundamental social and political relations virtually untouched.

The ferocious severity of the laws on debt was only slightly mitigated. The execution of the laws was delayed for thirty days, during which the creditor was obliged to feed the debtor 'adequately'. But that was not much comfort for a man who could not pay his debts, and in the end the creditor still had the right to make the debtor a *nexus*, that is, to enslave him.

The fact that the Twelve Tables wrote this down for the first time meant that these harsh laws were literally 'set in stone'. This was a finished recipe for a further intensification of the class struggle in Rome, which would later enter onto an unprecedented level of ferocity.

A further concession was made when, in the year 450 BC, several plebeians were appointed to the new decemvirate, but this solved nothing, since the patricians still dominated. The peasantry was being ruined by constant wars with the neighbouring nations. Compelled to make good their losses by borrowing money from patrician creditors, they were liable to become bondsmen if they defaulted on their repayments.

None of the problems were addressed by the decemvirate, which became increasingly violent and tyrannical. To make matters worse, when its term of office expired, its members refused to leave office or permit successors to take office.

The conduct of the decemvirs had brought matters to the verge of civil war, and finally provoked an uprising in 449 BC. At first the ruling class resorted to the old trick of prevarication. But when the common soldiers saw that the endless discussions of their problems were getting nowhere, they decided to take drastic action. Led by an ex-tribune called Marcus Duillius, they simply left the city and moved to the Sacred Mount, and the whole of the civilian population followed them. They said that they would only return on condition of being protected by tribunes of their own. The scene is vividly conveyed in the words of Livy:

> The plebeian civilians followed the army; no one whose age allowed him to go hung back. Their wives and children followed them, asking in piteous tones, to whom would they leave them in a City where neither modesty nor liberty were respected? The unwonted solitude gave a dreary and deserted look to every part of Rome; in the Forum there were only a few of the older patricians, and when the senate was in session it was wholly deserted.[11]

The angry citizens taunted the magistrates, asking them: "Are you going to administer justice to walls and roofs?"[12] It was an incredible situation. A city that shortly before had been bustling with vibrant life stood empty, its streets as silent as a desert. One can envisage a factory without capitalists, but never a factory without workers. The

---

11 Livy, *History of Rome*, Vol. 1, Book 3, p. 197.

12 Ibid.

same was true in ancient Roman society. The ruling class was suddenly seized by panic.

Faced with the prospect of losing the people who did all the work in peacetime and all the fighting in the wars, the decemvirate backed away. It is always the same story: faced with losing *everything*, the ruling class will always be prepared to give *something*. This threat tore concessions from the ruling class, which attempted to defuse the conflict by compromise.

At last, the decemvirs gave way, overwhelmed by the unanimous opposition. They said that since it was the general wish, they would submit to the authority of the Senate. "All they asked for was that they might be protected against the popular rage; they warned the Senate against the plebs becoming by their death habituated to inflicting punishment on the patricians."[13] As always, the concessions of the ruling class were dictated by fear.

The people regained the right to elect their tribunes. This caused panic among the patricians. Livy writes: "Great alarm seized the patricians; the looks of the tribunes were now as menacing as those of the decemvirs had been." The tribunes did take action against some of the most hated patricians, such as Appius Claudius, a particularly extreme reactionary.

When he took the field against the Volsci, his soldiers would not fight, and he had every tenth man in his legions put to death. For these acts he was brought to trial by the tribunes M Duillius and C Sicinius. Seeing that conviction was certain, he committed suicide.

However, the ruling class need not have worried. Most of the people's tribunes were like our modern reformists, as the following words of Duillius show quite well:

> M Duillius the tribune imposed a salutary check upon their excessive exercise of authority. "We have gone," he said, "far enough in the assertion of our liberty and the punishment of our opponents, so for this year I will allow no man to be brought to trial or cast into prison. I disapprove of old crimes, long forgotten, being raked up, now that the recent ones have

13 Ibid., pp. 205-6.

> been atoned for by the punishment of the decemvirs. The unceasing care which both the consuls are taking to protect your liberties is a guarantee that nothing will be done which will call for the power of the tribunes."[14]

Livy adds:

> This spirit of moderation shown by the tribune relieved the fears of the patricians, but it also intensified their resentment against the consuls, for they seemed to be so wholly devoted to the plebs, that the safety and liberty of the patricians were a matter of more immediate concern to the plebeian than they were to the patrician magistrates.[15]

These lines might have been written yesterday! They accurately convey the conduct and psychology of the kind of individuals who, while trying to mediate between irreconcilable class interests, invariably abandon the struggle for the interests of the poor and oppressed and assume responsibility for defending the interests of the rich and powerful.

The new oligarchy

Despite the sharp conflict between the upper layers of the plebs and the old aristocracy, these two social groups, as the chief holders of property, had far more in common than they had with the poorest plebeians. By degrees, the old patrician aristocracy came to understand that the tribunes could be useful to control the excesses of the masses, in whose eyes they enjoyed great authority.

The plebs' leaders succeeded in obtaining concessions from the patricians by leaning on the masses, and the patricians were usually flexible enough to give concessions and reforms in order to preserve their class rule and privileges. Eventually, this led to a process of fusion that created a new oligarchy of *nobiles*, determined not by birth but by wealth and the possession of political power.

As a concession to the plebs (that is, to the wealthy plebeians), it was agreed that in future, one of the two consuls would always be a

14 Ibid., p. 206.

15 Ibid.

plebeian. By 351 BC the censorship was also opened to plebeians, and later it was agreed that a censor must always be a plebeian. This meant that the patricians had understood that in order to keep the masses in check, it was necessary to buy off their leaders by giving some of them access to positions of power.

About this time a new temple was established at Rome – the Temple of Concord. A kind of concord had indeed been established in Rome, but not between rich and poor. As Michael Grant points out:

> The effect of these changes was to create a new ruling class, no longer an entirely patrician aristocracy but a nobility consisting of those men, patricians and plebeian alike, whose ancestors had included consuls or censors or dictators – which is what the term 'noble' came to mean. And within the next century plebeian clans such as the Marcii and Decii and Curii, in addition to those who had come from Tusculum and elsewhere, succeeded in establishing themselves among the leaders of this new oligarchy of nobles.[16]

16 Grant, *History of Rome*, p. 68.

3. *The Rise of Rome*

The Roman state was born out of war, and was in an almost perpetual state of war with its neighbouring tribes. The struggle with tribes like the Volsci, the Aequi and the Sabines were a matter of national survival for Rome. The wars against these peoples gave the Roman citizens' army a great deal of experience. It perfected its tactics. A new spirit was engendered in the Roman people, a spirit hardened by the trials and tribulations of war. The traditional Roman virtues: valour, discipline and submission to the state, thus reflects the real conditions in which Rome was forged.

At the same time, the class contradictions at the heart of Roman society found their reflection within the army. After all, the plebs constituted the overwhelming majority of the troops. On more than one occasion the plebs turned this weapon against the patricians by refusing to fight or sabotaging recruitment. Livy notes that the Roman commanders in the field were sometimes more afraid of their own men than they were of the enemy. This brings to mind the words of the Duke of Wellington when passing review of his troops on the eve of the Battle of Waterloo: "I don't know what effect they will have on the enemy, but by God, they frighten me!"

Livy writes:

> This disaffection amongst the plebs was fanned by their tribunes, who were continually giving out that the most serious war was the one going on between the senate and the plebs, who were purposely harassed by war and exposed to be butchered by the enemy and kept as it were in banishment far from their homes lest the quiet of city life might awaken memories of their liberties and lead them to discuss schemes for distributing the State lands amongst colonists and securing a free exercise of their franchise. They got hold of the veterans, counted up each man's campaigns and wounds and scars, and asked what blood was still left in him which could be shed for the State. By raising these topics in public speeches and private conversations they produced amongst the plebeians a feeling of opposition to the projected war.[1]

Livy thus attributes the mutinous mood in the army to the agitation of the tribunes. But it is more likely that the discontent was already present, and the tribunes were merely giving it a voice: a sufficiently serious crime from the standpoint of the Senate. Again, the crafty patricians took the necessary measures to pacify the plebs. The Roman generals were careful to allow the soldiers to plunder the town of Anxur, where 2,500 prisoners were taken:

> Fabius would not allow his men to touch the other spoils of war until the arrival of his colleagues, for those armies too had taken their part in the capture of Anxur, since they had prevented the Volscians from coming to its relief. On their arrival the three armies sacked the town, which, owing to its long-continued prosperity, contained much wealth. *This generosity on the part of the generals was the first step towards the reconciliation of the plebs and the senate.*
>
> *This was followed by a boon which the senate, at a most opportune moment, conferred on the plebeians. Before the question was mooted either by the plebs or their tribunes, the senate decreed that the soldiery should receive pay from the public treasury. Previously, each man had served at his own expense.*[2]

---

1 Livy, *History of Rome*, Vol. 1, Book 4, p. 285.

2 Ibid., p. 286, emphasis added.

Livy describes the scenes of rejoicing at the unexpected generosity of the Senate, which was preparing for war with the powerful Etruscan city state of Veii, and needed to avoid a conflict with the soldiers:

> Nothing, it is recorded, was ever welcomed by the plebs with such delight; they crowded round the Senate-house, grasped the hands of the senators as they came out, acknowledged that they were rightly called 'Fathers', and declared that after what they had done no one would ever spare his person or his blood, as long as any strength remained, for so generous a country. They saw with pleasure that their private property at all events would rest undisturbed at such times as they were impressed and actively employed in the public service, and the fact of the boon being spontaneously offered, without any demand on the part of their tribunes, increased their happiness and gratitude immensely. The only people who did not share the general feeling of joy and goodwill were the tribunes of the plebs. They asserted that the arrangement would not turn out such a pleasant thing for the senate or such a benefit to the whole community as they supposed. The policy was more attractive at first sight than it would prove in actual practice. From what source, they asked, could the money be raised, except by imposing a tax on the people? They were generous at other people's expense.[3]

The concerns of the tribunes were well founded. The Senate did impose a tax, and the tribunes publicly announced that they would defend anybody who refused to pay it. Livy records that the Senate emptied the treasury of bronze coins to keep the army happy, an aim which they succeeded in achieving – for the time being.

From the first conflicts with more backward Latin tribes, Rome was preparing for greater things. The later wars were waged against more advanced opponents such as the Etruscan colony of Veii. It was in this war that Camillus first compelled the Romans to accept continuous military service. Previously, the peasant soldiers had been allowed to interrupt their military service for harvesting. Now Camillus ended this tradition, replacing it with pay. The campaign against Veii was

3 Ibid., p. 287.

successful and marks a turning point. For the first time, the soldiers of Rome had conquered a great Etruscan city-state.

These conquests prepared the way for the inexorable expansion of Rome. The defeat of Veii in 396 BC removed an important obstacle in the path of this expansion. Overnight, it almost doubled the territory of Rome. Land in the newly-conquered regions, linked by the excellent Etruscan road system, could be given to the Roman citizen-farmer/soldier as individual allotments. This system of obtaining land through conquest was a very important element in the history of the Roman Republic, but the biggest question of all was: *who would get control of this conquered land?* It proved to be the central question of the entire history of the Republic.

Gauls and Samnites

However, in 387 BC the seemingly inexorable advance of Roman arms received a sudden and shocking reverse. This was a period of huge migrations, which transformed the face of Europe forever, and only ended in the centuries following the fall of the Roman Empire in the West.

By the eighth and seventh centuries BC, the migration of the Celtic-speaking peoples was in full swing. They spread as far as Spain in the West to Britain in the North, and the banks of the Danube in the East. They occupied what is now France and gave it its name: Gaul.

From there, in the fifth century they gradually spread across the Alps and drove out the Etruscans who were settled there. From this time on the North of Italy was called Gaul this side of the Alps (Cisalpine Gaul). The Gauls who occupied the valley of the Po had developed the art of war to the point where they possessed a formidable military machine. They had the first cavalry to use iron horse shoes and their infantry was skilled in the use of finely-tempered slashing broad-swords.

Few could resist the mass onslaught of these ferocious warriors, their bodies painted and tattooed, their horses decorated with the skulls of fallen enemies. To make their attack more terrifying, they accompanied the charge with a deafening cacophony of trumpets and war-cries that struck terror into the hearts of the most hardened Roman soldiers.

In the late fourth century BC, one group of Gauls called Senones drove southwards from the Po Valley into the Italian peninsula in the direction of Rome. In 387 BC, at the confluence of the Tiber and Allia rivers, only eleven miles from the city, they were met by an army of 10-15,000 Romans – the largest force Rome had ever put into the field. What followed was the greatest catastrophe in Roman history.

The Roman phalanx of heavily-armed spear-carrying troops was overwhelmed by the faster-moving Gaulish cavalry and infantry, which rushed on them with an unstoppable impulse, shouting their terrifying war-cries. The Roman ranks were shattered and the army routed. Most of its soldiers plunged into a nearby river in a desperate attempt to save themselves and were drowned. Rome was left defenceless in the face of the enemy.

The Gauls entered the city and camped in the streets of Rome. Meeting no opposition, they murdered, plundered and burned, although they lacked the siege weapons to take the Capitoline Hill, where the last of the Roman defenders had barricaded themselves. The Gauls finally got tired of the siege, and were eventually persuaded by bribery to leave the city, for which, in any case, they had no use. But the memory of this horrifying experience remained to haunt the Romans long after the events had receded into that misty area of consciousness where historic memory becomes blurred by myth and legend.

The Roman historians have left us the story that the terrified Romans emptied their temples of gold to pay the Gauls to leave the city. The gold was brought to the place appointed by the Gauls, but when the amount that the Romans had with them was not equal to the weights brought by the Gauls, the Gallic leader, Brennus, threw his sword onto the scales, uttering the chilling words: "*Vae victis*" – "Woe to the conquered."

This story may or may not be founded on fact, but it left a strong imprint on the national psychology of the Romans forever, and in particular coloured their attitude to the people of Gaul, who later learned the true horror behind the words that Roman legend attributes to Brennus.

Despite this setback, Rome soon revived and continued its march to domination, extending its sphere of influence into the fertile plains of Campania. This brought them into conflict with one of the most warlike of all the Latin peoples and dragged Rome into the longest and most bitter wars in its history.

The Samnites were peasants and herdsmen, living in the barren limestone uplands of the Apennines in central Italy. They were barbarians at a stage of social and economic development not unlike the one that characterised Rome in its initial stages. As happened with the Gauls and many other barbarian tribes in antiquity, pressure of a growing population and the lack of agricultural land to feed it brought about a mass migration.

The result was a headlong collision with Rome, which was strengthening its position on the fertile plains of Campania, now threatened by a wholesale Samnite invasion. The Romans constructed the Appian Road for the purpose of transporting large numbers of troops towards the theatre of military operations.

However, the Samnites proved to be tough opponents and Rome suffered more than one costly defeat in the course of three separate wars. The first lasted from 343 to 341 BC. The second (or Great) Samnite War lasted from 326 to 304 BC. And the third war lasted from 298 to 290 BC. This represented a titanic effort that seriously drained the resources of Rome. The second war alone lasted more than twenty years and in the first half of the war Rome suffered serious defeats. Only the second half saw Rome's recovery, reorganisation and ultimate victory.

Now for the first time Rome found itself involved with the powerful and wealthy Greek city-states of southern Italy, who had appealed to Rome for help against the Samnites. Victory in this costly war made Rome the master of the whole of Italy except for Sicily. The final defeat of the Samnites therefore decided the fate of Italy and changed world history. It also gave a powerful impulse to the class struggle in Roman society.

Class contradictions in Rome

The first period of the Roman Republic was characterised by a continuous expansion that established the hegemony of Rome in all Italy after the victory over the Samnites. After the long wars of defence against neighbouring Latin tribes and marauding Gauls, the Romans passed over to wars of offence and conquest.

In the process, the Roman army had been transformed. It was far bigger than before, growing from two to four legions of 4-6,000 men. Michael Grant describes this:

> Each legion was a masterpiece of organisation, more mobile than the Greek phalanx which had served as the original model because a legion contained an articulated group of thirty smaller units (maniples), each of which could manoeuvre and fight separately on its own, in rough mountainous country as well as on the plains, either in serried ranks or open order, thus combining compactness with flexibility.[4]

The Romans perfected a kind of warfare that was well suited to the peculiarities of a citizens' army: the disciplined legions, fighting with the throwing spear and the short sword, created a formidable military machine that swept all before it. These new weapons were probably introduced during the Samnite wars. They completely changed the nature of warfare.

The withering hail of javelins, followed by a charge and the employment of the short stabbing sword wielded from behind a solid barrier of shields, has been likened to the combination of the musket and bayonet in eighteenth century warfare. No other army could withstand it. The lighter and less costly equipment of the new legions (referred to as 'manipular legions') also allowed for the effective mobilisation of an even larger layer of the population, beyond the wealthier plebeians who had formerly made up the old phalanx system.

The main factor that ensured the success of Roman arms was therefore the free peasantry that formed the backbone of the

4 Grant, *The History of Rome*, p. 54.

Republic and its army. Under the early *gens* system, land was held in common by the *gens* itself. But with the break-up of the *gentes*, and the emergence of private property of the land, a class of free small peasants was created. Alongside the class of small peasants (*assidui*) there was the poorest layer of society, the *proletarii* – the 'producers of children'. But it was the class of small proprietors that supplied the troops for military service.

The Roman peasant was a free citizen who had something to fight for. He had the right to bear arms and the duty of military service. The very word for 'people' comes from the Latin *populus*, which originally meant 'a body of warriors', and is related to the word *populari*, to devastate, and *popa*, a butcher.

The ruling class understood the need to ensure that Rome's plebeian soldiers would continue to fight. Appius Claudius, known as Caecus, 'the Blind' – which he was in his old age – was a patrician who became censor in 312 BC. His main aim appeared to have been to improve the position of discharged soldiers, who by this time were increasingly landless peasants flocking to Rome.

No reformer had ever before taken up the cause of the Roman proletariat. His intentions may have been motivated by genuine concern, but more likely his main aim was to avoid disturbances in the capital. These measures, however timid, irritated the Senate, which took steps to undermine and sabotage them.

The third and last Samnite war began in 298 BC and lasted for eight years. This ferocious conflict ended in victory but also in financial exhaustion. The plebeians of middle rank who spent years fighting in the army had returned home to find themselves ruined. The influx of cheap grain from the conquered lands undermined them. So, despite all the laws passed to protect them, a large number of small peasants fell into debt. A new period of instability ensued.

Within the community from the very beginning there were the elements of class contradiction. But the rapid increase of inequality and the encroachments on the rights of the plebs by the wealthy patricians placed a growing strain on the social cohesion of the Republic.

The wealthy classes encroached on the common lands and oppressed the plebs in different ways, causing rising tension between the classes. The constant need to defend the Roman state against external enemies provided the patricians with an invaluable instrument to keep the plebs in check, as Hegel points out:

> In the first predatory period of the state, every citizen was necessarily a soldier, for the state was based on war; this burden was oppressive, since every citizen was obliged to maintain himself in the field. This circumstance, therefore, gave rise to the contracting of enormous debts – the patricians becoming the creditors of the plebeians. With the introduction of laws, this arbitrary relation necessarily ceased; but only gradually, for the patricians were far from being immediately inclined to release the plebs from the cliental relation; they rather strove to render it permanent. The laws of the Twelve Tables still contained much that was undefined; very much was still left to the arbitrary will of the judge – the patricians alone being judges; the antithesis, therefore, between patricians and plebeians, continues till a much later period. Only by degrees do the plebeians scale all the heights of official station, and attain those privileges which formerly belonged to the patricians alone.[5]

Here the inner workings of every state in history are laid bare, exposing the organised violence and class oppression that lies beneath the thin veneer of 'impartiality' and 'justice' that is expressed in the Majesty of the Law, and serves as a fig-leaf to obscure the crude reality of the state as an organ for the oppression of one class over another:

> In order to obtain a nearer view of this Spirit, we must not merely keep in view the actions of Roman heroes, confronting the enemy as soldiers or generals, or appearing as ambassadors – since in these cases they belong, with their whole mind and thought, only to the state and its mandate, without hesitation or yielding – but pay particular attention also to the conduct of the plebs in times of revolt against the patricians. How often in insurrection and in anarchical disorder was the plebs brought back into a state of tranquillity by a mere form, and cheated of the fulfilment

5 Hegel, *Lectures on the Philosophy of History*, p. 286.

> of its demands, righteous or unrighteous! How often was a Dictator, e.g., chosen by the senate, when there was neither war nor danger from an enemy, in order to get the plebeians into the army, and to bind them to strict obedience by the military oath![6]

The campaign for land reform was repeatedly interrupted by the threat of foreign invasion, the patricians making good use of the external threat to defuse the class struggle. How well the old idealist Hegel understood the workings of class society! And how brilliantly he exposed the tactics with which the rulers of the state make use of the 'external enemy' to fool the masses and whip up patriotic sentiment in order to divert their attention from the self-evident fact that their worst enemies are at home.

The Punic Wars

The history of class society is studded with wars and revolutions. Pacifists and moralists may lament this fact. But, sad to say, even the most superficial examination of history shows that it has never been guided by moral considerations. It is as inappropriate to approach history from a moralistic standpoint as it would be to do this in relation to the workings of natural selection in the evolution of species. We may regret that carnivorous animals are not vegetarians, but our feelings on the subject will not affect the ways of nature in the slightest degree.

It is self-evident that wars and revolutions have an important – even a decisive effect – on human history. They are, to use the Hegelian expression, the *nodal points* where quantity becomes transformed into quality, the boundaries that separate one historical epoch from another. Thus we refer to the period before and after 1789, 1815, 1914, 1917, 1945 and so on.

At these critical points, all the contradictions that have been slowly accumulating emerge with explosive force, impelling society forward – or back. In the case of the Roman Republic, we see a dialectical process in which war leads to a change in the mode of production,

6 Ibid., p. 288.

and the change in the mode of production leads to a change in the nature of war and the army itself.

The formative period of the Roman Republic was an age of almost permanent warfare: wars against the Etruscans, the Latins, the Gauls, the Samnites, the Greek colonies in Italy, Epirus (modern day Albania and Greece) and finally, against Carthage. This last episode was a decisive turning point in Roman history. Carthage was the main trading power in the Western Mediterranean. It possessed a great part of the coast of northern Africa and southern Spain and had a footing in Sicily and Sardinia.

It was the Carthaginians' involvement in Sicily that first brought them into conflict with Rome. An appeal for aid against the city-state of Syracuse from a group of mercenaries based at Messana (modern-day Messina) was eagerly taken up by the Senate as a pretext for Roman expansion onto that wealthy island.

The Romans became involved in the affairs of Sicily, where the Carthaginians were already well installed. A complex web of alliances and trade interests caused a chain reaction that led inexorably to war between the two powers for control of the island.

Roman historians like Polybius liked to portray this as a defensive war, but there is little evidence to support the idea that at this stage Carthage was a serious threat to Rome. The fact is that Rome was now an aggressive power that was fighting to achieve total domination of the whole of Italy – including Sicily.

Thus, a conflict with Carthage was inevitable. But this conflict was to turn Rome into a power, not just in Italy, but throughout the Mediterranean. And if we recall that the word *mediterraneus* in the Latin language signifies "the centre of the world", then what is meant is a world power, in the understanding of those times.

There were three wars with Carthage, known as the Punic Wars (264-241, 218-201 and 149-146 BC). In comparison to these conflicts, all previous wars seemed like child's play. This was a deadly, bloody slogging match, which lasted decades. The human and economic cost of the war was immense. In the First Punic War alone, in a five-year period, the census of Roman citizens fell by about

40,000, one-sixth of the total population. And these figures do not include Rome's allies, who suffered big losses at sea.

The First Punic War ended in 241 BC with the Treaty of Lutatius, under which Carthage evacuated Sicily and agreed to pay an indemnity of 3,200 talents of silver. But though the Romans won the first war with its most powerful enemy, the conflict was not resolved. Carthage soon rebuilt its power, drawing on the rich silver mines of Spain. A second sixteen-year war followed – a war that is forever associated with the name of Hannibal.

The Romans had watched with alarm as the Carthaginians consolidated their power in Spain. This was dangerous and had to be stopped at all costs. The Romans needed a pretext to intervene in Spain and they got one when Carthaginian forces led by Hannibal besieged the city of Saguntum (the modern Sagunto), which was under Roman protection. The Romans claimed that there was an agreement that the Carthaginian army should not go south of the Ebro River, and that Hannibal had broken this agreement.

Whether the claim made by Rome was true or false is a question of third-rate importance. One must never confuse the causes of war with the diplomatic pretexts or accidental factors that provoke the commencement of hostilities.

The First World War was not caused by the assassination of Archduke Ferdinand in Sarajevo, as the old history books used to claim. It was the inevitable result of the conflict of interests between the rising imperialist power of Germany and the older, established imperialist powers of Britain and France, which had carved up the world between them. Here we have an analogous case from the world of antiquity.

Polybius recognised the fact that:

> Some of those authors who have dealt with Hannibal and his times, wishing to indicate the causes that led to the above war between Rome and Carthage, allege as its first cause the siege of Saguntum by the Carthaginians and as its second their crossing, contrary to treaty, the river whose native name is the Iber [Ebro]. I should agree in stating that

> these were the beginnings of the war, but I can by no means allow that they were its causes…[7]

This is very true. The Romans were determined to prevent Carthage from restoring her economic and military power, and therefore used this incident as a pretext to send an army into Spain.

They made the Carthaginians an offer they could not accept (another typical diplomatic trick to start a war). They demanded that either the Carthaginians hand over Hannibal for punishment or else accept war with Rome. Hannibal had in fact been trying to avoid a war with Rome, because he was not yet ready. But once he understood that war was inevitable, he boldly seized the initiative. He went onto the offensive.

The Romans never imagined he would take the step of invading Italy. Even less did they imagine he would lead his army out of Spain, march through Gaul and cross what seemed to be an impassable barrier – the Alps – to enter Italy from the North. But he did all these things, and took the Romans by surprise. And surprise can be a decisive element in war.

Rome suddenly found itself invaded by a foreign army fighting on Italian soil. This extraordinary general, with very little support from outside, harried the Roman armies and came within a hair's breadth of destroying Roman power altogether.

Hannibal calculated that his relatively small army would be supported by an uprising of the Latin peoples who were under Roman domination (though technically allies). He did get support from the Gauls of Northern Italy. But in general the Latin peoples remained loyal to Rome.

Thus, although his spectacular military victories at Trebbia, Trasimene and Cannae brought Rome to its knees, he lacked sufficient strength to deliver the knockout blow. The Romans could always rebuild their armies out of the remaining peasant population, while Hannibal, deprived of outside help, could not afford to lose men. Therefore, in the long run, even Hannibal's great talent as a general could not bring victory.

---

7 Polybius, *The Histories*, Book 3, p. 15.

Learning from their earlier mistakes, the Romans simply avoided direct battles and waited for the Carthaginian forces to exhaust themselves. Then a Roman army led by Scipio invaded Spain and conquered it. After this, Rome turned its attentions to Carthage itself.

They organised an intrigue with Carthage's African vassals and got them to rise up against their masters. This revolt compelled Hannibal to return to Africa to defend Carthage. Once again, the might of Rome prevailed. In the end Carthage was decisively beaten at the battle of Zama.

After this, the Romans no longer felt any need to pretend that their wars were of a defensive character. They had developed a taste for conquest. But this was merely a reflection of a fundamental change in property relations and the mode of production.

The final Punic War was deliberately provoked by Rome. The war party was led by Cato, who always ended his speeches in the Senate with the celebrated slogan: *"delenda est Carthago"* – *Carthage must be destroyed*. After a three-year siege in which the inhabitants suffered terrible famine, the city was taken by storm. In a display of extreme vindictiveness, the Romans broke their promises to the Carthaginians and sold the population into slavery. They then demolished the city stone by stone and cursed the site with the intention that it would never be inhabited again.

The same year (146 BC) they destroyed Corinth, another trading rival. By order of the Senate, the city was razed to the ground, its entire population was sold into slavery and its priceless art treasures were shipped off to Rome. The destruction of Corinth was partly to prevent social revolution – the Romans always preferred to deal with oligarchic governments, whereas Corinth was a turbulent democracy.

The defeat of Carthage changed the destiny of Rome. Until it was compelled to take to the sea in the war with Carthage, Rome had never been a sea power. Carthage had always blocked her way. Now, with this mighty obstacle removed, Rome was free to launch herself on a career that was to end in complete domination of the Mediterranean.

The Roman victory added new territories to its growing empire, including the prosperous Greek and Phoenician colonies on the coast of Spain. This gave a further impetus to the class of Roman merchants, involved in trade in the Mediterranean. Spain opened up her valuable iron and silver mines, which were also worked by slave labour in terrible conditions.

Rome simply took over this business from Carthage. It also led to a further development of trade and exchange and therefore the rise of a money economy. Thus, war played an important role in bringing about a complete transformation of the mode of production – and therefore of social relations – in Rome.

Effects on the army

The armies of Rome were victorious on all fronts. But in the midst of these foreign triumphs, intense contradictions were developing at home, where a new and even more ferocious war was about to break out – a war between the classes. Stripped of all non-essentials *this was a war for the division of the loot.*

This was already pointed out by Hegel, who wrote: "*The Roman state, drawing its resources from rapine, came to be rent in sunder by quarrels about dividing the spoils.*"[8] This is a very precise, and wholly materialist, account of the basis of the class struggle in Rome at this time.

The Punic Wars also marked a change in the nature of the Roman army. Until now the army was based on the property-owning citizens and was drawn mainly from the mass of free peasants. But in the course of the Punic Wars, when the fate of the Republic was in the balance, it was no longer possible to maintain the old situation and the property qualifications were greatly reduced.

For the first time, a large number of proletarians between the ages of eighteen and forty-six were recruited into the army and served for an average of seven years and were paid for out of the public funds. This was a further step in the transformation of the Roman army

8 Hegel, *The Philosophy of History*, p. 309, emphasis added.

from a citizens' militia to a professional army. It created a new type of general in the person of Scipio Africanus, the first Roman general who was named after his military conquests.

With every military conquest, Rome acquired a huge amount of land confiscated in the conquered territories. This land became the property of the Roman state – the *ager publicus* (public land). But since the state itself was in the hands of the patricians, in practice they treated the *ager publicus* as their own property and leased it out to people of their own class. The mass of propertyless plebeians had no access to the conquered lands, and this was a constant source of intense discontent.

The discontent of the plebeian soldiers was further intensified by the fact that the length of compulsory military service was continually being increased as the wars became longer. Initially, the citizens' militia was fighting defensive wars on its own territory. But the Samnite Wars, which were fought a long way from home, had extended over half a century, involving almost all the states of Italy.

The long periods of military service often meant that the Roman soldier returned home to find his farm in ruins, and himself and his family deep in debt. The long years of war led gradually, on the one hand, to the rise of slavery and the big estates, and on the other hand, to the rapid increase of a landless population of proletarians.

The tendency of the Senate to treat the lands of the conquered territories as their personal property has already been noted. But after the long and bloody slugging match with Hannibal, there was a feeling that the Senate had saved Rome, and the military victory over Rome's most dangerous enemy greatly boosted the Senate's authority and undermined any potential opposition – at least for a time. Victory meant Roman control over vast new territories with immense riches. As the third century passed into the second, the Senate strengthened its grip on the new territories by the appointment of governors, who had a virtual licence to coin money at the expense of the provinces.

It is important to note that the class struggle in ancient Rome was not identical with the struggle between plebeians and patricians. That was a difference of rank – roughly the same as the difference between 'commoners' and 'nobles'. But there were also wealthy plebeians – who invariably took the side of the patricians against the plebeian masses.

Thus, the old struggles of plebeians against patricians became transformed into the struggle of rich against poor, a struggle which would acquire an explosive and revolutionary character in the period following the end of the Punic Wars.

4. The Slave Economy

The underlying motor force of history is the development of the productive forces, or to put it another way, the development of humankind's power over nature. In the last analysis, the viability of a given socio-economic system will be determined by its ability to provide people with food, clothing and shelter. It is obvious that in order to think beautiful thoughts, invent clever machines, develop new religions and philosophies, one first has to eat.

Long before Marx, the great Aristotle wrote that philosophy began "when practically all the necessities of life were already supplied."[1] And Hegel pointed out that:

> The first glance at History convinces us that the actions of men proceed from their needs, their passions, their characters and talents; and impresses us with the belief that such needs, passions and interests are the sole springs of action – the efficient agents in this scene of activity.[2]

Marx and Engels explained at great length that the connection between the economic base of a given society and the immense superstructure of the state, laws, religious beliefs, philosophical

1 Aristotle, *Metaphysics*, Vol. 1, p. 13.

2 Hegel, *Lectures on the Philosophy of History*, p. 20.

tendencies and schools of art, literature and music is not a direct and mechanical one, but an extremely complex and contradictory dialectical relation. However, in the last analysis, the causes of all great historical transformations must be traced back to changes in the mode of production, which give rise to profound modifications in society.

On one occasion the English socialist Ernest Belfort Bax challenged Engels to deduce the appearance of the Gnostic religious sect in the second century from the economic conditions in Rome at the time. The question showed a complete lack of understanding of historical materialism on Bax's part, but Engels was patient and answered that one could not do such a thing, but suggested that "by tracing the matter further back you might arrive at some economic explanation of what he granted was an interesting side problem in history."[3]

It is impossible to understand the fall of the Roman Republic unless we take the trouble to "trace the matter back" to its origins, which are the direct result of a change in the mode of production, which in turn produced profound changes in the relations between the classes in Roman society, the nature of the state and the army. The decisive change in this case was the rise of slavery, which led to the liquidation of the class of free peasants that was the backbone of the Republic and its army. All subsequent developments are contingent on this fact.

Each stage in the development of human society is marked by a certain development of the productive forces, and a higher development of labour productivity. This is the secret wellspring of all progress. Greece and Rome produced marvels of art, science, law, philosophy and literature. Yet all these intellectual marvels were based, in the last analysis, on the labour of the slaves. Subsequently, slavery entered into decline and was replaced by feudalism, where the exploitation of labour assumed a different form. Finally, we arrive at the capitalist mode of production, which remains dominant, although its contradictions are now clear to all.

To us, slavery appears as something morally repugnant. But then we are left with a paradox. If we ask the question: where did all our

---

3 Bax, 'Meetings with Engels', *Reminiscences of Marx and Engels*, p. 306.

modern science and technology, art and philosophy come from, we are forced to answer: Greece and Rome (we leave aside the important contributions later made by the Arabs, who preserved and developed the ideas of antiquity and transmitted them to us). That is to say, the achievements of those civilisations were the products of slavery.

The transition of the Roman economy from one based on free peasant labour to one dominated by slavery undoubtedly raised the productive powers of society, and was accompanied by a notable advance of art, literature and culture. Before the Punic Wars, the Romans were not at all interested in the fine arts. Learning was not highly regarded, and the top statesmen devoted most of their energies to agriculture. This was very different to Athens.

Among the Romans, fine talk was regarded with suspicion. They tended to speak in practical terms of what they had to do, preferring substance to style. Fine writing was no better regarded: the literature of the early Republic was confined to purely factual annals. But the latter phase of the Republic was characterised by the rise of new literary trends and philosophical schools: poets like Catullus and Lucretius became fashionable. This reflected a change in the lifestyle and outlook of the ruling class.

Despite all the barbarous and bloody features that naturally arouse indignation and disgust, each stage of social development marks an advance on the road to the final emancipation of the human race, which can only be achieved on the basis of the fullest development of the productive forces and of human culture. It was in that sense that Hegel wrote that it is not so much *from* slavery as *through* slavery that humankind reaches emancipation.

The rise of slavery

With the destruction of Carthage in 146 BC, Rome controlled the whole of North Africa, Greece, Southern Gaul and Spain. Wealth was pouring in from all sides. But it was ultimately these conquests that undermined the foundations of the Republic.

Before the Punic Wars started, a new oligarchy was formed when the tribunes went over to the side of the Senate. The wealthy plebeians gradually fused with the old aristocracy to form a powerful nobility of big property owners. The first two Punic Wars greatly strengthened the hold of this oligarchy on Roman society. This was the social and political reflection of a fundamental change in the mode of production, from an economy based on free labour and small peasant agriculture to an economy based on slave labour and big landed estates (*latifundia*).

Until the Punic Wars, slavery was not the decisive mode of production. True, there were probably always some slaves in Rome, and the phenomenon of debt slavery was present from the earliest recorded times. But in the beginning the number of slaves working in the fields was far less than that of the free peasants, and the lot of slaves was not as bad as in later times. The slave worked alongside his master and was almost like a member of the family. Slaves could be freed through manumission and this was a fairly common occurrence. In *The Foundations of Christianity*, Karl Kautsky writes:

> From the material point of view the situation of these slaves was not too hard to start with; they sometimes found themselves well enough off. As members of a prosperous household, often serving convenience or luxury, they were not taxed unduly. When they did productive work, it was often – in the case of the wealthy peasants – in common with the master; and always only for the consumption of the family itself, and that consumption had its limits. The position of the slaves was determined by the character of the master and the prosperity of the families they belonged to. It was in their own interest to increase that prosperity, for they increased their own prosperity in the process. Moreover the daily association of the slave with his master brought them closer together as human beings and, when the slave was clever, made him indispensable and even a full-fledged friend. There are many examples, in the ancient poets, of the liberties slaves took with their masters and with what intimacy the two were often connected. It was not rare for a slave to be rewarded for faithful service by being freed with a substantial gift; others saved enough to purchase their freedom. Many preferred slavery to freedom; they would rather live

as members of a rich family than lead a needy and uncertain existence all by themselves.[4]

The rise of the big estates changed all that. The mode of production was transformed. The rising population of the towns meant an increased demand for bread and an increased market for other agricultural products. On the other hand, the destruction of Carthage meant that Italy was now the main producer of wine and olive oil. The small peasant subsistence agriculture was now rapidly displaced by large-scale intensive agriculture, producing not for the use of the landowner and his household but for a large market using new techniques: crop rotation, the use of manure and new deep-cutting ploughs and the selection of seeds.

In southern Italy there were big ranches for the raising of cattle and sheep. In turn there were new industries for the working of wool and leather and the production of meat and cheese. Only the biggest estates could do this, since they alone had access to both the upper and lower pastures required for seasonal migration. Naturally, they were worked by slave labour.

The use of large-scale slave labour probably began in the mines. Victory in the Punic Wars meant that Rome now had possession of the valuable silver mines in Spain that had previously been exploited by the Carthaginians. Since the Romans had a huge supply of extremely cheap slaves, who could literally be worked to death, these mines could show a very decent profit for a relatively small outlay. The Spanish silver mines became among the most productive of antiquity, as ancient authors confirm. Diodorus writes:

> In the beginning, ordinary private citizens were occupied in the mining and got great riches, because the silver ore did not lie deep and was present in great quantity. Later, when the Romans became masters of Iberia [Spain], a crowd of Italians appeared at the mines, who won great riches through their greed. For they bought a throng of slaves and handed them over to the overseer of the mines. […] Those slaves that

4 Kautsky, *The Foundations of Christianity*, p. 29.

> have to work in these mines bring incredible incomes to their masters: but many of them, who toil underground in the pits day and night, die of the overwork. For they have no rest or pause, but are driven by the blows of their overseers to endure the hardest exertions and work themselves to death. A few, that have enough strength and patience to endure it, only prolong their misery, which is so great it makes death preferable to life.[5]

By degrees the free peasants found themselves displaced by slave labour, as Mommsen explains:

> The burdensome and partly unfortunate wars, and the exorbitant taxes and taskworks to which these gave rise, filled the measure of calamity, so as either to deprive the possessor directly of his farm and to make him the bondsman if not the slave of his creditor-lord, or to reduce him through encumbrances practically to the condition of a temporary lessee to his creditor. The capitalists, to whom a new field was here opened of lucrative speculation unattended by trouble or risk, sometimes augmented in this way their landed property; sometimes they left to the farmer, whose person and estate the law of debt placed in their hands, nominal proprietorship and actual possession. The latter course was probably the most common as well as the most pernicious; for while utter ruin might thereby be averted from the individual, this precarious position of the farmer, dependent at all times on the mercy of his creditor – a position in which he knew nothing of property but its burdens – threatened to demoralise and politically to annihilate the whole farmer-class.[6]

A fundamental change was taking place in Italy itself. The huge influx of slaves meant that slave labour was now extremely cheap. There was no way the free Italian peasantry could compete with it. Italy was now full of big landed estates worked by slave labour, as described by Mommsen:

5 Diodorus Siculus, Book 5, Chapters 36-38, quoted ibid., p. 33.

6 Mommsen, *History of Rome*, Vol. 1, p. 349.

> The human labour of the field was regularly performed by slaves. At the head of the body of slaves on the estates (*familia rustica*) stood the steward (*vilicus*, from *villa*), who received and expended, bought and sold, went to obtain the instructions of the landlord, and in his absence issued orders and administered punishment.[7]

Incidentally, as can be seen from the above quotation, our word 'family' comes from the word for a collection of slaves. He continues:

> The whole system was pervaded by the utter unscrupulousness characteristic of the power of capital. Slaves and cattle were placed on the same level; a good watchdog, it is said in a Roman writer on agriculture, must not be on too friendly terms with his "fellow slaves". The slave and the ox were fed properly so long as they could work, because it would not have been good economy to let them starve; and they were sold like a worn-out ploughshare when they became unable to work, because in like manner it would not have been good economy to retain them longer.[8]

Expropriation of the peasantry

The basic branch of production of the Roman Republic was agriculture. In spite of the high level of urbanisation in Roman society, 70 per cent of the population of Roman Italy lived in the countryside.[9] Other parts of the economy, such as mining, crafts and trading, were dependent on this.

The small peasants produced mainly for self-consumption. Only the surplus, if there was any, could be sold. Production for exchange was not developed until after the Punic Wars. All this changed with the rise of the big estates (*latifundia*) and the large-scale use of slave labour. Gradually the old order was subverted by slave labour that ruined the free Roman peasantry.

A vast gulf opened up between the wealthy elite and the mass of poor Romans, not to speak of the slaves. The great landowners

7 Ibid., Vol. 2, p. 434.

8 Ibid., p. 437.

9 Hunt, *Ancient Greek and Roman Slavery*, p. 50.

continued to buy up the small landholdings, and where the peasants proved obstinate, simply seized their land without even the pretence of a sale.

According to Mommsen, there was not a single free farmer left in Etruria by the year 134 BC.[10] The following extract from 'The Complaint of the Poor Man against the Rich Man', ascribed to the Roman rhetorician, Quintilian (c. 35 – c. 100 AD), describes the spread of the *latifundia* in the complaint of an impoverished peasant:

> I was not always the neighbour of a rich man. Round about there was many a farm with owners alike in wealth, tilling their modest lands in neighbourly harmony. How different is it now! The land that once fed all these citizens is now a single huge plantation, belonging to a single rich man. His estate has extended its boundaries on every side; the peasant houses it has swallowed up have been razed to the ground, and the shrines of their fathers destroyed. The old owners have said farewell to their tutelary gods and gone far away with their wives and children. Monotony reigns over the wide plain. Everywhere riches close me in, as if with a wall; here there is a garden of the rich man's, there his fields, here his vineyard, there his woods and stacks of grain. I too would gladly have departed, but I could not find a spot of land where I would not have a rich man for my neighbour. Where does one not come up against the rich man's private property? They are not content any longer to extend their domains so far that they are bounded by natural boundaries, rivers and mountains, like whole countries. They lay hold even of the furthest mountain wildernesses and forests. And nowhere does this grasping find an end and a limit until the rich man comes up against another rich man. And this too shows the contempt the rich have for us poor, that they do not even take the trouble to deny it when they have used violence on us.[11]

There are certain parallels between the transformation of the mode of production in the Roman Republic after the Punic Wars and the rise of capitalism in Europe, in particular with the 'enclosure' of common

---

10 Mommsen, *Roman History*, Vol. 3, p. 108.

11 Quoted in Kautsky, *The Foundations of Christianity*, p. 39.

lands and the clearing of the peasants from their former homes, which took place continuously from the sixteenth century. Indeed, the word 'capitalism' is sometimes used when speaking of this phase of Roman development. But, though there are certain analogies, the comparison is not exact.

It is true that an extensive market developed throughout the Mediterranean during the period of Rome's expansion. Commodities, including not only luxuries but staples such as grain and olive oil, were traded widely through Italy and the Mediterranean world, and with this growing trade came the development of merchant capital, that is the buying and selling of products as commodities for the realisation of what Marx calls exchange-value.

Further, the development of merchant capital began to react in turn on production itself. Agricultural manuals, written at the time by great landowners, repeatedly state that the landowners' aim should be to maximise profitability by producing as much and as great a variety of goods as possible. In his famous *De agricultura,* Cato the Elder states explicitly: "The master should have the selling habit, not the buying habit."[12]

The development of commerce and commodity production in any form stimulates the circulation and concentration of money. On this basis, usury, the lending of money at interest, can thrive. And it thrived to a never-before-seen extent under the Roman Republic.

Often, the great slave owners would also be the biggest usurers, on account of their accumulation of money through trade and naked plunder. In addition to squeezing the small producers dry, rich Romans would lend money to merchant fleets in return for interest. In essence this was the investment of a quantity of value in the form of a sum of money, in the expectation of receiving a greater sum of money at a later date: usurers' capital.

The picture that emerges from all of these elements is of the formation not only of a class of dispossessed proletarians but also the concentration of both land and money in the hands of a class

12 Cato, *On Agriculture,* p. 9.

of great estate holders, producing for the market. Marx even went so far as to say that the *latifundia* were devoted to the production of surplus-value. But in spite of all this, Marx rejected the notion of 'Roman capitalism', because the capitalist *mode of production*, that is the manufacture of commodities by free wage labour, never developed to a significant extent, in stark contrast to Europe in the Middle Ages.

Marx took up the comparison between ancient Rome and capitalist development in Europe on several occasions throughout his published and unpublished works. In one letter, he explicitly warned against equating any and all expropriation of the peasantry by big landed property with the development of the "capitalist economic order", taking up the Roman example as a case in point:

> In several parts of *Capital* I allude to the fate which overtook the plebeians of ancient Rome. They were originally free peasants, each cultivating his own piece of land on his own account. In the course of Roman history they were expropriated. The same movement which divorced them from their means of production and subsistence involved the formation not only of big landed property but also of big money capital. And so one fine morning there were to be found on the one hand free men, stripped of everything except their labour power, and on the other, in order to exploit this labour, those who held all the acquired wealth in possession. What happened? The Roman proletarians became, not wage labourers but a *mob* of do-nothings more abject than the former 'poor whites' in the southern country of the United States, and alongside of them there developed a mode of production which was not capitalist but dependent upon slavery.[13]

Marx comments in *Capital* that wherever they develop, merchant and usurer's capital have a "more or less dissolving influence everywhere on the producing organisation", but "whither this process of dissolution will lead, in other words, what new mode of production will replace

13 Marx, 'Letter to the Editor of the *Otecestvenniye Zapisky*', 1877, *Marx and Engels Selected Correspondence, 1846-1895,* pp. 354-5, emphasis in original.

the old, does not depend on commerce, but on the character of the old mode of production itself."[14]

A key difference between the Europe of the first century BC and the sixteenth century AD was the level of development of crafts and industry. Urban craft production was extremely underdeveloped in Rome, even in comparison to other ancient societies.

Slave labour tended to drive out free labour, destroying not only the class of free peasants but also preventing the development of handicrafts, which were undermined by the industries run by gangs of slaves in the cities and on the *latifundia*. Kautsky develops the same point:

> If the slaves were cheap, their industrial products would be cheap too. They required no outlay of money. The farm, the *latifundium* provided the workers' foodstuffs and raw materials, and in most cases their tools too. And since the slaves had to be kept anyway during the time they were not needed in the fields, all the industrial products they produced over and above the needs of their own enterprise were a surplus that yielded a profit even at low prices.
>
> In the face of this slave-labour competition it is no wonder that strong free crafts could not develop. The craftsmen in the ancient world, and particularly so in the Roman world, remained poor devils, working alone for the most part without assistants, and as a rule working up material supplied to them, either in the house of the client or at home. There was no question of a strong group of craftsmen such as grew up in the Middle Ages. The guilds remained weak and the craftsmen were always dependent on their clients, usually the bigger landowners, and very often led a parasitic existence on the verge of sinking into the *lumpenproletariat* as the landowner's dependents.[15]

The changes in the mode of production in the Roman Republic after the Punic Wars required greater and greater use of slave labour. This forced Rome into war after war as it sought to replenish its supply of

---

14 Marx, *Capital*, Vol. 3, *MECW*, Vol. 37, p. 330.

15 Kautsky, *The Foundations of Christianity*, pp. 35-6.

slaves. This abundant supply of cheap labour explains why there was no incentive to invest in labour-saving technology. It also explains the brutal treatment of the slaves and the subsequent mass revolts that broke out.

Contradictions of a slave economy

In this period we see a considerable strengthening of the ruling oligarchy, which increased its grip on society and the state. Together with the old aristocratic families we see the rise of a new class of rich merchants and usurers. But in the last analysis, all the wealth of these layers was derived from the products of agriculture. Since land was the main source of all wealth, everybody strove to get land, and to add to the land they already possessed. But in order for it to be profitable, someone had to work the land. This was provided by slave labour.

The Carthaginians had developed slavery on a large scale, and the Romans learned it from them. When they seized the provinces owned by Carthage in Sicily, Sardinia, Spain and North Africa, they also took over the large-scale farms they found there, and developed and extended them further.

In the slack times between harvesting and spring ploughing, the slaves were put to work weaving, tanning and leather working, making wagons and ploughs, and pottery making of all sorts. But they produced not only for the individual farm, but also for sale, marking the development of commodity production. The only cost to the slave-owner was the price of purchasing the slave in the first place, and the minimal costs of keeping him or her alive afterwards. Kautsky writes:

> There could be no question at that time of any technical superiority of large-scale agriculture; on the contrary, slave labour was less productive than the labour of the free peasants. But the slave, whose labour power did not have to be spared and who could be sweated to death without a second thought, produced a greater surplus over the cost of his subsistence than the peasant, who at that time knew nothing of the

> blessings of overwork and was used to a high standard of living. There was the further advantage that in such a commonwealth the peasant was constantly being taken from the plough to defend his country, while the slave was exempt from military service. Thus the sphere of economic influence of such large and warlike cities saw the rise of large-scale agricultural production with slaves.[16]

The wars that provided cheap slaves ruined the Roman free peasants, who were the backbone of the army. The ruined peasant was forced to resort to banditry or else join the army of unemployed lumpenproletarians in Rome or other cities. This social disintegration led to an unprecedented wave of crime and banditry, which furnished a new source of slaves in the form of convicted criminals. Prisons were unknown, and criminals were either crucified or sentenced to forced labour.

Although slavery enormously raised the productive powers of society, it contained a contradiction. It signified an increase in the productivity of labour in the aggregate, but the labour productivity *per unit* of an individual slave was far lower than that of a free peasant.

The labour of an individual slave has a low level of productivity because it is forced labour. *Slave labour only becomes profitable when it is employed on a vast scale*. What is important is the aggregate of production, where individual slaves are literally worked to death and quickly replaced by others. Thus, the conditions of the slaves worsened continually. The big estates or *latifundia* were worked by gangs of slaves during the day, branded with a hot iron and shackled together in gangs. They were locked up at night in common, frequently subterranean labourers' prisons. Cato used to say: "A slave must either work or sleep."

Just as the nomenclature of 'capitalist' is not really adequate to describe the functions of the Roman slave owners, so the word 'proletariat' is misleading when applied to the dispossessed peasants forced to flee to the cities. There is a fundamental difference between the modern proletariat and that of the ancient world.

---

16 Ibid., p. 34.

The modern working class is the only really productive class (together with the peasantry, insofar as it still exists), but the Roman proletariat did not work – it had an entirely unproductive and parasitical character. The modern proletariat feeds society, whereas the Roman proletariat was fed *by* society – that is to say, by the slaves, who were the real productive class.

The basis of modern capitalism is the accumulation of capital for the purpose of re-investment in the means of production. Such a conception would have been totally incomprehensible to a Roman slave-owner. The existence of a mass of cheap slave labour made such an idea unnecessary.

Slavery also inhibited the development of industry and technology. The modern capitalist invests a large part of his profit for improving technology in order to get an advantage over his competitors. The case with the Roman slave-owner was very different. For the reasons already stated, only the crudest tools could be put into the hands of the slaves on the large estates. The mule was developed in the slave states of the Southern USA because the slaves could not be trusted with a horse, which was too delicate to survive in their hands. Only the crudest, most resistant implements and tools could be entrusted to the slaves. Marx had pointed this out. He says the following of "production by slave power":

> This is one of the circumstances that makes production by slave labour such a costly process. The labourer here is, to use a striking expression of the ancients, distinguishable only as *instrumentum vocale* [instrument with a voice], from an animal as *instrumentum semi-vocale*, and from an implement as *instrumentum mutum*. But he himself takes care to let both beast and implement feel that he is none of them, but is a man. He convinces himself with immense satisfaction, that he is a different being, by treating the one unmercifully and damaging the other *con amore* [with love]. Hence the principle, universally applied in this method of production, only to employ the rudest and heaviest implements and such as are difficult to damage owing to their sheer clumsiness. In the slave-states bordering on the Gulf of Mexico, down to the date of the Civil War,

> ploughs constructed on old Chinese models, which turned up the soil like a hog or a mole, instead of making furrows, were alone to be found. [...] In his *Sea Board Slave States*, Olmsted tell us: "I am here shown tools that no man in his senses, with us, would allow a labourer, for whom he was paying wages, to be encumbered with; and the excessive weight and clumsiness of which, I would judge, would make work at least ten per cent greater than with those ordinarily used with us. And I am assured that, in the careless and clumsy way they must be used by the slaves, anything lighter or less crude could not be furnished them with good economy, and that such tools as we constantly give our labourers and find our profit in giving them, would not last out a day in a Virginia cornfield – much lighter and more free from stones though it be than ours. So, too, when I ask why mules are so universally substituted for horses on the farm, the first reason given, and confessedly the most conclusive one, is that horses cannot bear the treatment that they always must get from Negroes; horses are always soon foundered or crippled by them, while mules will bear cudgelling, or lose a meal or two now and then, and not be materially injured, and they do not take cold or get sick, if neglected or overworked. But I do not need to go further than to the window of the room in which I am writing, to see at almost any time, treatment of cattle that would ensure the immediate discharge of the driver by almost any farmer owning them in the North."[17]

One of the most striking contradictions of the ancient world is that, having laid down what Marx called the historical preconditions for capitalist production, having seemingly reached the threshold of capitalism, it always drew back from the edge and failed to develop a genuine capitalist economy. Take just one example: the Greek engineer, Hero of Alexandria, invented a steam engine that worked in the first century AD. But they regarded it as a mere curiosity – a toy. Its productive potential never occurred to them. Why should it?

Thus, for the whole period of the slave economy, no great advances were made in technology and productivity remained on a low level. This in turn greatly limited the scope for the reinvestment of the

17 Marx, *Capital,* Vol. 1, *MECW,* Vol. 35, p. 207, note.

profits made by the slave owners. The ancient market remained relatively limited by the fact that the great majority of the ancient world continued to produce for their own consumption on their own lands.

Beyond the acquisition of land and usury, the slave owners, like the feudal lords who succeeded them, were not in the least interested in accumulating for investment. The purpose of accumulation was for their personal enjoyment and consumption on a most lavish scale. This explains the extravagantly luxurious lifestyle of the wealthy Romans, their sumptuous banquets and so on.

The description of the extraordinary banquets, parties and orgies that have come down to us, the consumption of such things as stuffed lark's tongues and pearls dissolved in wine, are the end result of the labour of the slaves, along with extravagant games and festivals, silk dresses, colossal public buildings and – last but not least – the free handout of grain to the unemployed mob in Rome.

Since the slave owner had no use for productive investment in labour-saving machinery, he could use his entire surplus (apart from the fixed costs and replacements of tools, cattle and slaves) for his personal consumption. There was some investment in trade and usury, but in the end, this too could not be applied in any other way than in consumption.

In some trades the number of free workers might increase in absolute terms, because of the increasing demand for luxuries, like paintings, statues and objects of art, as well as silk clothes, expensive perfumes and ointments etc. But all this luxury was squeezed from the blood, sweat and tears of an army of slaves:

> The modern capitalist is marked by the drive to heap up capital; the noble Romans of the Empire, the time at which Christianity arose, were marked by love of pleasure. The modern capitalists have accumulated capital to an extent that dwarfs the riches of the richest ancient Romans. The Croesus of all of these was said to be Nero's freedman Narcissus, with a fortune of some 20 million dollars. What is that compared to the billions of a Rockefeller? But the expenditures of the American billionaires, no matter

how reckless they are, are not to be compared with those of their Roman predecessors who served dishes of nightingales' tongues and dissolved precious pearls in vinegar.[18]

These wealthy parasites lived for pleasure, since there was nothing else they could do with the surplus extracted from the slaves. The extravagances of the ruling class were deplored by conservatives like Cato the Elder (234-149 BC), who also denounced the debilitating effects of Greek culture on the Roman mind.

"We know," says Pliny in the thirty-third book of his *Natural History*, "that Spartacus (the leader of a slave uprising) did not allow gold or silver in his camp. How our runaway slaves tower above us in largeness of spirit!"[19]

Slavery – The motor-force of Roman expansionism

A new contradiction arose out of the constant demand for more slaves to make up the shortfall, as large numbers of slaves were worked to death. As slavery can only be profitably employed on a massive scale, and since slaves do not reproduce in sufficient numbers, a constant renewal of slave labour can only be achieved through war or other violent means. Therefore, new wars were constantly needed to replenish the supply of cheap slaves.

The owners of large estates were always naturally in favour of war, as the most effective way to get cheap slaves, and of seizing new territories. This gave a powerful impetus to Roman expansionism. After the Punic Wars, the wars waged by Rome often assumed the character of large-scale slave hunts. A steady flow of cheap slaves played a fundamental role in stimulating the slave economy. War was therefore a necessary element in the Roman slave economy.

All the wars of the period ended in the capture of a vast number of prisoners, which swelled the army of slaves working in the mines and big estates on Roman territory. To cite just one example, in the Romans' third war against Macedonia, in 169 BC seventy cities

18 Kautsky, *The Foundations of Christianity*, pp. 41-2.

19 Pliny, *Natural History*, Book 33, quoted ibid., p. 46.

in Epirus alone were sacked and 150,000 of their inhabitants sold as slaves.

Appian tells us that on one occasion in Pontus prisoners of war were sold at four drachmas (less than a dollar) apiece. When Tiberius Gracchus raided Sardinia, he took as many as 80,000 captives to be dragged to the slave market at Rome, where the expression "as cheap as a Sardinian" became a proverb.

By the end of the Republic, slaves were present at all levels of social life. They were put to work on the construction of public buildings, aqueducts and roads. They also worked as carpenters and blacksmiths who repaired the farm tools and carts. Others looked after the cattle, sheep and pigs.

The wool from the sheep was spun and made into items which were used by the Roman army and navy. Roman farm products such as wine, oil, tools and meat were exported to other countries. The slaves kept accounts, cooked the master's feast and read him Greek poetry (which they sometimes composed) after it. Finally, they fought and died in the arena.

Slave revolts

Slavery in general is not possible without a reign of terror. The conditions of the slaves on the big estates worsened continually in the later Republic. The slave had no rights and had to accept whatever conditions the master offered. They could be forced to work, kept in barracks and fed only as much as was needed to keep them alive.

Whereas a free wage-worker (in theory at least) can choose his employer, and withdraw his labour to get higher wages or better conditions, this is impossible for a slave. The only alternative was to escape, but a slave who escaped from his master or refused to work would be put to death.

The only real restraint on ill-treatment or neglect was similar to that involved in looking after a horse or an ox. If a slave died it was a dead loss to the owner, who would have to pay out money for a replacement.

If there was a scarcity of slaves, this might be an argument for treating them well. However, in a period when Roman armies were conquering the world, slaves were cheap and there was no reason to treat the slaves in anything approaching a humane manner. In an age of unending wars and civil wars, the price of slaves fell continuously, as captives flooded the market.

There was a Roman proverb: "so many slaves – so many enemies". That is why Plato, Aristotle and the Carthaginian, Mago, warned masters against bringing together slaves of the same nationality, lest they should combine and stage conspiracies against their masters.

The slave-owners were always anxious about the possibility of a slave uprising. The free Romans lived permanently like a man sitting on a volcano, waiting for it to erupt. Therefore, any expression of insubordination was punished with extreme cruelty. This explains why even petty offences could be met with arbitrary and sadistic punishments.

Since, in the eyes of the law, slaves were private property, the master's power over the slave (*dominica potestas*) was absolute. He was allowed to torture, degrade, beat without cause, and even kill a slave when he was old or sick. A slave could not legally hold property, make contracts, or marry, and could testify in court only under torture.

If a slave tried to run away, he could expect to be whipped, burned with iron, or even killed. Many cases of extreme cruelty have been recorded. When a slave of Vedius Pollio broke a crystal dish, he had him thrown into a pool of lampreys to be eaten alive by the fish.

For neglect of duty or petty misconduct slaves were often punished by flogging. In more serious cases, slaves were sold to be gladiators. Since nothing was so much dreaded throughout all Italy as an uprising of the slaves, any attempt on a master's life or taking part in an insurrection was punishable with death for the criminal and his family in a most agonising form – crucifixion.

Indeed, after the defeat of Spartacus' uprising, Pompey erected 6,000 crosses along the Appian Way to Rome, on each of which a survivor of the final battle was nailed. In fact, the word *crux* (cross) was used among slaves as a curse.

In spite of all these repressive measures – indeed one could say *because* of them – there were several large-scale slave revolts, of which the uprising led by Spartacus is the best known. But there were several other cases.

The first recorded slave revolt took place in 135-132 BC, in Sicily. The origins of this uprising can be traced to the great changes of property ensuing upon the final expulsion of the Carthaginians, about the middle of the Second Punic War. An army of speculators from Italy rushed into the island and, to the general distress of the Sicilians, bought up large tracts of land at a low price, or became the occupiers of estates which had belonged to Sicilians who had supported Carthage and had been forfeited to Rome after the execution or flight of their owners.

The Sicilians of the Roman party, by contrast, became rich out of the distress of their countrymen. After the ravages of war, Italy was in need of grain. The abundance of cheap slaves which came from the war could be used to produce it and take advantage of the sure market.

Sicily was therefore flooded with slaves, employed to grow grain for the great landowners to export to Rome. The slaves were so ill-fed by their masters that they began to take to robbing the poorer Sicilians; and the masters were glad that their slaves should be maintained at the expense of others. After seventy or eighty years, these pressures broke out in the First Servile War.

Roman sources give us some idea of the kind of treatment that provoked this uprising, which was accompanied by the most horrible atrocities. The ancient historian Diodorus Siculus specifically named Damophilus, together with his wife, as one of the cruellest:

> Purchasing a large number of slaves, he treated them outrageously, marking with branding irons the bodies of men who in their own countries had been free, but who through capture in war had come to know the fate of a slave. Some of these he put in fetters and thrust into slave pens; others he designated to act as his herdsmen, but neglected to provide them with suitable clothing or food. […]

> His wife Metallis, who delighted no less in these arrogant punishments, treated her maidservants cruelly, as well as any other slaves who fell into her clutches. And because of the despiteful punishments received from them both, the slaves were filled with rage against their masters, and conceiving that they could encounter nothing worse than their present misfortunes began to form conspiracies to revolt and to murder their masters.[20]

Tormented beyond endurance, the slaves took their revenge. Damophilus and Metallis were both murdered. But their daughter, who had treated the slaves kindly, was spared, and this detail was noted by the Roman historian as proof that the slaves were not naturally bloodthirsty, but only desired to avenge themselves for the unspeakable torments inflicted on them.

When the slave army captured the town of Enna we are told that they killed 'many'. In general, the Roman historians stress the injuries the slaves inflicted on the free citizens. But we must be on our guard here, since it was in the interests of these historians to blacken the name of the slaves as much as possible in order to justify the bloody reprisals they later inflicted on the defeated rebels.

We know almost nothing of the leader of this revolt, except that he was a freeborn slave named Eunus, and seems to have been born in Syria. Styling himself 'King Antiochus', Eunus was reputed to be a magician, evidently because the Romans were embarrassed that a mere slave or freedman could defy their power, and therefore attributed magical powers to him (similar nonsense was written about Spartacus). He led the slaves of the eastern part of Sicily. The same historian informs us:

> In three days Eunus had armed, as best he could, more than 6,000 men, besides others in his train who had only axes and hatchets, or slings, or sickles, or fire-hardened stakes, or even kitchen spits; and he went about ravaging the countryside. Then, since he kept recruiting untold numbers of slaves, he ventured even to do battle with Roman generals, and on

20 Diodorus Siculus, Books 34/35, *In Twelve Volumes*, Vol. 12, pp. 79-81.

> joining combat repeatedly overcame them with his superior numbers, for he now had more than 10,000 soldiers.[21]

At the same time, in the western part of the island, a slave manager or *vilicus* named Cleon, himself a slave (also, naturally, accredited with religious and mystical powers) gathered together a slave army.

It is interesting that Cleon was a manager or overseer of slaves, that is to say, a man who was recognised by his master as having sufficient intelligence and strength of character to be put in charge of other slaves. History knows many similar examples of this kind of thing. It is known, for example, that most army mutinies were organised and led by sergeants or other non-commissioned officers. Such men tend also to be the natural leaders of the working class.

Diodorus continues:

> Meanwhile a man named Cleon, a Cilician, began a revolt of still other slaves. And though there were high hopes everywhere that the revolutionary groups would come into conflict one with the other, and that the rebels, by destroying themselves, would free Sicily of strife, contrary to expectations the two groups joined forces, Cleon having subordinated himself to Eunus at his mere command, and discharging, as it were, the function of a general serving a king; his particular band numbered 5,000 men.[22]

The Roman sources are reluctantly obliged to pay tribute to the bravery of the rebel slaves:

> Soon after, engaging in battle with a general arrived from Rome, Lucius Hypsaeus, who had 8,000 Sicilian troops, the rebels were victorious, since they now numbered 20,000. Before long their band reached a total of 200,000 [possibly this figure included women and children – *AW*], and in numerous battles with the Romans they acquitted themselves well, and failed but seldom.[23]

21 Ibid., p. 65.
22 Ibid., pp. 65-7.
23 Ibid., p. 67.

Significantly, news of the rebellion in Sicily sparked off uprisings of the slaves elsewhere – even in Rome:

> As word of this was bruited about, a revolt of 150 slaves, banded together, flared up in Rome, of more than a thousand in Attica, and of yet others in Delos and many other places. But thanks to the speed with which forces were brought up and to the severity of their punitive measures, the magistrates of these communities at once disposed of the rebels and brought to their senses any who were wavering on the verge of revolt. In Sicily, however, the trouble grew. Cities were captured with all their inhabitants, and many armies were cut to pieces by the rebels, until Rupilius, the Roman commander, recovered Tauromenium for the Romans by placing it under strict siege and confining the rebels under conditions of unspeakable duress and famine: conditions such that, beginning by eating the children, they progressed to the women, and did not altogether abstain even from eating one another.[24]

The Roman Senate was obliged to dispatch the Roman army to end the slave war. The Roman accounts that have come down to us describe Eunus as more cunning than able; but it should be remembered that these reports were written by his enemies who would not wish to depict him in a favourable light.

His lieutenant, Cleon, was given the credit for the many victories he won over the Roman forces; but this may just be spite on the part of the latter. This rebel chief must have been a man of considerable ability to have maintained his position so long, and to have commanded the services of those said to have been his superiors. Cleon fell in battle, and Eunus was made prisoner, but died before he could be brought to punishment.

This was the first of a series of three slave revolts in the Roman Republic. A second lasted from 104 until 100 BC. The leader of this slave revolt, named Salvius, led the slaves in the east of Sicily, while Athenion led the western slaves. It took Rome four years to suppress the revolt.

---

24 Ibid., pp. 67-9.

The Roman consul, Manius Aquillius, quelled the revolt only after great effort. In addition to these slave uprisings, and the great, last and most famous uprising led by Spartacus, the war against Aristonicus and his 'Heliopolites' in Asia Minor was also in reality a war of the landowners against insurgent slaves.

In some cases the free labourers made common cause with the slaves. In fact, at one point, the whole island of Sicily fell into the hands of the slaves. According to even the most moderate estimates, the active slave army amounted to at least 70,000 men capable of bearing arms.[25]

The only way of assuring the total submission of the slaves after such revolts was by applying the most ruthless and brutal methods. Thus, in every case, the revolt ended with a massacre of the slaves. In the capital of Sicily, 150 slaves were executed, in Minturnae 450, and in Sinuessa, as many as 4,000. After the suppression of the revolt in Sicily the consul Publius Rupilius ordered that every rebel slave who was captured be crucified – some 20,000 in all.

From its humble origins Roman society had been completely transformed in its economic and social relations, but the republic remained in the hands of an exclusive aristocratic club. The political superstructure no longer corresponded to the economic base. This contradiction had to be resolved, and it was resolved through the most savage class struggle.

25 Mommsen, *History of Rome*, Vol. 3, p. 104.

5. The Revolt of the Gracchi

The early Republic was an agricultural economy based upon subsistence farming. Its backbone was the class of free peasants who produced mainly for their own consumption, only exchanging the small surplus left over. In the early days of Rome money therefore played an unimportant role in the economic life of society.

But a long period of wars and foreign conquests radically transformed the Roman economy. With the emergence of Rome as a world power and the consequent expansion of trade on an international scale, money began to play a more important role, first as bronze, later as silver and gold. For the first time, exchange and money-relations began to dominate economic life.

This led to the disintegration of the old social forms. The rise of a money economy put an end to the relative equality of the early days of the Republic, and in its place we see an increasing polarisation between rich and poor that no longer corresponded to the old tribal divisions – between plebeians and patricians, noblemen and commoners.

Together with trade and money, a new 'aristocracy' of speculators, tax farmers, merchants and the like arose on the basis of money, production for exchange and the slave economy: the *equites*. The name, *equites* ('knights', derived from *equus*, a horse), was originally given to those citizens who could afford a horse and provided the cavalry in the army, but now began to refer to all those with an estate worth more than 4 million sesterces.

With the emergence of these new relations of production, the day of the free peasant was over, and so was the old Republic with its stern morality and simple soldierly virtues. Gone was the famous frugality of the Romans. Very often the new men of money were commoners, and even freedmen (former slaves). These 'new men' had no aristocratic pedigree, but they had wealth and showed it off ostentatiously.

These *nouveaux riches* dressed in silk, drank fine foreign wines and employed educated Greek slaves to recite Homer at their lavish banquets, even if neither they nor their guests understood a single word. Conservatives like Cato the Elder complained bitterly about this ostentation, but, as we have already seen, by this time old Cato was regarded as a crank when he dressed himself up in a rough peasant's tunic and went to work in the fields alongside his slaves. Such things were now seen as anachronisms.

Although in economic terms the *equites* and the old landed nobility had similar interests as defenders of private property, in political terms there were still important differences between them. The power of the old aristocracy was based on its control of the Senate, but increasingly the *equites* began to exercise a decisive influence on Roman politics.

As these 'new men' gradually accumulated vast sums of wealth, so they increasingly felt themselves to be a power in the land. They constantly jostled with the old patrician nobility for political power, creating new tensions and antagonisms within the Roman Republic.

Despite the concessions that the old nobility had been forced to give to the 'new men' in the previous period, the latter were still poorly represented in the offices of state. The government was still in the hands of a closed circle of privileged families. About 2,000 men from fewer than twenty *gentes* controlled the state and took the lion's share of the huge amounts of loot from the wars.

A good example of this is the Scipio family, which in less than a hundred years had gained no fewer than twenty-three consulships.

This was a permanent source of friction between the *equites* and the senatorial class. These great aristocratic families kept in their cupboards the wax masks of their ancestors who had held consular office. These masks were paraded in the streets at their funerals, when there were pompous speeches in praise of the dead man and all his ancestors.

Rome was now effectively divided into three rival centres of power, reflecting the interests of different classes: the official state power, the Senate, controlled by the predominantly patrician aristocracy; the voting-assemblies or *comitia*, dominated by the wealthy citizens; and the informal popular assemblies (*contiones*), where the poorest sections of the populace gathered: the proletariat, including street-boys, Jews, Egyptians and the city rabble in general. The political life of the Republic now becomes much more complicated.

A struggle opened up between defenders of the aristocracy and its opponents, whose most radical wing, the *populares*, tried to lean on the masses, as the French middle-class Jacobins did at the time of the French Revolution. We could describe the *populares* as the Roman 'popular party', although no formal parties existed in Roman society as such. Nevertheless, a distinct section of leaders, leaning on the plebeian masses, opposed themselves to the conservative faction, which would later be described as the *optimates*, or 'the best'.

The *contiones*, although they had no legal powers to decide anything, in practice controlled the streets. And the power of the street in Rome was growing. The urban poor formed a lumpenproletariat of dispossessed peasants, embittered by their expropriation and always ready to riot.

Plutarch describes the popular agitation in Rome at this time. In his *Life of Tiberius Gracchus,* he writes of the common people expressing their discontent by "setting up writings upon the porches, walls, and monuments",[1] demanding that the poor citizens be reinstated in their former possessions. This was the explosive background to the emergence of the Gracchi.

---

1 Plutarch, *Lives*, Vol. 4, 'Tiberius Gracchus', p. 324.

The agrarian question

The period that led to the fall of the Republic was characterised by a ferocious struggle between the classes, along with fierce power struggles between ambitious generals and politicians. There is an official history of this period, but there is also a secret history. In *Capital*, Marx wrote:

> For the rest, it requires but a slight acquaintance with the history of the Roman republic, for example, to be aware that its secret history is the history of its landed property.[2]

It was standard practice for the Romans to confiscate part of the land of conquered cities and states. This was made public land, which was occupied by tenants who paid rent, usually in produce, to the state. From the earliest times the patricians held the lion's share of the public lands, known as the *ager publicus*. In Rome's Italian territories the holding of public lands tended to become a monopoly of the wealthy.

No matter by what dubious means this land had been acquired, once it had been occupied for a certain length of time it was considered as the real property of the occupier, confirming the old saying that possession is nine-tenths of the law. In this way, gradually, the people were robbed of the public lands, and this was the focal point of all the great class battles in the later Roman Republic.

There were repeated attempts to pass laws regulating the distribution of public lands – the result of the struggle of the poorer classes to gain some share in the *ager publicus*. Since these lands were occupied without lease, from a strictly legal point of view, this should not have been difficult. But the law, especially as regards property, has always favoured the rich and powerful. And since most agrarian legislation challenged the wealth and privileges of the powerful, it remained a dead letter. The wealthy classes were determined to keep the lands they held, and they controlled the state and drew up the laws. Even the agrarian laws that were passed were often flagrantly disobeyed or simply ignored.

---

2 Marx, *Capital*, Vol. 1, *MECW*, Vol. 35, p. 93, note.

The most famous of early agrarian laws were the Licinio-Sextian laws (367 BC), which limited the amount of public land any citizen could hold and the number of sheep and cattle he could pasture on it. Some public lands were distributed to poor citizens, but by about 233 BC these laws had already fallen into disuse, and the situation of the poor peasants had become increasingly difficult.

The next serious attempt to solve the agrarian problem was the *Lex Sempronia Agraria* of 133 BC. This will be forever associated with the name of one of the most remarkable figures in Roman history: Tiberius Sempronius Gracchus.

Gracchus was not a plebeian but an outstanding member of the Roman aristocracy, whose father had held high office. Tiberius and his brother Gaius, known to history as 'the Gracchi', came from a prestigious patrician family. They were the sons of Sempronius Gracchus and Cornelia, the daughter of Scipio Africanus, the famous general who had defeated Hannibal.

With such a pedigree, Gracchus would normally be destined to take his place with the ruling aristocracy and hold high office in the state. But instead, he broke with his class and became the most celebrated leader of the Roman poor – the proletariat. Despite his impeccable aristocratic credentials, Tiberius Gracchus was destined to launch himself on a course that would destroy the social and political equilibrium of the Republic.

This is not the only case in history where outstanding members of the ruling class come over to the side of the revolution. In *The Communist Manifesto* Marx and Engels point out:

> … in times when the class struggle nears the decisive hour, the progress of dissolution going on within the ruling class, in fact within the whole range of old society, assumes such a violent, glaring character, that a small section of the ruling class cuts itself adrift, and joins the revolutionary class, the class that holds the future in its hands.[3]

3 Marx and Engels, *The Communist Manifesto*, *The Classics of Marxism: Volume One*, p. 12.

We see the same process in other periods also. Marx points out that in the period of the decay of feudalism, a section of the nobility went over to the bourgeoisie. So in a period of intense class struggle in the Roman Republic, certain individuals broke away from their class and attempted to represent the interests of the oppressed classes.

It may be argued that the Gracchi did not have a consistently revolutionary policy, that they vacillated and attempted to compromise, and that this eventually led to defeat. But when we consider that these men had no selfish reason to do what they did, and that they gave their lives fighting for the cause, surely they deserve to be remembered for their courage and not for their weaknesses.

Tiberius Gracchus was clearly a man of high principles and extraordinary talent, a fact that was grudgingly accepted even by his critics. Seventy-five years after Gracchus' death, Cicero considered him to be among the best orators Rome had ever produced, but he also saw him as a dangerous demagogue. He wrote: "I only wish that Tiberius Sempronius Gracchus [...] had possessed political intentions as good as [his] oratorical talents", and he added: "If so, [his] renown would have been the most splendid in the world."[4]

To us today his proposals for reform do not seem excessively radical, but they had revolutionary implications. It was almost unheard of for Roman politicians to deal with social or economic problems and such problems seldom played any part in senatorial debates. The idea that a senator or politician might represent a particular social class was completely alien to the Romans. Tiberius was the first one to address the growing problems in the city of Rome itself, and tried to solve the economic crisis in the countryside by rallying the oppressed masses.

Gracchus clashes with the Senate

How did this man become a revolutionary? Probably there are several different reasons. Cicero wrote: "He took the office because he was so infuriated with the nobility".[5] His clash with the Senate seems to

4 Cicero, *On Government*, p. 254.

5 Ibid.

have its origins in an incident during the Numantian war in Spain (143-133 BC), when the name of Tiberius Sempronius Gracchus first comes to our attention.

He apparently became interested in the land question when he travelled to Spain, and observed the decline of smallholdings in Etruria. Plutarch writes:

> ... while Tiberius was travelling through Etruria on his way to Numantia, he saw for himself how the country had been deserted by its native inhabitants, and how those who tilled the soil or tended the flocks were barbarian slaves introduced from abroad; and that it was this experience which inspired the policy that later brought so many misfortunes upon the two brothers.[6]

He saw with his own eyes how the Italian smallholders, whom Rome depended on to provide men for her army, were declining in numbers, undermined by competition from the huge farms worked by armies of slaves. The smallholdings were everywhere in decline, although they had by no means disappeared by this time. Tiberius Gracchus drew the conclusion that the destruction of the class of free peasants would undermine Rome itself.

As a member of an aristocratic family, Tiberius Gracchus could have expected a distinguished senatorial career, following in his father's footsteps to both the consulship and the censorship. But his reputation was undermined by a reckless decision he took in Spain. In the Numantian campaign, Tiberius served with distinction as quaestor, and earned the respect of the Spaniards for his bravery and honesty. Such was his reputation for honesty and fairness that the Numantines insisted on negotiating with a man who had treated the Iberians better than other Romans, who frequently reneged on their promises.

But his conduct gave rise to an incident that changed his life and the course of Roman history. In order to save the army of the consul Gaius Hostilius Mancinus, which was trapped and facing certain

---

6 Plutarch, *The Makers of Rome*, 'Tiberius Gracchus', p. 161.

destruction, Tiberius staked his reputation by concluding a treaty with the Spaniards – without first consulting the Senate. Plutarch credited Tiberius Gracchus with saving the lives of 20,000 Roman citizens through this agreement. But there was a problem. The Senate had not been consulted about this deal and promptly rejected it and sent the commander Mancinus in chains back to Numantia in 136 BC.

The actions of the Senate mortified Tiberius. A Roman aristocrat was brought up to prize above all else his *dignitas*, a more complicated idea than dignity in English. It means not just dignity, but status and honour. Tiberius had given his word to the Spaniards, and the Senate broke it. He considered this a dishonourable action, which not merely betrayed the Numantines, but also disgraced him.

Tiberius' brother-in-law Scipio Aemilianus did his best to shelter him from the dishonour of the Numantian affair, but to no effect. This betrayal had a profound effect on Gracchus, who took deep and lasting offence at the Senate. This set in motion a chain reaction which exercised a fatal influence on Roman history for more than a century.

Tiberius Gracchus became the mortal enemy of the Senate and the Roman aristocracy. He entered the political arena, and in 133 BC he shocked the Roman system by standing not for the office of magistrate, but for the office of Tribune of the Plebs. This was a bold and fateful step to take.

The tribunate carried with it important powers: the power to veto and to propose law. But the ruling class had always assumed that it could buy off the tribunes and use them to police the masses. They never thought that such an office would be held by a significant political figure such as Tiberius Gracchus, or that it would be used in a serious attempt to change society. They were wrong.

The moment Gracchus stood for the office it was clear that he was seeking to use his power to rival that of the consuls. In so doing, he was acting according to the letter of the law, but he was doing things that were not in the original script. This was extremely dangerous. It was as if the modern Labour leaders were to make use of the machinery of formal parliamentary democracy to pass laws to expropriate the capitalists. That also is not in the script!

This action set Tiberius Gracchus on a collision course with the Senate. The hatred felt by the aristocracy towards him was so intense because they saw him as a traitor to his class. He was the first member of the Roman senatorial class to break ranks. His actions offended the strong spirit of solidarity that always exists within the ruling class. They wanted to destroy him utterly. For his part, he was looking for a fight.

Tiberius Gracchus was no doubt a courageous and sincere man, convinced of the need for a change. He was a social reformer, an idealist who was influenced by the philosophical doctrines of the Stoics of the brotherhood of man. His critics said that he had spent too much time listening to Greeks. As we have noted, according to his contemporaries, he was an excellent orator. The following speech recorded by Plutarch is probably not authentic but invented by Plutarch (this was standard procedure with the ancient writers). But it undoubtedly conveys the spirit, if not the letter, of his agitation:

> "The savage beasts", said he, "in Italy, have their particular dens, they have their places of repose and refuge; but the men who bear arms, and expose their lives for the safety of their country, enjoy in the meantime nothing more in it but the air and light; and, having no houses or settlements of their own, are constrained to wander from place to place with their wives and children."
>
> He told them that the commanders were guilty of a ridiculous error, when, at the head of their armies, they exhorted the common soldiers to fight for their sepulchres and altars; when not any amongst so many Romans is possessed of either altar or monument, neither have they any houses of their own, or hearths of their ancestors to defend. They fought indeed and were slain, but it was to maintain the luxury and the wealth of other men. They were styled the masters of the world, but in the meantime had not one foot of ground which they could call their own.[7]

7 Plutarch, *The Lives of Noble Grecians and Romans*, 'Tiberius Gracchus', p. 675.

Despite the implacable opposition of the aristocracy, Tiberius Gracchus obtained some important backers for his candidature to the tribunate, including a number of key senators and ex-consuls. This may reflect the power of old family ties and personal friendships, or maybe they simply did not take his populist propaganda very seriously.

In the same way, members of the British establishment did not take seriously the communist convictions of Burgess, Maclean and Philby because they were members of the upper class and had been educated at Eton and Cambridge – until they turned out to be Soviet spies. And if the senators had looked more closely at his programme for taking office, they might have seen that he was very serious indeed.

Tiberius Gracchus was elected tribune in 133 BC on a platform of distributing land to the urban poor and limiting the land that each individual could hold. This was hugely popular with the poor but – in spite of significant concessions to the wealthy landowners – it provoked the anger of the patrician reactionaries who blocked his proposed reforms. This sharpened the class conflict, giving it a revolutionary character.

The Sempronian Law

The support that Gracchus got at first from the most powerful of Rome's politicians may indicate that at least a section of the ruling class understood that land reform was both necessary and overdue. His original proposals were not very radical. Many of the *latifundia* were actually situated on public land, which they rented for ridiculously small sums from the state, if they paid anything at all. In his *Life of Tiberius Gracchus*, Plutarch writes:

> Of the land which the Romans gained by conquest from their neighbours, part they sold publicly, and turned the remainder into common; this common land they assigned to such of the citizens as were poor and indigent, for which they were to pay only a small acknowledgement into the public treasury. But when the wealthy men began to offer larger rents,

> and drive the poorer people out, it was enacted by law, that no person whatever should enjoy more than 500 acres[8] of ground. This act for some time checked the avarice of the richer, and was of great assistance to the poorer people, who retained under it their respective proportions of ground, as they had been formerly rented by them. Afterwards the rich men of the neighbourhood contrived to get these lands again into their possession, under other people's names, and at last would not stick to claim most of them publicly in their own. The poor, who were thus deprived of their farms, were no longer either ready, as they had formerly been, to serve in war or careful in the education of their children; insomuch that in a short time there were comparatively few freemen remaining in all Italy, which swarmed with workhouses full of foreign-born slaves. These the rich men employed in cultivating their ground of which they dispossessed the citizens.[9]

Tiberius devised a plan to distribute land to the urban poor and landless peasants. The Licinian laws were easily circumvented and they had been turned into a dead letter, but they had never been revoked. Tiberius Gracchus therefore could argue that his proposed reforms were based upon law.

The *Lex Agraria* proposed by Gracchus in 133 BC reaffirmed the provisions of the Licinio-Sextian laws and added to the maximum allowance an extra amount for each son. He proposed to limit the amount of land a man could own to no more than 500 *iugera* (300 acres). To conciliate the big landowners, he offered to allow the current holders of public land to keep 500 *iugera* as their undisputed property, plus another 250 *iugera* for each of two sons.

Any wealthy man with at least two sons would therefore be allowed to keep 1000 *iugera*, twice the limit set down by the Licinio-Sextian laws. The remaining public land was to be redistributed in plots of thirty acres to families of smallholders. The intention was to create thousands of new landowners, from whom Rome would recruit soldiers for her armies. The plots, once granted, were supposed to

8 The Licinian law limited holdings to 500 *iugera*, roughly 300 modern acres.

9 Plutarch, *Lives*, Vol. 4, 'Tiberius Gracchus', pp. 323-4.

be inalienable. They could not be sold or transferred to new owners, other than by inheritance from father to son.

In compensation for their losses, the occupants of public land were to receive full title to the land they retained. This was a huge concession to the rich, who would be allowed to keep a large amount of public land, in addition to any other lands they already outright owned, which would have remained untouched. In effect, the old Licinio-Sextian law on the land would have been superseded, and the big landowners would have their vast estates legitimised.

This was intended to make the reforms palatable to the rich landowners. By this measure Tiberius Gracchus hoped to reduce the opposition of the wealthy landowners to his reform. But this was a vain hope. Despite the moderate nature of his proposals, the wealthy classes were bitterly opposed to everything Tiberius Gracchus stood for. Plutarch describes their rabid hostility:

> But though this reformation was managed with so much tenderness, that, all the former transactions being passed over, the people were only thankful to prevent abuses of the like nature for the future, yet, on the other hand, the moneyed men, and those of great estates, were exasperated, through their covetous feelings against the law itself, and against the lawgiver, through anger and party-spirit. They therefore endeavoured to seduce the people, declaring that Tiberius was designing a general redivision of lands, to overthrow the government, and throw all things into confusion.[10]

How familiar these lines sound today! Nowadays, the ruling class would use the mass media to launch a campaign against the 'threat to democracy' posed by socialism. We saw this in the hysterical campaign in the media in the USA, which recently tried to present a very timid attempt to reform the health system more or less as an attempt to push through a socialist revolution and "sovietise American medicine". This fact shows how little has changed in over 2,000 years of class struggle. The names and circumstances have changed, but the psychology of the ruling class has not.

---

10 Ibid., p. 325.

Aristocratic reaction

For the conservative aristocrats who sat in the Senate, even minor political differences seemed to be matters of fundamental principle. They saw any attempt to restrict their powers as an attack on the Republic. It was particularly intolerable that those who were agitating for reform were men from their own class. Tiberius Gracchus knew he would have to face a stiff fight. Similar land reform had been proposed roughly ten years earlier by Gaius Laelius, but these proposals were shipwrecked on the rock of senatorial opposition.

Naturally, the most strenuous opposition came from those who held large quantities of public land. They faced losing the lion's share of their public lands, and some of them had no great private estates to fall back on. Many senators were themselves large landowners holding vast tracts of public land.

They furiously opposed the reform as a radical attack on the principle of private property. They also understood that a land redistribution that would involve settling 70,000 families on public land would create a mass base of clients loyal to Tiberius. For such men, Gracchus' law could represent a serious threat. Among these opponents, the most implacable was Publius Cornelius Scipio Nasica, a former consul, who was one of the principal holders of public land.

The new land reform bill was carefully drafted. But Gracchus took a revolutionary step when he presented the bill directly to the Plebeian Council (*concilium plebis*). He did not submit the law for review to the Senate. This was not strictly required by law but it was the usual practice.

Why did Tiberius Gracchus proceed in this way? The reason is unclear. Did he want to take his revenge on the Senate, treating them with contempt for having betrayed him over the Numantia affair? It seems more likely that he sought to by-pass the Senate where he would meet stiff opposition, and appeal directly to the people.

Whatever his reasons were, the senators were outraged. They did everything in their power to block the bill's progress. When voting day arrived, the party of the rich prevented a vote by the simple expedient of seizing the voting urns. The masses confronted them and were preparing for a fight.

Rome now seemed on the brink of revolution. But once again the situation was saved by the cunning of the ruling class and the vacillations of the leaders of the popular party. Two distinguished men of consular rank, Manilius and Flavius, threw themselves to their knees before Tiberius and implored him to stop the proceedings and instead take the matter to the Senate.

Tiberius agreed out of respect for their rank. This shows the limitations of his outlook. Despite his undoubted sincerity, he had not yet given up all hope of convincing the Senate of the correctness of his proposals. Tiberius appealed to the Senate. What was the result? There was no result because the aristocracy dominated the proceedings. The masses were demobilised and the initiative, at least for now, was lost.

Intervention of the masses

We can only explain the conduct of Tiberius Gracchus by the fact that he was not proposing a revolution against the Senate, but a reform that was calculated to prevent revolution and save the Republic through an agrarian reform that would save the small peasantry. But for the wealthy and powerful such proposals sounded like a call to subvert all property, undermine the state and provoke a general revolution. Feeling themselves threatened, the aristocrats armed a large number of their followers and slaves. They were preparing for a showdown.

Stirred up by the prospect of land, large numbers of country people flocked to Rome to vote for the bill, which was easily passed in the plebeian assembly. The Senate struck back. They bribed another tribune, Marcus Octavius, to veto the bill.

This was a scandalous move, because this man was using his position to frustrate the will of the people he was supposed to represent. The tribunate had never been intended for this purpose. But the office of tribune was being corrupted and turned into the tool of the senatorial order. The tribune's veto seemed to spell the end of the reform.

One might have expected Tiberius Gracchus either to retreat or seek to do some kind of deal with the Senate. But this time he did no such thing. Instead, he passed onto the offensive. First he offered Octavius (who, it seems, was himself the owner of public land) to compensate him out of his own pocket for any losses he incurred, on condition that he would drop his veto on the bill. Octavius refused.

Then Gracchus proposed that unless he withdrew his veto, Octavius should be removed from office. What he was demanding was *the right of recall*. In a desperate attempt to avoid a head-on confrontation, Tiberius tried to appeal to Octavius before the popular assembly. Plutarch describes the scene very vividly:

> When the people were met together again, Tiberius placed himself in the rostra, and endeavoured a second time to persuade Octavius. But all being to no purpose, he referred the whole matter to the people, calling on them to vote at once, whether Octavius should be deposed or not; and when seventeen of the thirty-five tribes had already voted against him, and there wanted only the votes of one tribe more for his final deprivation, Tiberius put a short stop to the proceedings, and once more renewed his importunities; he embraced and kissed him before all the assembly, begging with all the earnestness imaginable, that he would neither suffer himself to incur the dishonour, nor him to be reputed the author and promoter of so odious a measure. Octavius, we are told, did seem a little softened and moved with these entreaties; his eyes filled with tears, and he continued silent for a considerable time. But presently looking towards the rich men and proprietors of estates, who stood gathered in a body together, partly for shame, and partly for fear of disgracing himself with them, he boldly bade Tiberius use any severity he pleased. The law for his deprivation being thus voted, Tiberius ordered one of his servants, whom he had made a freeman, to remove Octavius from the rostra, employing his own domestic freed servants in the stead of the public officers. And it made the action seem all the sadder, that Octavius was dragged out in such an ignominious manner. The people immediately assaulted him, whilst the rich men ran in to his assistance. Octavius, with some difficulty, was snatched away, and safely conveyed out of the crowd; though a trusty servant of his, who had placed himself in front of his master that he might assist his

> escape, in keeping off the multitude, had his eyes struck out, much to the displeasure of Tiberius, who ran with all haste, when he perceived the disturbance, to appease the rioters.[11]

In these lines we can clearly see the class forces at work. The two opposing forces, the aristocracy and the masses, are pulling in opposite directions. It is a clash of mutually incompatible interests. In the middle we have the social reformer, Tiberius Gracchus, who has set in motion forces beyond his control.

He begins to fear that the situation is slipping out of his hands and pleads with the other side to see reason. But the other side is obdurate and will not budge an inch. The masses, enraged, intervene and force the issue. For the time being, the Senate is forced to retreat.

After Octavius refused to withdraw his veto for the second time, and was promptly voted out of office and dragged from the speaker's podium, he was replaced with another candidate. Another Roman historian, Appian, describes the euphoria of the people in this moment:

> Gracchus became immensely popular by reason of the law and was escorted home by the multitude as though he were the founder, not of a single city or race, but of all the nations of Italy. After this the victorious party returned to the fields from which they had come to attend to this business. The defeated ones remained in the city and talked the matter over, feeling aggrieved, and saying that as soon as Gracchus should become a private citizen he would be sorry that he had done despite to the sacred and inviolable office of tribune, and had sown in Italy so many seeds of future strife.[12]

Sabotage by the Senate

When Tiberius Gracchus persuaded the Plebeian Council to impeach the tribune, he committed an unconstitutional act that was absolutely without precedent. Cicero later used this disagreement between two

11 Ibid., pp. 328-9.

12 Appian, *Roman History*, Vol. 3, *The Civil Wars*, Book 1, pp. 28-9.

tribunes as an example of the wonderful flexibility of the Roman constitution:

> "The tribunes have too much power", you say. Yes, that is undeniable. But the power of the popular Assembly has a much more cruel and violent potential. Yet, in practice, that potential sometimes makes for greater mildness when there is a leader to keep the Assembly under control. [...] For no board of tribunes, surely, would ever be so outrageously constituted that not a single one of its members remained sane! Indeed, what caused the overthrow of Tiberius Sempronius Gracchus was the fact the he had an opponent on his own board, whose veto he brushed aside and whose powers he took away. For that, indeed, is what brought about his downfall: his removal of one of his own colleagues from office, because he had exercised his right of veto against Tiberius Gracchus.[13]

The Senate had suffered a setback, but was by no means prepared to concede defeat. Tiberius' agrarian law was finally passed without opposition and a new tribune was elected to replace the deposed Octavius. But the Senate still held a strong card in its hand: *its control over finances.*

A commission was set up to supervise the distribution of land to the people. However, the Senate sabotaged the measure by withholding the funds that were necessary to help stock the new smallholdings. Without money to provide the basic necessities, the plots distributed under the reform would not be viable farms.

Tiberius Gracchus now took a drastic step, which brought the struggle between the two factions to a head. Attalus, king of Pergamon, who had died childless, bequeathed his treasury to the Roman state. Tiberius Gracchus proposed that this wealth be divided up between the citizens of Rome in order to fund the land commission and help set up farms for new settlers. In effect, he confiscated a large amount of money in order to finance the work of the agrarian commission.

Thanks to this measure, the commission could begin distributing land. But such an action was in complete disregard for tradition,

13 Cicero, *On Government*, p. 205.

which gave the Senate control of all overseas affairs. Although nowhere was this explicitly stated by Roman law, Tiberius' action was a direct challenge to the Senate.

And that was not all. He also proposed to reduce the length of military service, and to introduce the right of appeal against the verdicts of juries (up to then composed exclusively of senators). In short, he was trying to reduce the powers of the Senate by every means possible.

The reactionaries in the Senate were alarmed by the passage of the bill, the deposition of the tribune and the confiscation of Attilus' legacy. They were even more alarmed by the mass following Tiberius was acquiring among the poor. The Senate was forced to accept the situation, but was only playing for time. The reactionaries had no intention of limiting themselves to peaceful and legal means.

The murder of Tiberius Gracchus

The seizure of the Pergamene treasury in defiance of the Senate was a turning point. Tiberius Gracchus had made powerful enemies. Many of his former allies now broke away, once they saw he was serious about his intentions. He was now in a dangerous position.

There were plenty of people out to destroy him. The fundamental issue at this point was no longer the land reform. The question was: *Who rules Rome?* There was now an open clash between the Senate and the Plebeian Council. The situation was completely polarised: on one side were Tiberius Gracchus and his supporters, the poor peasants and proletarians, on the other, the senators, the patricians, and the big landowners.

There were two rival centres of power in society, a situation resembling what Lenin called dual power: On the one hand, the Senate, which was in the hands of the slave-holding aristocracy; on the other, the Plebeian Council, representing the free masses. This contradiction could not be settled by laws and constitutions, by speeches and votes. It could only be settled by violent struggle.

The reactionaries now saw their opportunity. Tiberius' term as tribune was nearing its end. Once he no longer had immunity from prosecution as a tribune, he would be a dead man. The only way to prevent this was to stand for a new term of tribune. But for him to run for a second term as tribune was yet another unconstitutional action. He decided upon this desperate recourse.

As a matter of fact, his chances of winning the re-election for the tribunate were very poor. A large part of his base was in the rural areas, where the peasants were busy with the harvest. His powerful political allies had abandoned him and he had lost the support of his fellow tribunes. But the senators did not want to take any chances.

These tactics used by counter-revolutionaries of every period are well known. The reactionaries accuse their enemies of wishing to install a 'tyranny'. They agitate around this false accusation in order to incite violence, while at the same time publicly adopting a defensive stance: "We will not be the ones who cast the first stone. We are only trying to defend the existing order and institutions of society, and protect the rights of the citizens."

While posing as the injured party that was trying to 'defend' themselves, the aristocracy was in fact preparing a violent aggression against Gracchus and the popular party. The Roman ruling elite decided that their only hope was to behead the mass movement: to kill Tiberius Gracchus. But since Tiberius was too powerful to attack directly, his opponents decided to play a waiting game.

The reactionary forces began to prepare the ground carefully. They gathered around Publius Nasica, the Pontifex Maximus, who was in charge of religious observances and, by chance, Tiberius' cousin. They began by provoking a riot in the Senate:

> They created uproar in the Senate, and Nasica demanded that the consul must act now to protect the state and put down the tyrant. The consul answered in conciliatory fashion that he would not be the first to use violence, and would put no citizen to death without a regular trial.[14]

There was violence also in the Plebeian Council, where the reactionaries were attempting to gain support by bribery or other

14 Plutarch, *The Makers of Rome*, 'Tiberius Gracchus', p. 171.

means. The masses on the other hand attempted to make use of their existing rights to express their grievances, and this led to open fights in the assembly, with the supporters of Gracchus attempting to physically expel the aristocrats and their supporters.

The Gracchan faction held the Capitol where the voting assemblies met. According to Appian, Nasica led a mob of nobles and senators armed with clubs to the Capitol where Tiberius Gracchus was addressing his supporters.

As a supreme irony, the unsuspecting supporters of Gracchus gave way as a sign of respect for the senatorial rank. This polite gesture was answered by a show of naked force. The frenzied reactionaries attacked the meeting and battered Tiberius Gracchus' brains out on the steps of the Temple of Fidelity. The scene is described by Plutarch:

> The senators' followers were armed with clubs and staves, which they had brought from their houses. The senators themselves snatched up the legs and fragments of the benches which the crowd had broken in their hurry to escape, and made straight for Tiberius, lashing out at those who were drawn up in front of him. His protectors were quickly scattered or clubbed down, and as Tiberius turned to run, someone caught hold of his clothing. He threw off his toga and fled in his tunic, but then stumbled over some of the prostrate bodies in front of him. As he struggled to his feet, one of his fellow tribunes, Publius Satyreius, as everybody agrees, dealt the first blow, striking him on the head with the leg of a bench. Lucius Rufus claimed to have given him the second, and prided himself upon this as if it were some noble exploit. More than 300 men were killed by blows from sticks and stones, but none by the sword.[15]

For the first time in almost four centuries, there was open violence and bloodshed in Rome among members of the ruling elite. "All other disputes", wrote Plutarch, "although they were neither trivial in themselves nor concerned with trivial objects, were resolved by

15 Ibid., pp. 171-2.

some form of compromise, with the Senate making concessions through fear of the people and the people out of respect for the Senate."[16]

White terror

The terror that followed was similar to all other such episodes in history. The ruling class took its revenge on the defeated party with the utmost cruelty and ruthlessness. In the proscriptions that followed, the supporters of Gracchus were hunted down and killed like animals. The vengeful spite of the aristocratic party was vented even on the dead bodies of its enemies. Plutarch comments:

> They refused his brother's request for permission to take up the body and bury it at night: instead they threw it into the Tiber together with the rest of the dead. And this was not all. Some of Tiberius' supporters were banished without a trial, while others were arrested and executed, Diophanes the rhetorician among them. A certain Gaius Villius was shut up in a vessel with vipers and other poisonous snakes and put to death in this way.[17]

The bitterness at all levels of society is indicated by the rumour that the war hero Scipio Aemilianus had been murdered by his wife, Sempronia, who was the sister of Tiberius Gracchus, because of Scipio's refusal to condemn the murder of Tiberius Gracchus.

The rich senators, having killed Gracchus, found that it was not the end of the matter. Powerful class forces had been unleashed from below. Such was the strength of the movement that the Senate was forced to accept at least a partial implementation of Tiberius' reforms.

But this was only a means of controlling the masses and eventually overturning those very same reforms. The destruction of the small free peasants and the concentration of land in the hands of the wealthy was an unstoppable process.

---

16 Ibid., p. 172.

17 Ibid.

The murder of Tiberius Gracchus changed everything. It introduced violence onto the streets of Rome as a political weapon. All hopes of a political consensus died with Tiberius. There was now no question of compromise. Neither side paid any attention to the laws or the 'rules of the game'. It was a fight to the finish between the contending classes. Appian writes:

> So perished on the Capitol, and while still tribune, Gracchus, the son of that Gracchus who was twice consul, and of Cornelia, daughter of that Scipio who robbed Carthage of her supremacy. He lost his life in consequence of a most excellent design too violently pursued; and this abominable crime, the first that was perpetrated in the public assembly, was seldom without parallels thereafter from time to time. On the subject of the murder of Gracchus the city was divided between sorrow and joy. Some mourned for themselves and for him, and deplored the present condition of things, believing that the commonwealth no longer existed, but had been supplanted by force and violence.[18]

Although reaction was once more in the saddle in Rome, the murder had solved nothing for the aristocracy. Objectively, the problems of the poor and the dispossessed peasantry continued to worsen, providing a fertile soil for revolutionary agitation. Marx explains that the revolution sometimes needs the whip of the counter-revolution. The masses were enraged by the murder of Tiberius. They insulted the counter-revolutionary senators in the streets.

Tiberius' younger brother Gaius was put on trial, but defended himself energetically and was cleared. By contrast, Nasica, the murderer of Tiberius, was disgraced and forced into exile, posted to the new province of Asia (in modern-day Turkey), where he died under suspicious circumstances.

The aristocratic party concentrated its attacks on the agrarian reform, determined to remove the last remaining barrier to its seizing all the remaining land. But the Senate did not feel strong enough to reverse Gracchus' land law. The popular party was

---

18 Appian, *Roman History*, Vol. 3, *The Civil Wars*, Book 1, p. 35.

equally determined to keep the laws that defended what was left of the free peasantry.

Faced with the sullen anger of the people, the Senate retreated and named a land commission to carry out some of the reforms that Tiberius had demanded. For a time, it even seemed to be succeeding. By 125 BC, 7,000 citizens were added to the list of those liable for military service, when compared to the census figures of 131 BC.

The Senate was forced to buy peace for a while by squeezing the provinces with high taxes. While keeping the merchants and the urban poor quiet by a combination of concession and repression, the slave-owning aristocracy continued to concentrate more land into its hands. They plundered Italy shamelessly, ruining the small peasants and driving them out, creating an economic and social disaster. Small farms in Italy, says Mommsen, "disappeared like raindrops in the sea."[19]

Many dispossessed Italians began to drift into Rome, agitating for greater rights. This added to the political ferment in the city. In 126 BC the tribune Iunius Pennus passed a law expelling non-citizens from Rome. This measure was really targeted at evicting the Italian agitators. To what extent it was ever enforced against the rich foreign merchants and traders is unclear. It is obvious that many of them circumvented this law, which was directed against the poor non-Roman citizens.

Italian discontent became so dangerous that in 125 BC consul Marcus Fulvius Flaccus proposed to grant full citizenship to the Latins and Latin privileges to all Italians in preparation of eventual full citizenship.

But this met with opposition on two fronts. The senators saw the mass of Italians as a threat to their political authority, as they had no hold of political patronage over them. And the Roman poor saw any increase of the number of citizens as a threat to their privileges as Roman citizens. The measure stood little chance of success, but just to make sure, the Senate sent Flaccus off to Massilia to fight the Saluvii.

---

19 Mommsen, *History of Rome*, Vol. 3, p. 170.

Unable to win by force, the Senate temporarily resorted to intrigue and bribery. They offered to increase the ration of corn and to give land to the landless Roman citizens (at the expense of the Italian peasants). But this was only meant to buy time while they prepared behind the scenes to deal with their enemies in the traditional way.

Later the class struggle assumed a violent form again, with new conflicts on the streets and murders. The ruling class, not yet sure of the situation, had to tread with care. They allowed the distribution of public land to proceed and proposed that the people should elect a new commissioner to succeed Gracchus.

The struggle therefore continued, but there was a situation of deadlock between the classes. A class of no more than 2,000 wealthy families decided everything. But the whole state was now in a palpable state of decline. The upper class showed itself as utterly degenerate and unfit to hold power, while the masses sought a way out of the crisis.

Gaius Gracchus

The people had learned to challenge the authority of the Senate. Tiberius had turned the popular party into a viable political movement. After his murder it was impossible to make the constitution of the Republic work effectively. How could the laws work when the people understood that the legal code was only the formal expression of the class interests of their masters? Tiberius Gracchus had tried to base himself on the people. He failed, but there would be others willing to try it again.

Gaius Gracchus, the brother of the murdered Tiberius, assumed leadership of the popular party. Like his brother he advocated a programme that was aimed at breaking the power of the aristocracy. He was a political agitator who started a hundred years of civil war that brought the Roman Republic to the point of exhaustion. He enjoyed immense popularity with the masses, and equally was hated by the rich and powerful:

> All the most distinguished men in Rome without exception joined forces to oppose him, but such an immense multitude poured into the city from various parts of Italy to support his candidature that many of them could find no lodging; and since the Campus Martius was too small to hold them, they climbed up to the attics and housetops to declare their support for Gaius.[20]

Despite Gaius' popularity, the aristocrats succeeded in gerrymandering the elections to the post of tribune, so that he came fourth, instead of first, as expected. But no trickery could prevent his meteoric rise.

The agrarian law of Tiberius Gracchus was being applied in a reactionary manner, at the expense of the Italian peasants. This created a profound sense of grievance amongst Rome's Italian allies. As we have seen, a prominent member of the Gracchan camp, Fulvius Flaccus, argued strenuously that the Italians should be granted Roman citizenship as compensation for any disadvantages they should suffer from agrarian reform, and Gaius agreed. The Italian question finally proved to be his undoing.

The Senate tried to get rid of Flaccus by sending him off as consul to Gaul to protect the Roman allies of Massilia (now Marseilles) who had appealed for help against the Celtic tribes. The manoeuvre backfired. He later returned in triumph, having won victories over the Gauls. In the meantime, Gaius Gracchus had finished his term of office as quaestor in Sardinia, and returned to Rome to take the place of his brother. Nine years after his brother's murder, at the age of about thirty, Gaius was elected as people's tribune in 123 BC.

Gaius' main base was the city poor, the proletariat, which looked to him to provide them with their rations and land. He planned to expand his base, forming a broad opposition based on the city masses, the wealthy *equites* and the Italians.

The programme initiated by the younger Gracchus was even more far-reaching than that of his brother. He demanded that the soldiers should be supplied with clothing at the public expense, with no

20 Plutarch, *The Makers of Rome*, 'Gaius Gracchus', p. 177.

deduction from their pay, and that nobody under the age of seventeen should be conscripted. He also demanded a reduction in the price of grain sold to the public.

He had a law passed adding to the 300 members of the Senate another 300 drawn from the class of *equites*, although this law does not seem to have been put into effect. He launched an ambitious programme of public works, such as roads and harbours, which mainly benefited the equestrian class. By such means he succeeded in splitting the *equites* away from the Senate.

With this broad coalition, Gaius was able to remain in office for two years, during which he pushed through a lot of legislation. He reaffirmed Tiberius' land laws and established smallholdings in Roman territory abroad, creating new colonies, including one on the old site of the destroyed city of Carthage.

He proposed to divide up the public lands among the poor citizens. But once again he was met with sabotage. The Senate allowed the new tenants to sell their new land, which the wealthy bought up. This was a regular feature, by which the Senate turned every attempt at reform into a dead letter.

Every time newly acquired lands were assigned to the poor, they simply passed into the hands of the wealthy landholders. In the meantime, large-scale slave labour drove all before it, tearing up the laws and mercilessly displacing free peasant labour throughout Italy.

The aristocracy was able to control the assembly of all Roman citizens (*comitia tributa*) because, with each tribe controlling a single block vote determined by the majority, the voting power of the urban proletariat was concentrated within four tribes. On the other hand, the rural tribes numbered thirty-one.

The landowners could therefore register themselves, together with their freedmen and clients, and this body of interests could usually dominate the assembly, since the small farmers seldom travelled to Rome in great numbers and never stayed there for long. Originally this system had been devised to prevent the interests of the farmers being swamped by those of the urban masses. But now it was a weapon in the hands of the slave-owning aristocracy.

In order to please the *equites*, Gaius awarded them the right to contract for the collecting of the enormous taxes due from the newly created province of Asia. It was further agreed that members of the equestrian class should hold judgement in court cases over provincial governors accused of wrong-doings. This was clearly an attempt to cut down the power of the Senate, as it restricted its power over the governors, many of whom were *equites*, filling their pockets at the expense of the provinces.

Gaius wished to expand the franchise to give the vote to the Italians, in order to increase his basis of support. But these measures were controversial and exposed the contradictions within the popular camp. The reactionaries then skilfully utilised anti-Italian feeling to divide the masses and thus the city poor united with the Senate to defeat this proposal.

The lumpen rabble did not want to share their privileges as Roman citizens with anybody. Since this, "seemed to these people, so to speak, like a partnership which gave them a claim to share in sundry very tangible profits, direct and indirect, they were not at all disposed to enlarge the number of the partners."[21]

The struggle between the classes had reached the point of deadlock, as Mommsen points out:

> It was clear that the Senate was not powerful enough to wrest either from the merchants or from the proletariate their new privileges; any attempt to assail the corn-laws or the new jury-arrangement would have led, under a somewhat grosser or somewhat more civilised form, to a street-riot in presence of which the Senate was utterly defenceless.[22]

In 121 BC Gaius Gracchus stood for yet another term as tribune, just as his brother had done. Once again, the Senate conspired against him. They put forward their own candidate, Marcus Livius Drusus, with a demagogic programme intended to undermine Gracchus' standing as a champion of the people.

21 Mommsen, *History of Rome*, Vol. 3, p. 153.

22 Ibid., p. 154.

They put into circulation malicious rumours about Gaius to undermine his credibility. But the most serious weakness was the loss of popularity resulting from the failed proposal to extend Roman citizenship to the Italians. As a result, Gaius lost the vote for his third term in office.

Gaius Gracchus' angry supporters, some of them apparently carrying weapons, held a mass protest demonstration on the Aventine Hill, with Flaccus at their head. This was used as an excuse for sending the consul Lucius Opimius to the Aventine Hill, backed by militia, legionary infantry and archers, 'to restore order'. He carried an order from the Senate to take action against anyone "endangering the stability of the Roman state".

That was all he needed. What followed was a massacre in which the Gracchan movement was drowned in blood. It appears that realising the hopelessness of the situation Gaius ordered his personal slave to stab him to death. His headless corpse was thrown into the Tiber. In the bloody proscriptions that followed as many as 3,000 of his followers were arrested and strangled in prison.

Why the Gracchi failed

The fatal weakness of the Gracchan Revolution was the fact that what we call the Roman proletariat was not a proletariat in the Marxist sense, but to a very great extent a declassed lumpenproletariat.

The unemployed mob in Rome hated the rich nobles, but in the last analysis, they were dependent on the exploiting classes, living off the wealth created by the slaves in the form of state handouts of free grain. The Roman proletariat benefited from the exploitation and oppression of the Italians, and therefore were implacably opposed to recognising them as Roman citizens.

They were able to stage riots, and sometimes played a revolutionary role, but in the end they also turned out to be fodder for the camp of reaction, which skilfully played on their prejudices. A large number of plebeians, jealous of their privileges as Roman citizens, turned against Gaius. This fatal split in the popular camp was what emboldened the reactionaries, who again went onto the offensive.

As we have seen, the aim of the Gracchi was to distribute land to the free citizens, revive the peasantry, and populate Italy with free peasants instead of slaves. They demanded that this public land should be redistributed to the poor. Nevertheless, their proposals did not remove the central contradictions.

The new class of smallholders could not compete with the big estates of the rich run on the basis of slave labour, especially if they were to be regularly taken away from their farms to perform military service. In essence, this was an attempt to put back the clock. It flew in the face of economic necessity.

Just as under modern capitalism all the attempts to bolster small businesses and prevent the spread of monopolies by anti-trust laws have proved futile, so in the Roman Republic, the efforts to re-create a class of small farmers proved to be ineffective. The tendency towards the concentration of the ownership of land in the hands of a small number of slave-owners was unstoppable.

The different classes in society – the urban 'proletariat', the small peasants, and the propertied classes, divided between equestrian money men and the old nobility – were not capable of providing any way out of the impasse Roman society faced. The result was a long and inglorious agony of the Republic that led inexorably to Caesarism and the Empire.

The Republic was dying on its feet because its social basis had ceased to exist. This fact expressed itself in continuous political crises and convulsions in the capital, party strife, revolutions and counter-revolutions. Paradoxically, the peasants were not the only ones affected by debt. Behind their outward splendour and overbearing pride, many Roman senators were in debt. The rise of a money economy served to disintegrate the old social relations and the political power that rested upon them.

The old system was dead but there was nothing viable to put in its place. The class struggle in Rome during this period assumes a particularly feverish and convulsive character. One party succeeds another without offering a definitive solution.

The freedmen were given votes in order to make their patrons masters of the streets. Politicians appeared in the streets and the forum at the head of private armies of freedmen numbering hundreds or even thousands to intimidate the Senate into passing certain laws. The political struggle had reached the point where only armed force could restore some kind of order and equilibrium. The stage was set for the irruption of the army into politics.

6. *Marius and Sulla*

The crushing of the Gracchan movement removed the possibility of the Roman masses overthrowing the Senate and reconstructing Roman society themselves. But the old ruling class remained incapable of ruling as it had done in the past.

As we have seen, the simmering hostility between the senatorial and equestrian classes came to a head in 123 BC, when Gaius Gracchus passed the *Lex Judicaria*, which prescribed that the jurors (*judices*) should be chosen from the *equites*, and not the Senate. From this time on the gulf between the Senate and the *equites* widened every year. Hitherto the jurors had been chosen from the ranks of the nobles, who therefore had control of the courts, and made unscrupulous use of their power.

This was especially the case in the courts which were established to try governors for extortion in the provinces. The voracious *publicani*, Roman tax-farmers who plundered the provinces, were mainly drawn from the *equites*. Usually the governors connived with them in this thievery, in exchange for bribes. But occasionally, a governor would clash with them either out of honesty or self-interest, and they could be threatened with prosecution, fines or exile. The question of who controlled the courts therefore affected the fundamental interests of an important section of the equestrian class.

In a situation where the contending classes have fought themselves to a standstill, and where neither side is able to win a decisive victory, the state apparatus, in the form of the army, begins to raise itself above society and acquire a certain degree of independence. In the Roman Republic this process was assisted by the fact that the army had an increasingly mercenary character, reflecting the destruction of the free peasantry that had been the backbone of the old citizens' militia.

After the crushing of the Gracchan movement, the class struggle resolved itself into mere party strife in which ambitious politicians and generals representing one or another clique of the possessing classes struggled to get control of the state. There now appeared a whole series of rival generals, each manoeuvring for power. The constant wars against the Cimbri, the Teutones and other tribes conferred increasing power and prestige to these generals, who supported first one party, then another.

The first of these generals with political ambitions was Gaius Marius, the son of a poor day-labourer who got rich as the result of lucky speculation and married into the ancient patrician gens of the Julii. His military victories over the Africans, Germans, Cimbri and Teutones further increased his prestige. "Marius stood aloof from parties not much less than from society", Mommsen informs us.[1] This adventurer had one foot in each class and intrigued and manoeuvred between all of them. But his main base was the army, which he reorganised to suit his own purposes.

Prior to this, the army was open only to citizens with property. The different branches of the army (cavalry, heavy infantry, etc.) were likewise determined by the amount of property one possessed. But the changes in the class composition of Roman society rendered these distinctions irrelevant.

Marius first obtained the consulship in 107 BC, and his reforms of that year were a big step towards transforming the army from a citizens' militia into a professional standing army, separate and apart from society, with its own identity and interests. The soldiers' first

1 Mommsen, *History of Rome*, Vol. 3, p. 240.

loyalty was not to the Senate and the people of Rome but to their own commander – the man who would guarantee them their pay, plunder and glory. It was also a step towards a dilution of the rank of Roman citizen, since the army was open to Latins and other non-Romans, and Marius even gave Roman citizenship away on the battlefield, which he had no constitutional right to do.

From now on, the army was open to the non-propertied classes and what part of the army one served in was determined not by property but only by duration of service. A section of the urban proletariat was drafted into the army, far from Rome and the popular assemblies. In this way the Roman class struggle was effectively exported abroad and directed at Rome's enemies.

All distinctions of armour were abolished, all wore the same uniform and all recruits were uniformly trained. The result was a general improvement in the fighting qualities and discipline of the troops, who had a new sense of identity – a new *esprit de corps*. The Roman army became a formidable and disciplined fighting force. But the reforms had another, more sinister import. Mommsen observes:

> The republican constitution was essentially based on the view that the citizen was also a soldier, and that the soldier was above all a citizen; it was at an end, so soon as a soldier-class was formed. To this issue the new system of drill, with its routine borrowed from the professional gladiator, necessarily led; the military service became gradually a profession. Far more rapid was the effect of the admission – though but limited – of the proletariat to participate in military service; especially in connection with the primitive maxims, which conceded to the general an arbitrary right of rewarding his soldiers compatible only with the very solid republican institutions, and gave to the able and successful soldier a sort of title to demand from the general a share in the movable spoil and then from the state a portion of the soil that had been won.[2]

The little detail that the training of the soldiers was copied from that of gladiators is significant of a profound change in the nature of the

2 Ibid., p. 246.

army. Gladiatorial combat, which played such a significant role in the national psychology of Rome in the later Republic and Empire, was probably invented by the Etruscans as a religious ritual involving human sacrifice. But it is possible that the Romans copied this bloody practice from the Samnites. Indeed, they used the words 'gladiator' and 'Samnites' synonymously. The gladiator was more often than not a slave, and although some of them acquired the status of pop stars (as long as they stayed alive), the profession in general was looked down upon as unworthy of free men.

The Roman soldier was now a professional killer, just like the gladiator, part of a well-oiled machine, held together by military discipline and a common interest in conquest and plunder: "His only home was the camp, his only science war, his only hope the general", writes Mommsen.[3] The Roman legion was now completely severed from civil society, and, although it carried on its banners the proud title SPQR (*Senatus Populusque Romanus* – the Senate and the People of Rome), in practice ambitious Roman generals could, and did, use it as a weapon *against* both the Senate and the Roman people.

Thus, the basis for Caesarism had been laid:

> They had now the standing army, the soldier-class, the body-guard; as in the civil constitution, so also in the military, all the pillars of the future monarchy were already in existence: the monarch alone was wanting.[4]

The very existence of a standing professional army is a threat to democracy. A standing army that is cut off from society is always a potential instrument for a coup d'état. This was demonstrated by the experience of the Roman Republic. That is why many centuries later the Paris Commune inscribed in its programme the demand for the abolition of the standing army and its replacement by the armed people – a citizens' militia. And this demand is at the very heart of the programme of workers' democracy as explained by Lenin in *State and Revolution* and included in the Bolshevik Party Programme of

3 Ibid., pp. 246-7.

4 Ibid., p. 247.

1919. The history of the Roman Republic is a salutary warning in this respect.

Caesarism

The Republic was being torn apart by class struggle. A series of demagogues arose, always willing to rouse the city poor in Rome to riots and disorders. Such men were the street orator Gaius Servilius Glaucia, known as the Roman Hyperbous, and his more able colleague, Lucius Appuleius Saturnius, whom even his enemies recognised as a fiery public speaker. Marius flirted with the *populares*, who were not averse to a deal with the victorious general who had the power of the legions at his back.

Here we have one of the elements of what we now call Bonapartism, and its ancient equivalent, Caesarism: *a tendency to balance between the classes, to lean on the lumpenproletariat to strike blows against the ruling class, while manoeuvring to seize power, using the army*. The populist leaders struck a deal with Marius to carve up public offices between them.

It is said that Marius himself was not above soliciting votes or even buying them. He certainly used the services of discharged soldiers to help his campaign with a little physical force. By a combination of bribery and assassination, Marius succeeded in getting himself elected consul, while Glaucia was made praetor and Saturninus a tribune of the plebs.

Marius obtained the loyalty of his men by promising them land. This could only be done through conquests. Partly it consisted of confiscated Carthaginian lands. Other land was taken from the Gallic territory in northern Italy. But soon all the legally available land was divided up. This fact was an important impulse to future Roman expansion, as was the resources to bribe the population of the capital with free grain. Together with the constant need to replenish the stock of cheap slaves, it became a self-enforcing process, propelling Rome to new wars of conquest.

In Rome itself the struggle between the conservative and populist factions continued. The latter demanded subsidies for the poor that would have bankrupted the treasury. The aristocracy resisted, but the Senate was under the pressure of the masses, who regularly rioted in the streets. Saturninus demanded that the Senate act, "or else thunder will be followed by hail". But behind the scenes the aristocratic party was preparing a counterstroke. Arms were distributed to the sons of the rich, and they began to attack supporters of the popular party.

As on previous occasions, the populists were superior in numbers, but they were not properly armed or trained. They were therefore unprepared for such an onslaught. They broke open the doors of the prisons and even appealed to the slaves to fight for their freedom. But it was too late. As we have seen so many times in history, small, well-organised armed groups with good captains can defeat an unarmed and disorganised mass without too much difficulty. And in the moment of truth, they found that they could not rely on 'friendly' generals to save them.

Marius, who had leaned upon the populists to gain power for himself, now abandoned them and sided with the aristocracy to put down the masses. A fierce battle was fought in the great marketplace. The supporters of the popular party were defeated and took refuge in the Capitol, where fighting was seen for the first time in history. But they were forced to capitulate when the water supply was cut off.

Probably Marius would have preferred to spare the lives of his former allies, who could be useful to him in future intrigues, but matters were no longer in his hands. Without waiting for orders, the reactionary 'gilded youth' of Rome climbed the rooftops of the courtyard where the supporters of the popular party were effectively imprisoned and, tearing the tiles from the roofs, stoned their helpless victims to death.

The victory of the reactionaries was complete and devastating. Overnight, the popular party was utterly crushed, its leaders butchered. There followed yet another reign of terror, in which the ruling class took revenge for its humiliation at the hands of the masses: trials, executions, bans and proscriptions decimated the populists. In the past, the *equites* had supported the Gracchi, but now, terrified of the threat from the masses, they rallied to the banner of reaction that always unites the propertied classes against the poor and dispossessed.

The state rises above society

In the end the conflict had solved nothing. Roman society was now split into two bitterly antagonistic camps of rich and poor. On the one hand, the equestrian merchants and moneylenders formed a single reactionary bloc with the aristocratic slaveowners; on the other side stood the mass of dispossessed Roman citizens, the proletarians. But the peculiarity of the situation was this: that neither side could win a final and decisive victory over the other. Under such circumstances, the state – armed bodies of men – tends to rise above society and acquire a large degree of independence.

Engels explained the role of the state thus:

> The state is therefore by no means a power forced on society from without; just as little is it "the reality of the moral idea", "the image and reality of reason", as Hegel maintains. Rather, it is a product of society at a particular stage of development; it is the admission that this society has become involved itself in an insoluble self-contradiction and is cleft into irreconcilable antagonisms which it is powerless to exorcise. But in order that these antagonisms, classes with conflicting economic interests, shall not consume themselves and society in fruitless struggle, a power, apparently standing above society, has become necessary to moderate the conflict and keep it within the bounds of 'order'; and *this power, arisen out of society but placing itself above it and increasingly alienating itself from it*, is the state.[5]

Unable to rule as it had in the past, the Roman ruling class had to rely increasingly on rule by the sword to keep the masses in check. The murders of Saturninus and Glaucia were followed by a long night of reaction in which the rights of the proletariat were abolished or restricted, laws were changed and progressive reforms liquidated.

---

5 Engels, *The Origin of the Family, Private Property and the State*, pp. 155-6, emphasis added.

However, the class struggle was not abolished, only driven underground. The discontent of the masses festered. Some resorted to individual terrorism. Cicero alleges that they succeeded in assassinating the hated Quintus Metellus by poisoning him. Others took refuge with foreign enemies of Rome, such as King Mithridates of Pontus, who was preparing war against Rome.

Reaction was firmly in control, but contradictions were breaking out in the camp of the victors. Having utilised the services of the *equites* to crush the proletariat, the aristocratic party in the Senate now proceeded to turn on its erstwhile allies. The confidence of the aristocrats had grown, their old overweening pride reasserted itself. Freed of the fear of the masses, they asserted their right to rule the roost without consideration for their junior partners, whom they saw as upstart *nouveaux riches*.

The class lines did not completely comply with the lines of party affiliation. There were certainly those in the Senate who supported the *equites*. Men like Lucius Marcius Philippus defended the rights of the equestrian class. The conflict between the senatorial and equestrian orders boiled down to who would plunder the provinces.

Some of the senatorial class were prepared to share the plunder with the *equites*. Others were greedier or else blinded by the class hatred of the old Roman aristocracy for the new class of moneyed upstarts, such as Marcus Aemilius Scaurus (c. 159 – c. 89 BC), one of the most prominent leaders of the *optimates,* and Marcus Livius Drusus (155-108 BC), who opposed the reforms of Gaius Gracchus.

While squabbling among themselves, the ruling class always kept a wary eye on the masses, whom they attempted to keep happy with free handouts of grain (plundered from the unfortunate provinces) and promises of land (likewise taken from the provinces). Slowly the provinces were being crushed by the burdens imposed by the capital.

The class of small peasants was already extinct in Umbria and Etruria, although it maintained a precarious foothold in areas like the Abruzzi valley. Italy was being bled by Rome and denied of its rights. This provoked a revolt of the Italians against Rome.

The Italians revolt

The intolerable burdens imposed by a parasitical capital city eventually drove the provinces to revolt. The political upheavals in Rome gave the Italians some hope of redress, but this led nowhere. The provincials first allied themselves to the *populares*, then to the *optimates*, but to no avail. No matter which party ruled at Rome, the provinces were always the losers.

Nowhere is the parasitic nature of Roman society more clearly illustrated than in this systematic plundering of the productive provinces by the unproductive centre. The cities of Italy were theoretically independent allies of Rome, but in practice Rome dominated them, demanding tribute and soldiers.

By the second century BC, between one half and two-thirds of the soldiers in Roman armies were from their Italian allies. Rome also controlled the allies' foreign policy and their relations between one another. In compensation, the allies received a slice of the booty and lands taken in the course of Rome's conquest in the Mediterranean. But as time went on, the burden of the impositions grew.

As we have seen, the Romans' policy of land distribution was carried out unjustly and at the expense of the Italians. This led to huge and increasing inequality of land ownership and wealth. Appian writes that this led to the "Italian race [...] declining little by little into pauperism and paucity of numbers without any hope of remedy".[6] For nearly two centuries they had shared dangers and victories with the Romans; they now eagerly demanded all their privileges.

In 91 BC, the tribune Marcus Livius Drusus, the son of the aristocratic leader of the same name, courageously took up the banner of reform. Like the Gracchi, he was noble, wealthy, and popular, and he hoped to settle the question peacefully and fairly. But his attempt to reform the courts alienated the *equites*, his agrarian and corn laws earned him the hostility of the big landowners, and his attempt to admit the Italians to the rights of Roman citizenship aroused the jealousy of the Roman city rabble.

6 Appian, *Roman History*, Vol. 3, *The Civil Wars*, Book 1, p. 19.

In an exact repeat of what had happened with the Gracchi, his laws were passed, but the Senate pronounced them null and void. He was denounced in that body as a traitor, and was struck down by an assassin in the same year. The death of Drusus drove the Italians to despair.

Eight states entered into a defensive alliance and what had begun as a movement for equality and Roman citizenship began to evolve into a war for separation. The rebels formed a federal republic to which they gave the name Italia, with Corfinium, in the Pelignian Apennines, as its capital. All Italians were to be citizens of Corfinium, and here was to be the place of assembly and the Senate House.

This Italian rebellion is known as the Social War (from *socii*, meaning 'allies'). The lead was given by the Samnite tribes, followed by other Latin tribes from the Liris and the Abruzzi down to Calabria and Apulia. Soon all of central and southern Italy was in arms against Rome. Only the Etruscans and Umbrians stuck with Rome. Here the landed and moneyed aristocracy ruled, and the class of independent small peasants had disappeared.

This war was at first disastrous to Rome. The Italians overran Campania, defeated the Romans several times, and entered into negotiations with the Northern Italians, whose loyalty to Rome began to waver. In the face of this challenge to its power, Rome took decisive action. The consuls, Lucius Julius Caesar and Publius Rutilius Lupus, both took the field. Each had five lieutenants, among whom were Gaius Marius and Lucius Cornelius Sulla.

The Social War was the last expression of the vigour of the class of small peasants that had once been the backbone of the Roman republic. The revolt was partly national in character – the Italians were a separate people (or rather, peoples) who spoke languages different to Latin. But there were also elements of class warfare – particularly on the issue of debt.

The free Italian peasantry, undermined by slave labour and the rise of the big *latifundia*, were being crushed under the weight of debt. They demanded the liquidation of all outstanding debts.

The war dragged on for five bloody years. But in the end the Italians suffered defeat. Their revolt had served to unite all the classes in Rome against them. The radical demands on debt pushed the *equites* into the arms of the aristocratic party, and their differences were forgotten in the fight against the common enemy. The city rabble was implacably opposed to sharing their privileges with the Italians and enthusiastically supported the war.

As usual, the Roman ruling class used a combination of cunning and brutality to get what it wanted. It decided to make concessions. Towards the close of the year 90 BC, the consul Caesar introduced the Julian Law, by which Roman citizenship was extended to all those Italians who had not yet revolted. This law was supplemented in the following year by the *Lex Plautia Papiria*, which allowed every citizen of an Italian town the franchise, if he handed in his name to the praetor at Rome within sixty days.

Yet another law, the Calpurnian Law, permitted Roman magistrates in the field to grant Roman citizenship to all who wished it. These laws had the desired effect. They succeeded in dividing and disorganizing the rebellion. The Samnites and Lucanians held out till the bitter end, but were finally crushed by Marius.

The end of the Social War did not bring peace to Rome. Far from being satisfied with the concessions, the new Italian citizens were embittered and resentful. Ultimately, they had fought for freedom from oppression. What they gained was oppression of the same kind as the rest of the plebeian masses.

In Rome, the Senate was torn apart by violent personal rivalries. All classes were affected by the prevailing austerity. The huge expense of the war had drained the treasury, and many were plunged into bankruptcy.

The Social War had tilted the balance of forces sharply toward reaction. The Senate, whose ranks had been depleted by the long period of wars and revolutions, was filled up by the admission of 300 new senators – all of them naturally loyal to the ruling aristocratic clique.

The voting system was reorganised so as to give a crushing preponderance to the propertied classes: those with estates greater than 100,000 sesterces in value possessed almost half the votes. In practice this meant that the poorer classes were excluded from the franchise.

The war also led to the rise of powerful generals like Sulla and Marius. The Roman army was now an army of mercenaries. The soldiers were loyal only to their general and indifferent to politics or the interests of the Republic.

In 88 BC the reactionary Sulla led six legions into Rome itself, in defiance of all laws and traditions of the Republic. His men murdered two tribunes who annoyed them. Very soon Sulla, the representative of the aristocratic party, was master of Rome. This was a fatal precedent. For the first time the army decided the outcome of the political struggle, as Mommsen remarks:

> The first military intervention in civil feuds had fully demonstrated, not only that the political struggles had reached the point at which nothing save open and direct force proves decisive, but also that the power of the bludgeon was of no avail against the power of the sword. It was the conservative party which first drew the sword, and which accordingly in due time experienced the truth of the ominous words of the Gospel as to those who first have recourse to it.[7]

Once more the triumphant reactionaries abolished progressive legislation. The Sulpician Laws, intended to enhance the voting power of the new enfranchised citizens, were pronounced null and void and their author, Publius Sulpicius, was condemned to death. His head was sent to Sulla as a present.

Nothing was done for the debtors, except to enforce the already existing rules for the maximum rate of interest. The people's tribunes were forbidden even to appear before the people unless the Senate gave permission. To the social and political crisis was added an economic slump. Rome was now in the grip of a deep commercial and monetary crisis.

---

7 Mommsen, *History of Rome*, Vol. 3, p. 321.

Mithridates

In the spring of 88 BC, King Mithridates of Pontus in the East invaded the wealthy province of Asia, which disrupted trade and drained the coffers of the Republic. So unpopular were the Romans with the oppressed provinces that as soon as Mithridates' troops entered Greece, most of the smaller Greek states – the Achaeans, Laconians and Boeotians – joined them.

As we have seen, the economic system depended upon a steady supply of slaves, and that depended on successful foreign wars, in which entire cities were sold into slavery to guarantee a continuous supply of cheap slaves for the mines of Spain or the *latifundia* of Italy. But when the Romans met with serious resistance, as in the wars of Mithridates, the flow of slaves dried up, and the disruption of trade immediately provoked a crisis. This was, in fact, the most serious financial crisis that Rome had ever experienced.

The *equites* were discontented with the rule of the oligarchy that had not been able to prevent these ruinous wars and the economic crisis that accompanied them. They had, of course, supported the aristocrats when the latter suppressed the masses.

But now they began to move into opposition again. There were clashes between the two sides at election time, in which swords were drawn and blood ran in the Forum. On one occasion it is said that 10,000 people were killed.[8]

Mithridates understood that the best way to strike at Rome was to disrupt its trade. His fleet commanded the eastern Mediterranean, and he controlled most of Greece and Asia. Delos, the centre of Roman trade in the eastern Mediterranean, was occupied and nearly 20,000 men, mainly Italians, were put to the sword.

Mithridates skilfully combined military methods with revolutionary measures such as the cancellation of debts and even the liberation of the slaves. This made him a formidable enemy. After a hard struggle, the Roman armies eventually defeated those of Mithridates. But even here the corrupt spirit of degeneration was manifest.

---

8 Ibid., p. 382.

War had ceased to be a patriotic duty for free citizens and had become a simple business affair, an opportunity to plunder and rob. The troops serving in northern Greece under the Roman general Flaccus mutinied against their commander, accusing him of embezzling the soldiers' spoils. The accusation must have had some basis because Flaccus was deposed by the army and executed. Needless to say, after the Roman victory, the slaves were brought back to their previous position and the debts cancelled by Mithridates were reintroduced.

The Marian terror

The struggle between the parties in Rome acquired an increasingly ferocious character. Lucius Cornelius Cinna, who had distinguished himself as an officer in the Social War, would become the most visible head of the *populares.* When he set about trying to resurrect the democratic reforms of Sulpicius, the Senate deprived Cinna of his consular office. Others were pronounced outlaws and fled to Africa. But these measures did not calm things down; quite the opposite.

The spirit of the soldiers at this time was inclined to be revolutionary and democratic except when individual generals succeeded in purchasing their loyalties. Therefore, when Cinna appealed to the soldiers stationed in Italy against the unconstitutional proscription against him, he got an immediate response.

The army of Campania recognised him as consul and marched on the capital. He invited the exiles back. More importantly, as he marched on Rome Cinna freed the slaves, whom he armed and included in his rebel army. He ordered his soldiers to break open the *ergastula*, the buildings where the landowners shut up their field-labourers for the night.

Cinna issued a proclamation offering freedom to any slave who should desert to him. As a result, many slaves left the city to join the rebels. In desperation, someone suggested that the Senate should offer freedom to any slave who joined the army, but this was too much for the Senate to swallow.

Many others flocked to his standard, and his army soon grew to 6,000, along with forty ships. He was joined by Marius, who was made commander of the rebels in Etruria. Rome was besieged. The armies of the Senate just melted away. Defeat now stared it in the face.

The Senate was forced to capitulate ignominiously, only asking that there should be no bloodshed. This was a vain hope, given the extremely inflamed and embittered mood of the populace. No sooner did the rebels enter the city than they launched a bloody reign of terror, in which Marius played the leading role.

The noted general, now over seventy years of age, was driven by the thirst for revenge against all those who had engineered his downfall. As Mommsen put it, Marius repaid every sarcasm with a stroke of the dagger.

The victors decided not to waste time prosecuting individual senators but to deal with their enemies by a far simpler method: they decided to kill all the members of the ruling party and confiscate their property. The city gates were closed to stop them from escaping.

For five days and nights the slaughter went on uninterruptedly. Even after this, the executions continued throughout Italy. A large number of Rome's wealthiest citizens were put to death in what became known as the Marian terror.

In theory, the republican laws and constitution remained. But what use are laws and constitutions when all the important questions are settled by armed force? After Marius died in 86 BC, Cinna, the head of the popular party, ruled for four years as consul and regularly nominated himself and his colleagues without consulting the people, although he continued to lean on them for support. In effect, he made himself dictator of Rome.

Cinna naturally abolished the reactionary laws introduced by Sulla. He gave the freedmen (freed slaves) the vote in order to turn them into a fixed clientele. He introduced measures to ease the position of debtors. A new law on debt reduced the level of every private claim to one-fourth of its nominal amount and cancelled three-quarters in favour of the debtors.

To please the Roman proletariat, he removed the restrictions on the free distribution of grain. In this way the Roman people accepted the loss of their political power in exchange for material benefits. The era of 'bread and circuses' was born.

The real basis of Cinna's regime was the army. The *equites*, who might have backed him, were alienated by his measures on behalf of debtors, which hit them in the most sensitive part of their anatomy – the purse.

The smashing of the aristocratic party produced a situation of relative stability for about three years, until a new wave of agitation upset the status quo. Those members of the oligarchy who had survived the Marian terror fled to territory controlled by Mithridates. Sulla, the chief of the reactionary party, established something like a government in exile.

In the spring of 83 BC, Sulla landed in Brundisium at the head of his legions. As Sulla advanced northwards, he successfully bought the support of other generals, formerly associated with the populists. His soldiers mixed with theirs, fraternised, joked, got drunk together. Naturally, Sulla's troops, generously supplied with gold from their master's coffers, bought the drinks.

This was not a struggle for political ideas but simply for loot. The general who promised more loot got the army's backing. On this occasion, Sulla promised more. The armies of Rome once again melted away like snow in springtime. Bribed by Sulla's gold, they passed over *en masse* to his side.

The Marian army was routed and forced to retreat, but not before putting to death all those prisoners who had so far escaped execution. Sulla finally entered Rome, where he made himself dictator and immediately instituted a White terror.

A regime of blood and iron was imposed. The Latin tribe of the Samnites, who had obtained a *de facto* independence under the popular government, was ruthlessly crushed and their cities given up to pillage. The Samnite nation, said Sulla, should be forever extirpated from the face of the earth.

Sulla's dictatorship

Sulla's government was supposed to represent the Roman aristocracy, but in fact its members were chosen mainly from defectors from the *populares* and wavering elements – the equivalent of the men who in the French Revolution were called 'the Marsh'.

He understood that the social base of the aristocracy was too narrow to guarantee stability to his regime, which, like that which it had overthrown, rested mainly on the army. Among the deserters from the popular party were Lucius Flaccus, Lucius Philippus, Quintus Ofella, and last but not least, Gnaeus Pompeus – later known as Pompey the Great.

Like his father, Strabo, the young Pompey was not originally a supporter of the oligarchy and had identified himself with the populists, even serving in Cinna's army. But in this age of cynical military adventurers, principles and ideas could change with every change of the wind. Men like Pompey were not the exception but the rule.

The fact that Sulla's dictatorship rested on the army is shown by his nomenclature: he did not call himself *Consul* but *Proconsul* – an office of a purely military character. He wrote to the Senate, explaining to them that in his modest opinion, they should hand all power to one man, who, again in his modest opinion, should be himself.

Since he had a large army at his back, the senators were in no position to argue. Here for the first time, the state – in the form of the army – lifted itself above society and dominated it without any restraint.

The title 'dictator' originally signified a magistrate appointed by the Senate during an emergency. It had fallen into disuse at the time of the wars with Hannibal. Now Sulla revived it, assuming supreme control of the state.

But the original idea was for a short-term period – not more than six months – after which the dictator would step down. What happened under Sulla was quite different. His dictatorship had no limits of any kind. It was rule by the sword, pure and simple.

In order to protect the oligarchy against the proletariat, Sulla established his personal dictatorship over the oligarchy. Although

Sulla spoke in the name of the Senate, and in fact represented the interests of the senatorial class (the oligarchy), *he expropriated them politically*, concentrating all power into his own hands.

Thus, *the ruling class lost power over its own state*. As Mommsen correctly comments: "the protector of the oligarchic constitution had himself to come forward as a tyrant, in order to avert the ever-impending *tyrannis*. There was not a little of defeat in this last victory of the oligarchy."[9]

Following the now familiar pattern, Sulla launched a campaign of proscriptions, arrests and executions of his enemies. Every day saw new political murders. The death toll amounted to at least 4,700 names, mostly members of the Marian party. On Sulla's instructions, their heads were piled up for public display at the Servilian Basin near the Forum.

But these bloody reprisals were not confined to those members of the Marian party directly implicated in the previous terror. The victims included *equites* who had sat in judgement on senators or had made money speculating on confiscated lands. There were about 1,600 such people on the proscribed lists.

Sulla's terror dragged on for months and spread all over Italy. Spies and informers were everywhere. People were denounced out of spite, personal hatred or plain greed. Some were murdered even before their name was placed on the proscribed list to justify murder *ex post facto*.

Naturally, Sulla and his family and friends did not neglect the opportunity to enrich themselves by getting their hands on the confiscated property of their enemies. One of his freedmen is said to have purchased property worth 6 million sesterces for just 2,000, while one of his subalterns is said to have accumulated an estate worth 10 million sesterces through speculation.

Sulla's terror was different in kind to anything that went before. The Marian terror was mainly the product of the desire for personal revenge. It was relatively haphazard in comparison to the systematic

9 Mommsen, *History of Rome*, Vol. 3, pp. 421-2.

campaign of Sulla with its cold, calculating cruelty. Sulla's confiscations amounted to the staggering value of 350 million sesterces. Many of the wealthiest men in the republic were ruined by this. Mommsen writes:

> It was altogether a fearful visitation. There was no longer any process or any pardon; mute terror lay like a weight of lead on the land, and free speech was silenced in the market-place alike of the capital and of the country-town. The oligarchical reign of terror bore doubtless a different stamp from that of the revolution; while Marius had glutted his personal vengeance in the blood of his enemies, Sulla seemed to account terrorism in the abstract, if we may so speak, a thing necessary to the introduction of the new despotism, and to prosecute and make others prosecute the work of massacre almost with indifference. But the reign of terror presented an appearance all the more horrible, when it proceeded from the conservative side and was in some measure devoid of passion; *the commonwealth seemed all the more irretrievably lost, when the frenzy and the crime on both sides were quite equally balanced.*[10]

When a ruling class is weakened and exhausted by long years of internecine struggle, we see how power can pass into the hands of a 'strongman' who rules in the name of the existing social order, but who in fact usurps power and reinforces it by creating a new state in his own image. Such a man was Sulla. His rise, however, also marked the beginning of a process of utter degeneration of Roman society in all spheres of life.

In the good old days of the Republic the army was not allowed to set foot in Rome, and as a consequence there was no army garrison in the capital. The revolutionary events of the previous period, however, persuaded the ruling clique of the need to take special measures. Sulla therefore took steps to strengthen the state as an organ of repression. For the first time he set up a real standing army, made up of specially selected professionals taken from the ranks of freed slaves and numbering around 10,000.

10 Ibid., p. 427, emphasis added.

Nowadays the state is surrounded by a mystique that has been built up over centuries. It is presented as a power standing above society (which it is) and above all class interests (which it is not). It is the Holy of Holies, and not to be questioned. But in Sulla's time the nature and role of the state was plain for all to see.

The force set up by Sulla was intended as a kind of bodyguard for the oligarchy, but this was not defence, as in the past, against a foreign enemy, but to defend the ruling class *against its own citizens.*

Here we already have the outline of the future *Praetorian Guard.* Here is the embryo of the Gestapo, the KGB, and all future special organs of state repression, where an armed force is created to defend the state against the people it is supposed to be defending.

Having concentrated power into his hands, Sulla ruthlessly crushed both the popular party and the *equites*. Ever since the time of Gaius Gracchus, the government had provided the proletariat with the distribution of free corn. Sulla abolished this. Gaius Gracchus had encouraged the growth of the equestrian class by developing the system of tax farming, whereby private individuals were able to fleece the wealthy provinces of Asia for their own benefit.

Sulla struck a heavy blow against these *publicani* by abolishing the system of middlemen and establishing fixed taxes for Asia, to be paid directly to the treasury at Rome. Gracchus gave the *equites* a privileged place in the legal system. Sulla abolished the equestrian courts and re-established the senatorial courts. In short, the equestrian order established by Gaius Gracchus was abolished by Sulla.

It is impossible to run society by repression alone, and the army is too narrow a base to achieve a stable regime. Therefore, Sulla needed a policy that would give him a social base. Following a line of action that was in theory acceptable to both conservatives and populists, he tried unsuccessfully to put the clock back by encouraging the creation of small farms through the colonisation of territories in Italy.

He ordered the breaking up of some big *latifundia*, to be settled by soldiers in his own army. Similar utopian schemes were advanced 2,000 years later by the Italian fascists – with just as little success. In the time of Sulla the big *latifundia* dominated agriculture just as the big monopolies dominate our own world. The day of the free small peasant was over, and all attempts to revive it were necessarily doomed to impotence.

Which class now held power? In theory all power now passed to the Senate. But in practice, this was only a show. Real power was concentrated in the hands of Sulla and the army. In a move ostensibly designed to strengthen it, Sulla introduced 300 new members into the Senate. These new appointees were grateful to Sulla for their promotion and loyal to him.

However, while preserving the outward forms of the old republican democracy, Sulla robbed them of any real content. Mommsen explains:

> The burgess-body remained formally sovereign; but so far as its general assemblies were concerned, while it seemed to the regent necessary carefully to preserve their names, he was still more careful to prevent any real activity on their part. Sulla dealt even with the franchise itself in the most contemptuous manner; he made no difficulty either in conceding it to the new burgess-communities, or in bestowing it on Spaniards and Celts *en masse*...[11]

Sulla did everything to consolidate his grip on power. But he had overlooked one small detail. The Roman army on which he relied had been entirely transformed. The soldiers no longer had any loyalty to the state, but only to their commanders. And this loyalty lasted only as long as the latter guaranteed the soldiers an acceptable amount of loot. In the course of the civil war, no fewer than six generals had been murdered by their own troops. The army now had a sense of its own power, and was not prepared to submit to anybody.

When Sulla attempted to assert his authority over the army, he immediately met with resistance from his own staff. Naturally, his main opponents were the people in whom he had placed the greatest trust: Gnaeus Pompeus, whom he had entrusted with the

---

11 Ibid., pp. 435-6.

conquest of Sicily and Africa and intended to make his son-in-law, and Quintus Ofella.

When Sulla, through the Senate, ordered Pompey to dismiss his army, the latter refused. The arrogant upstart Pompey told Sulla to his face that "more worshipped the rising than the setting sun".[12] Nevertheless, Sulla decided to attempt a compromise with Pompey. Ofella was not so lucky. It is typical of the cynicism of men like Sulla that while he had abolished the death penalty for political offences, he had Ofella cut down by his paid assassins in the marketplace anyway.

Plunder of the provinces

Under Sulla's dictatorship, the *populares* and the *equites* were deprived of all rights. But the ruling oligarchy was itself displaced from state power, which passed to the hands of Sulla and his clique. Sulla was a king in all but name. The fact that Sulla gave provincials the vote was an empty gesture, because the vote itself was meaningless. He gave the provinces an empty title and in exchange robbed them of very real wealth. But though Sulla kicked and humiliated them, he could not do without the very *equites* he had displaced from political power.

After decades of revolution and civil war, Rome's treasury was depleted. Sulla needed the moneylenders to raise more cash, but then a large part of the wealth flowed from the state's coffers straight back into the moneylenders' pockets. The war tax that Sulla imposed on Asia swelled to six times its original amount as a result of usurious interest rates. The usurers made huge fortunes and the provinces were stripped bare. People in the affected communities had to sell their public buildings, their jewels and their works of art; parents had to sell their children in order to satisfy the greed of these insatiable leeches.

The provinces were being crushed under an intolerable burden of taxation. Sicily and Sardinia had to hand over one-tenth of their production of grapes and wheat. There was also a land tax, import duties, and a hundred other impositions. The province of Judea had to pay a Temple tax.

---

12 Plutarch, *Lives*, Vol. 3, 'Pompey', p. 365.

Even more onerous was the quartering of troops and other such obligations, such as the free lodging of magistrates, clerks, lectors, heralds, physicians, priests and a host of other official functionaries. To these taxes and obligations must be added periodic forced sales and requisitions. All this provided enterprising Roman magistrates with a huge source of personal enrichment.

These things were the normal state of affairs for most of the provinces. But if the provincials dared to rebel against their tormentors, their plight would be far worse. Sulla compelled the cities of Asia who had joined Mithridates against Rome to pay to every common Roman soldier quartered in them the equivalent of forty times his daily wage (16 denarii), seventy times if he was a centurion. In addition to free food and lodging, the cities had to provide the soldiers with free clothing. To make matters worse, the soldiers were given the right to invite as many guests as they liked.

This does not exhaust the list of impositions. To it must be added the numerous local taxes for the maintenance of public buildings and the payment of all local services. Last, but not least, the system of tax farming greatly increased the burden of taxation, as greedy Roman middlemen took their slice of the wealth produced by the provinces. Even without the tax farmers, the Roman governors and magistrates plundered the provincials shamelessly. And new laws introducing new taxes were a regular occurrence.

It was necessary to look around for some new source of plunder. And the ancient civilisations of the East were the most tempting target for Roman avarice. Despite all her wealth, Rome's annual income was only two-thirds of that of the pharaoh of Egypt. The Ptolemies exploited the fabulous wealth of the Nile Valley and in addition benefited from Egypt's favoured position as an international commercial centre. Its turn would come soon.

The other source of wealth was slavery. Although the landowners had been politically expropriated by Sulla, they still retained their stranglehold on the key elements of the economic life of Rome and increased their wealth all the time. In Sulla's time, a modest fortune for a Roman senator would be 3 million sesterces, while 2 million was considered to be a decent equestrian fortune.

The landowners and money men were naturally the driving force behind the Republic's foreign policy. It was their pressure that led to the destruction of Carthage and Corinth, because they wanted to rid themselves of these trading rivals. Similarly, the slave trade was increased to unheard-of levels to meet the demands of the Roman landowners:

> All lands and all nations were laid under contribution for slaves, but the places where they were chiefly captured were Syria and the interior of Asia Minor.[13]

This was the heyday of slavery. Italy was now overrun by a mass of slaves. It is of course impossible to state the total number of slaves in Roman Italy with certainty, but historians consider a range of up to 2 million, out of a total population of 6 million at the end of the Republic, to be plausible. This would have meant that one in three inhabitants of Italy were slaves, giving a similar proportion of slave to free inhabitants as the southern slave states of the antebellum USA.[14]

Degeneration

The rule of Sulla was a golden age for the Roman upper classes. This was a period in which the rich became even more fabulously rich. This was shown by the lavish gladiatorial games that now became fashionable. Sulla himself, when he was praetor, exhibited a hundred lions at the games.

This was an age, like our own, characterised by a sharp and deepening contrast between rich and poor. Most people lived in stinking, narrow streets, where poor Romans inhabited overcrowded slums in rat-infested apartment blocks called *insulae* (literally, islands). The dwellings of the poor often only contained one or two

13 Mommsen, *History of Rome*, Vol. 3, p. 491.

14 See Madden, 'Slavery in the Roman Empire Numbers and Origins', *Classics Ireland*, Vol. 3, pp. 109-128.

rooms. There was no running water and conditions were squalid and unsanitary.

Some of these *insulae* were seven or more storeys in height. To reach an apartment, a poor tenant had to climb as many as 200 stairs. Most buildings were made of wood and were so badly built that they all too frequently collapsed or caught fire. That made them real death traps.

The contrast with the luxurious lifestyle of the rich could hardly be greater. The Roman nobility lounged in idleness in their splendid villas around the Bay of Naples tended to by armies of slaves. The inside of their houses was even more impressive than the outside, being hung with expensive curtains and tapestries. The great usurer, Crassus, had a townhouse famous for its old trees, which was valued at 6 million sesterces. By comparison the value of an ordinary dwelling in Rome was about 600.

Extravagant prices were paid for qualified domestic slaves – 100,000 sesterces for a good cook, for instance, or 200,000 for an educated Greek slave of the first rank. As in every other form of class society the ignorant rich masters could purchase the services of poets and philosophers.

Instead of the old woollen dresses, wealthy women wore silk that scarcely concealed their figures. Conservatives complained that the latest styles were only an excuse for people to walk around naked. Fortunes were made and lost at the gaming tables. Morals were looser than ever before. Divorce, previously almost unheard of in Rome, became commonplace.

So scandalous was the ostentation of the rich that Sulla passed the so-called sumptuary laws, which sought in vain to place some limit on the extravagances of the wealthy. The rulers of Rome were afraid of the reaction that such conduct might provoke among the less favoured population of Rome.

But the nobles felt themselves above the law. Their ostentation was a defiant reaction to the period when they had to suffer the indignities and persecutions of the rule of the *populares*. They were now the masters of the house! They would flaunt their wealth for all to see! No laws would stop them!

We see this phenomenon repeated many times in history – in France during the Thermidorian reaction, for example, or in seventeenth-century England after the Restoration of Charles II following the death of Oliver Cromwell.

To this moral decay we must add the decay of religion and the spread of mystical and irrational tendencies. The old Romans were not at all inclined to mysticism. The Roman religion was a religion of farmers with a rather provincial and prosaic outlook on life.

We see this healthy and thoroughly un-mystical outlook in all kinds of details. In the struggle against Carthage, the Romans had to learn how to fight on ships for the first time. They were not natural sailors. On one occasion, when they were about to go into battle with the Carthaginian navy, the priest announced that the auguries were unfavourable because the sacred chickens would not eat the grain he had offered them. The Roman captain's answer was: "If they will not eat, then let them drink!" So saying he threw the unfortunate birds into the sea and attacked the enemy – although, sad to say, not very successfully.

It is in the period of Sulla when for the first time we see the spread of mysticism in Roman society. Sulla himself had no ideology and little religion, but he was superstitious and believed in Fate. Of Sulla's beliefs, Mommsen writes:

> … it was that faith in the absurd, which necessarily makes its appearance in every man who has thoroughly ceased to believe in a connected order of things – the superstition of the fortunate player, who deems himself privileged by fate to throw on each and every occasion the right number.[15]

Both Caesar and Napoleon had a similar cast of mind to that of Sulla, and they constantly harped on about Destiny. There is always an element of the gambler in such military adventurers, and all gamblers are superstitious. It often appears that the outcome of a battle is decided by a lucky accident, like the lucky throw at dice.

15 Mommsen, *History of Rome*, Vol. 3, pp. 459-60.

But this is also a product of a specific period in history. As Hegel pointed out, necessity expresses itself through accident. The Men of Destiny throughout history have only been men who expressed an idea that had already become necessary by the working out of processes that take place behind the backs of men, and invisible to them.

Their 'luck' turns out to be no luck at all, but an optical illusion. The circumstances that determine whether they win or lose are prepared in advance. This does not cancel out the role of the individual in history. What it means is that the scope for individual action is severely limited by objective reality, which favours one outcome over all others. When history plays games with the destiny of men and women, it always plays with a loaded dice.

This rise of mysticism and irrationality in the later Roman Republic is also no accident. In a period when the productive forces are developing and society is going forward, people will believe in the existing gods, will accept unquestioningly the existing morality and obey the existing laws. But when a given social order is breaking down, when the productive forces stagnate and decline, then a different psychology can be observed.

There are symptoms of universal malaise, doubt and scepticism. The temples stand empty. Nobody believes in the old gods any more. Instead, we see the spread of mysticism, unbelief and superstition. Mommsen writes:

> Men had become perplexed not merely as to the old faith, but as to their very selves; the fearful crises of a fifty years' revolution, the instinctive feeling that a civil war was still far from being at an end, increased the anxious suspense, the gloomy perplexity of the multitude. Restlessly the wandering imagination climbed every height and fathomed every abyss, where it fancied that it might discover new prospects or new light amidst the fatalities impending, might gain fresh hopes in the desperate struggle against destiny, or perhaps might find merely fresh alarms. A portentous mysticism found in the general distraction – political, economic, moral, religious – the soil which was adapted for it, and grew with alarming

> rapidity; it was as if gigantic trees had grown by night out of the earth, none knew whence or whither, and this very marvellous rapidity of growth worked new wonders and seized like an epidemic on all minds not thoroughly fortified.[16]

This extract shows very clearly the depth of degeneration that had corroded the very spirit of the Roman Republic. The conclusion is clear.

The Republic now existed in name only. Unable to live, it was unwilling to die. It was only a matter of time until an appropriate executioner would be found to put it out of its misery. Exactly the same can be said of the capitalist system in the third decade of the twenty-first century. Reading Mommsen's comments on this period, we seem to be reading a description of our own troubled times.

16 Ibid., p. 525.

7. Spartacus

The crisis of Roman society necessarily affected the slaves. There was ferment among the slave population everywhere, and a whole series of revolts and uprisings, culminating in the first century BC, when a slave named Spartacus threatened the might of Rome. Spartacus (c.109-71 BC) was the leader, or possibly one of several leaders, of the massive slave uprising known as the Third Servile War.

Under his leadership, a tiny band of rebel gladiators grew into a huge revolutionary army, numbering about 100,000. In the end the full force of the Roman army was needed to crush the revolt. But despite his well-deserved fame as a great revolutionary leader and one of the most outstanding generals of antiquity, not much is known about Spartacus the man.

There were other leaders of the revolt whose names have come down to us: Crixus, Castus, Gannicus and Oenomaus – gladiators from Gaul and Germania. But of these even less is known. It is always the victors who write history and the voice of the slaves throughout the centuries can be heard only through the accounts of the oppressors.

What little information we have is from the writings of his mortal enemies. The surviving historical records are all written by Roman historians and therefore hostile. They are also often contradictory.

Trying to understand Spartacus from these sources is like trying to understand Lenin and Trotsky from the slanderous writings of the bourgeois enemies of the Russian Revolution.

Through this distorting mirror one can only catch tantalising glimpses of the real Spartacus. Plutarch writes:

> And seizing upon a defensible place, they chose three captains, of whom Spartacus was chief, a Thracian of one of the nomad tribes, and a man not only of high spirit and valiant, but in understanding, also, and in gentleness, superior to his condition, and more of a Grecian than the people of his country usually are.[1]

These words by an enemy present Spartacus in a personally favourable light, which requires an explanation. This is not hard to find. A man who defeated one Roman army after another and brought the Republic to its knees had to be possessed of extraordinary qualities. Only in this way could the Roman commentators begin to come to terms with the fact that 'mere slaves' had defeated their invincible legions.

Other Roman historians attempt to make him out to be of royal blood, for exactly the same reason. He is said to be endowed with superhuman attributes. His wife is said to have been a priestess, and so on and so forth. All this is clearly part of Roman propaganda that aims to present Spartacus as somebody very special, and in this way to try to reduce the sense of shame and humiliation felt by the master class when it had been defeated by farm labourers, kitchen skivvies and gladiators.

Spartacus' real origins are unclear as the ancient sources do not agree on where he came from, although he was probably a native of Thrace (now Bulgaria). He seems to have had military training and experience and may even have joined the Roman army as a mercenary. Plutarch also says Spartacus' wife, a prophetess of the same tribe, was enslaved with him.

In any case, he was enslaved and sold at auction to a trainer of gladiators in Capua. Appian says he was "a Thracian by birth, who

1 Plutarch, *Lives*, Vol. 3, 'Crassus', p. 212.

had once served as a soldier with the Romans, but had since been a prisoner and sold for a gladiator".[2] Florus says he "had become a soldier, and from a soldier a deserter, then a highwayman, and finally, thanks to his strength, a gladiator."[3]

The gladiators' revolt

At the time of Spartacus' uprising, the Roman republic was in a period of turmoil. The bloody dictatorships of Marius and Sulla were still fresh in the memory, while Roman territories were expanding east and west; ambitious generals could make a name fighting in Spain or Macedonia, then carve out a political career in Rome.

Battles were staged in the newly popular entertainment of gladiatorial combat. While successful gladiators were idolised, in terms of social status they ranked little above convicts; indeed, some gladiators were convicted criminals. Others were slaves. Slaves were liable to extreme and arbitrary punishment from their owners. While the death penalty for free Romans was rarely invoked and (relatively) humanely executed, slaves were routinely crucified.

Spartacus was trained at the gladiatorial school (*ludus*) near Capua, belonging to one Lentulus Batiatus. It was here that in 73 BC, Spartacus led a revolt of the gladiators, who armed themselves, overpowered their guards and escaped. This is how Plutarch deals with it in the section of his Roman History, *The Life of Crassus*:

> The insurrection of the gladiators and the devastation of Italy, commonly called the war of Spartacus, began upon this occasion. One Lentulus Batiatus trained up a great many gladiators in Capua, most of them Gauls and Thracians, who, not for any fault by them committed, but simply through the cruelty of their master, were kept in confinement for this object of fighting one with another. 200 of these formed a plan to escape, but being discovered, those of them who became aware of it in time to anticipate their master, being seventy-eight, got out of a cook's shop chopping-knives and spits, and made their way through the city, and

2 Appian, *Roman History*, Vol. 3, *The Civil Wars*, Book 1, p. 215.

3 Florus, *Epitome of Roman History*, pp. 244-5.

> lighting by the way on several wagons that were carrying gladiators' arms to another city, they seized upon them and armed themselves. And seizing upon a defensible place, they chose three captains, of whom Spartacus was chief…[4]

Armed with the knives in the cook's shop and a wagon full of weapons that they seized, the slaves fled to the slopes of Mount Vesuvius, near modern-day Naples. The news of the breakout encouraged others to follow. A steady flow of rural slaves soon joined the mutineers, whose numbers began to swell.

The group overran the region, raiding the farms for food and supplies. Thus the rebels began by winning small victories, which led to bigger things. Plutarch continues his account:

> First, then, routing those that came out of Capua against them, and thus procuring a quantity of proper soldiers' arms, they gladly threw away their own as barbarous and dishonourable.[5]

One can almost picture the exhilaration of these early victories and the joy with which the gladiators cast aside the hated uniform of their trade and dressed themselves as proper soldiers, not slaves.

This little detail reveals something far more important than weapons and equipment. It reveals a growing confidence, the rejection not only of the servile state but also of the servile mentality. We see the same thing in every strike and in every revolution in history, where the ordinary workers – the lineal descendants of the slaves – draw themselves up to their true height and begin to think and act like free men and women.

This slave mutiny was by no means a unique event. When the news of the outbreak reached Rome, it caused some concern, but neither surprise nor undue alarm. In the previous century, two slave revolts, both on Sicily, had been put down at the cost of tens of thousands of lives. There could be no doubt in the minds of the august senators,

4 Plutarch, *Lives*, Vol. 3,'Crassus', pp. 211-2.

5 Ibid., p. 212.

who held control of the whole world in their hands, that the outcome of this rising would be no different.

In the first instance, therefore, the Roman authorities did not rate Spartacus as highly as later commentators. The Senate did not even bother to send a legion to suppress the rebels, but only a militia force of about 3,000 under the praetor, Claudius Glaber. They clearly considered that this was a mere police operation and would be easily dealt with.

They thought this would be more than enough to suppress a small number of badly armed slaves. But Spartacus' camp had become a magnet for slaves from the surrounding area, several thousand of whom had joined him. Unlike the Roman soldiers and their officers, the slaves were fighting a desperate battle for survival. By contrast, the Roman generals underestimated the enemy and were unduly lax in the beginning.

It is a well-known fact that revolutionaries can only win by going onto the offensive and showing the greatest audacity. The Romans surrounded the rebels on Vesuvius, blocking their escape. The slaves found themselves besieged on a mountain, accessible only by one narrow and difficult passage, which the Romans kept guarded, "encompassed on all other sides with steep and slippery precipices."[6]

In an impressive tactical coup, Spartacus had ropes made from vines and with his men abseiled down a cliff on the other side of the volcano, to the rear of the Roman soldiers, and launched a surprise attack. Plutarch describes the situation:

> Upon the top, however, grew a great many wild vines, and cutting down as many of their boughs as they had need of, they twisted them into strong ladders long enough to reach from thence to the bottom, by which, without any danger, they got down all but one, who stayed there to throw them down their arms, and after this succeeded in saving himself. The Romans were ignorant of all this, and, therefore, coming upon them in the rear, they assaulted them unawares and took their camp.[7]

---

6 Ibid.

7 Ibid., pp. 212-3.

Claudius Glaber, expecting an easy victory over a handful of slaves, probably did not bother to take the elementary precaution of fortifying his camp. He did not even post adequate sentries to keep a lookout.

The Romans paid a heavy price for this neglect. Most of them were killed in their beds, including Glaber himself. This was an ignominious defeat for the Romans. The slaves now possessed weapons and armour. More importantly, they developed a sense that they could fight and win. This was the biggest gain.

Spartacus was an excellent military tactician, which tends to confirm the idea that he had served as an auxiliary soldier under the banners of Rome. If this is true, he would have been acquainted with the tactics of the Roman army, and this, together with the audacity that is a necessary quality for a revolutionary, made him a formidable enemy.

However, his army was mainly composed of poorly armed and untrained former slave labourers. This dictated his tactics, which were at first defensive. They hid out on the heavily wooded Mount Vesuvius until such time as they had been trained properly for the inevitable showdown with the Roman army.

Realising that time was running out before a new and more serious battle, Spartacus delegated to the gladiators the task of training small groups, who then trained other small groups and so on. In this way he was able to create from scratch a fully trained army in a matter of weeks. And what the slave army lacked in military experience they made up for with the heroism of people fighting for their very survival, with literally nothing to lose but their chains.

There were many skirmishes with the Roman army, all of which ended in victory. Publius Varinus, the praetor, was now sent against them with 2,000 men, whom they fought and routed. Then Cossinius was sent "with considerable forces", and narrowly missed being captured in person, as he was bathing at Salinae.[8]

He made his escape with great difficulty, while Spartacus acquired his baggage. The slaves followed the retreating Romans, slaughtering

8 Ibid., p. 213.

many. Finally, they stormed the Roman camp and took it, and Cossinius himself was killed. With every such victory, the morale of the rebels grew.

The reports to the Senate at Rome must have made grim reading. Slowly, the truth was beginning to dawn in the minds of even the most dull-witted aristocrat that here they were facing a most dangerous enemy – one that possessed a vast number of reserves, infiltrated in the very heart of the enemy camp. On every farm, in every household, there were slaves, each of whom was a potential rebel, to be watched with suspicion and fear.

After this successful battle, the fame of Spartacus grew. The message was clear to all: the Romans were no longer invincible. A large number of runaway slaves joined and soon the small band of rebels grew into an army. By some accounts, the slave army may have finally numbered as many as 140,000 escaped slaves, used to living in harsh conditions, hardened by years of heavy labour and with nothing to lose by fighting their former masters. Plutarch writes:

> Several, also, of the shepherds and herdsmen that were there, stout and nimble fellows, revolted over to them, to some of whom they gave complete arms, and made use of others as scouts and light-armed soldiers.[9]

In the end the word 'several' should read several tens of thousands.

Spartacus' army spent the winter of 73 BC camped on the south coast of Italy, all the time building up its numbers, armaments and morale. In the spring, it headed north; the audacious plan appears to have been to march the length of Italy, cross the Alps and escape to Gaul (present-day France, then largely outside Roman control). According to Plutarch:

> … wisely considering that he was not to expect to match the force of the empire, he [Spartacus] marched his army towards the Alps, intending, when he had passed them, that every man should go to his own home, some to Thrace, some to Gaul.[10]

9 Ibid.

10 Ibid.

Divisions among the slaves

The Senate, now thoroughly alarmed, sent two legions under the consuls, Lucius Gellius and Gnaeus Cornelius Lentulus Clodianus against the slaves. Spartacus now faced his greatest challenge so far: an army of two legions – 10,000 men – commanded by Cassius Longinus, the Governor of Cisalpine Gaul. The Romans scored one victory, when they defeated a Gaulish contingent led by Crixus. The reason for this setback was divisions in the ranks of the rebels.

It cannot have been easy to maintain unity and discipline in an army of slaves from different lands, speaking different languages and worshipping different gods. It required a leader of colossal stature to achieve this, and even he did not always succeed. Crixus and the Gauls had refused to march under Spartacus' leadership. It seems that Crixus wanted to stay in Italy, seduced by the prospect of plunder. Spartacus wanted to continue North to Gaul, as Plutarch points out:

> But they, grown confident in their numbers, and puffed up with their success, would give no obedience to him, but went about and ravaged Italy; so that now the Senate was not only moved at the indignity and baseness, both of the enemy and of the insurrection, but, looking upon it as a matter of alarm and of dangerous consequence, sent out both the consuls to it, as to a great and difficult enterprise.[11]

The Roman commentator understood the root of the problem. Some of the leaders of the rebels had become over-confident, intoxicated by their early successes. For this reason, Crixus left Spartacus, taking around 30,000 Gauls and Germans with him. This split was a disastrous mistake: Crixus was defeated by Publicola and fell in battle. The Gauls paid a terrible price for this and 20,000 of them were killed. This was the first warning of the dangerous consequences of divisions in the ranks of the slave army.

Despite the disastrous actions of Crixus, Spartacus held funeral games in honour of the Gallic leader, including gladiatorial combat

---

11 Ibid.

between captured Roman soldiers. This detail reveals a nobility of character and true leadership qualities. Later Spartacus first defeated Lentulus, and then Publicola, as Plutarch relates:

> The consul Gellius, falling suddenly upon a party of Germans, who through contempt and confidence had straggled from Spartacus, cut them all to pieces. But when Lentulus with a large army besieged Spartacus, he sallied out upon him, and, joining battle, defeated his chief officers, and captured all his baggage. As he made toward the Alps, Cassius, who was praetor of that part of Gaul that lies about the Po, met him with 10,000 men, but being overcome in battle, he had much ado to escape himself, with the loss of a great many of his men.[12]

This was a heavy blow to Roman prestige and it shook the confidence of the Senate. Not only had their army been massacred, but Spartacus had captured the *fasces*, the symbol of Roman authority (from which the word fascism is derived). At Mutina (now Modena) the slaves defeated yet another legion under Longinus. The leader of the slaves now seemed to be completely invincible.

What happened next is one of the great mysteries of history. The slaves were in sight of the Alps and could have crossed into Gaul and entered Germany, where they might have escaped from Roman rule, or even to Spain where another rebellion was raging. However, for some reason, the plan changed and Spartacus turned back: his army once more marched the length of Italy.

What was the cause of this change? We do not know. Perhaps they were put off by the logistics of getting an army across the Alps, or perhaps the slaves were intoxicated by success and drawn by the prospect of plundering the rich Italian cities. However, events were no longer moving Spartacus' way.

By now, Spartacus' army was swollen by a large number of camp-followers, including women, children, and elderly men who joined the rebels in the hope of escaping from a life of servitude. The non-fighting followers may have numbered some 10,000 people,

---

12 Ibid., pp. 213-4.

all of whom would have had to be fed. This must have considerably complicated his movements. Moreover, the Romans were no longer making the mistake of underestimating the qualities of their enemy.

When the Senate learned that Spartacus had scored new victories over the armies of the Republic, they were furious at the consuls, and ordered them to keep out of the conflict. Instead, they gave Marcus Licinius Crassus charge of the war. He was the richest man in Rome, a very ambitious politician and hungry for glory.

Crassus was no fool and he did not make the mistake of underestimating his opponents. His aim was to carefully build up his forces and avoid a decisive battle, confident that in the end the superior resources and wealth of Rome would wear down the rebels and create favourable conditions for a military victory.

However, many of those who joined him in the pursuit of glory did not share his understanding of the enemy they were confronted with. They were rich young fops who did not realise what they were up against. They must have set out after the slaves with the same spirit as they would embark on a fox hunt. Plutarch informs us: "a great many of the nobility went [as] volunteers with him, partly out of friendship, and partly to get honour."[13] Once again, this excessive over-confidence was a recipe for disaster.

While Crassus stayed on the borders of Picenum, expecting Spartacus would come that way, he sent his lieutenant, Mummius, with two legions, to observe the enemy's movements, but gave him strict orders upon no account to engage or skirmish. They were ordered to capture a small hill, but to do it as quietly as possible, so as not to alert the enemy.

Overconfident, on the first opportunity, Crassus' lieutenant joined battle, and was heavily defeated. They would have been annihilated, had it not been for the fact that Crassus immediately appeared, and engaged in a battle. It proved a most bloody one. A great many of his men were slain, and a great many only saved their lives by throwing

13 Ibid., p. 214.

down their arms and ignominiously running away. By contrast, writes Plutarch:

> Of 12,300 whom [Crassus] killed, two only were found wounded in their backs, the rest all having died standing in their ranks and fighting bravely.[14]

This bravery of the slaves contrasts with the cowardly conduct of the Romans in earlier battles, which compelled Crassus to revive the ancient Roman method of punishment: decimation. In an attempt to restore discipline, Crassus first rebuked Mummius severely. Then he armed the soldiers again, but in a humiliating gesture made them pay a deposit for their arms, to make sure that they would part with them no more.

He then selected 500 men who had been the first to run away and he divided them into fifty groups of ten, one of each was to die by lot, "with a variety of appalling and terrible circumstances, presented before the eyes of the whole army, assembled as spectators", as Plutarch relates.[15]

This terrible punishment had long fallen into disuse and by reviving it, Crassus wanted to show that he meant business. From this moment, every Roman soldier learned to fear his general more than he feared the slaves.

Defeat

At the end of 72 BC, Spartacus and his army set up camp in Rhegium (Reggio Calabria), near the Strait of Messina. Spartacus attempted to strike a deal with Cilician pirates to get the slaves across the Straits to Sicily. According to Plutarch:

> … he had thoughts of attempting Sicily, where, by landing 2,000 men, he hoped to new kindle the war of the slaves, which was but lately extinguished, and seemed to need but little fuel to set it burning again.

14 Ibid., p. 216.

15 Ibid., p. 214.

> But after the pirates had struck a bargain with him, and received his earnest, they deceived him and sailed away.[16]

This shows a sound grasp of tactics and strategy. If they could get to Sicily and stir up a new slave revolt there, they might be able to defend the island against Rome. Having failed to take the opportunity to cross the Alps, this was perhaps the only option left to him, other than a direct assault on Rome itself.

But the project failed because the pirates betrayed the slaves. It may be that Crassus' agents had bribed them, or simply that they feared that by helping the slaves they would bring the whole weight of the Roman army down on their heads. Whatever the reason, Spartacus' army now found itself trapped in Calabria.

We can imagine the terrible blow this represented for Spartacus and his followers. Once the plan to escape to Sicily fell through, the position of the slaves was desperate. At the beginning of 71 BC, eight legions under Crassus were thrown against them. They had their backs to the sea with nowhere to escape. Worse news was to come.

The assassination of Quintus Sertorius, who had been leading a rebellion in Spain, enabled the Roman Senate to recall Pompey from that province. And just to make sure, they also recalled Marcus Terentius Varro Lucullus from Macedonia. The Roman state, which had earlier shown such contempt for the slaves, was concentrating all its forces against them.

It seems that after a small skirmish, Spartacus had a Roman prisoner crucified. The Roman propagandists cited this as proof of the "barbarous and cruel nature" of the rebels. However, crucifixion was a normal punishment for slaves. And all history shows that the masters, not the slaves, always display the most barbarous cruelty.

It may be that this was a calculated act of defiance, since crucifixion was a particularly cruel and degrading method of execution not normally used on Romans. By this act, Spartacus was saying to his enemies: you think the lives of slaves are cheap, but we will make you pay dearly for your actions.

---

16 Ibid.

This report, like all the other reports published by the Romans, were intended to justify their bloody suppression of the slaves. But they really did not require any excuse to do what they were already determined to do. These slaves had to be taught a lesson that the whole world would never forget!

Ultimately, excessive confidence played a big role in the defeat of the rising, as Plutarch explains:

> Spartacus, after this discomfiture, retired to the mountains of Petelia, but Quintius, one of Crassus' officers, and Scrofa, the quaestor, pursued and overtook him. But when Spartacus rallied and faced them, they were utterly routed and fled, and had much ado to carry off their quaestor, who was wounded. *This success, however, ruined Spartacus, because it encouraged the slaves, who now disdained any longer to avoid fighting, or to obey their officers, but as they were upon the march, they came to them with their swords in their hands, and compelled them to lead them back again through Lucania, against the Romans, the very thing which Crassus was eager for.*[17]

The ever-cautious Crassus did not want an immediate battle with an enemy whose strength, courage and resourcefulness had defeated the Romans many times. Instead of attacking, he ordered his troops to build a wall across the isthmus, in an attempt to starve the slaves into submission. All the technological prowess of Rome was summoned to defeat the slaves. In the words of Plutarch:

> This great and difficult work he perfected in a space of time short beyond all expectation, making a ditch from one sea to the other, over the neck of land, 300 furlongs long, fifteen feet broad, and as much in depth, and above it built a wonderfully high and strong wall.[18]

By building this wall, he achieved two objects: keeping his soldiers from demoralising idleness and denying the enemy food and forage.

All this effort, however, was in vain. Despite these frightening odds, Spartacus yet again displayed an uncanny grasp of tactics. On

---

17 Ibid., p. 216, emphasis added.

18 Ibid., p. 215.

a stormy night, Spartacus ordered his followers to fill up part of the ditch with earth and boughs of trees, and so passed over with one-third of his army.

But this was just a last show of strength, one last burst of energy before the final collapse of the revolt. With this daring manoeuvre, he managed to break through Crassus' lines and escape towards Brundisium (now Brindisi), where Lucullus' army was landing.

When he saw that Spartacus had evaded him, Crassus was terrified that the slave army was going to march directly to Rome. In reality, that was probably the best option open to Spartacus, indeed the only option: to chance everything on one last desperate throw and strike at the enemy's head. But this was rendered impossible by a new outbreak of divisions in the ranks of the slaves.

Once again, part of Spartacus' army mutinied, abandoned their commander and set up a camp upon the Lucanian lake. And once again the lack of unity had disastrous consequences. Crassus fell upon the dissident slaves and beat them from the lake. He would have slaughtered them, except that Spartacus suddenly appeared, rallying the troops and checking their flight.

Despite his recent setback, it was clear to Crassus that the slaves were in a difficult position. Sensing that victory was within his grasp, Crassus began to regret his earlier action of writing to the Senate to call Lucullus out of Thrace, and Pompey out of Spain.

As a typical politician of that period, he saw war as a means of winning prestige and glory that would help him to win high office in the state. If the other generals were to arrive at the last moment, before the decisive battle, it would look as if they, and not Crassus, had won the war.

This is just what happened. Crassus won the decisive battle against Spartacus, but it was Pompey who got all the glory. Crassus was therefore anxious to be the one to give battle as soon as possible:

> For news was already brought that Pompey was at hand; and people began to talk openly, that the honour of this war was reserved to him, who would come and at once oblige the enemy to fight and put an end to the war.

> Crassus, therefore, eager to fight a decisive battle, encamped very near the enemy, and began to make lines of circumvallation; but the slaves made a sally and attacked the pioneers.[19]

Spartacus, seeing that fresh reinforcements were arriving from all sides, understood that there was no longer any possibility of avoiding a battle. Every moment that passed meant a strengthening of the Roman host.

As he watched fresh supplies coming from every side to the Roman camp, Spartacus had to bet everything on one last superhuman effort. In the words that Karl Marx later used to describe the heroic uprising of the Paris Commune, the slaves decided to "storm Heaven". He therefore gathered his army and strove to raise their fighting spirits for the coming battle.

We can only guess at his state of mind at this fateful moment, when the entire destiny of the rebellion rested on the outcome of one last battle. Displaying the extraordinary qualities of a great commander, he calmly set all his army in battle order. What followed then is one of the most moving incidents in history.

When his horse was brought to him, Spartacus drew out his sword and killed it in front of the slave army, saying: "If we win the day I shall have a great many better horses from the enemy, and if we lose, I shall have no need of one."[20] By this action, Spartacus not only showed great personal courage and complete disregard for his personal safety, but also sent out an uncompromising message to the slaves: we win this battle or we die.

For the last time the slaves fought with desperate courage, as even the Roman historians are compelled to admit. But the outcome of this battle was never in doubt. According to Roman accounts, Spartacus cut his way through the mass of fighting men and made directly for Crassus himself.

Amidst the deadly rain of blows, and covered in wounds, he did not reach his goal, but killed two centurions that fell upon him together.

19 Ibid., p. 216.

20 See ibid.

Finally, being deserted by those that were about him, he himself stood his ground, and, surrounded by the enemy, bravely defending himself, was cut to pieces. The Roman historian, Appian, describes the scene thus:

> Spartacus was wounded in the thigh with a spear and sank upon his knee, holding his shield in front of him and contending in this way against his assailants until he and the great mass of those with him were surrounded and slain.[21]

After the battle, the legionaries found and rescued 3,000 Roman prisoners in their camp – all of whom were unharmed. This civilised treatment of the Roman prisoners contrasts starkly with the fate meted out to Spartacus' followers. Crassus had 6,000 slaves crucified along the Appian Way between Capua and Rome – a distance of about 200 kilometres. Their corpses lined the road all the way from Brundisium to Rome. Since Crassus never gave orders for the bodies to be taken down, for years after the final battle all who travelled that road were treated to this macabre spectacle.

Around 5,000 slaves somehow escaped capture. These shattered remnants of the slave army fled north and were intercepted on the shores of the Silarus River in Lucania by Pompey, who was coming back from Roman Iberia.

The slaves, who by now must have been exhausted by all their exertions, were confronted by the fresh, well-trained and confident legions of the most prominent Roman general. He proceeded to slaughter them, and later used the butchering of a depleted and dispirited band of exhausted runaway slaves as a pretext to claim the credit for ending the slave war.

Pompey immediately wrote a letter to the Senate, claiming that, although Crassus had defeated the slaves in a pitched battle, he (Pompey) had put an end to the war. Subsequently, Pompey was honoured with a magnificent triumph for his conquest over Sertorius

---

21 Appian, *Roman History*, Vol. 3, *The Civil Wars*, Book 1, p. 223.

and Spain, while Crassus was denied the honour of a triumph that he so earnestly desired. Instead, he was compelled to accept a lesser honour, called an ovation.

Thus was Pompey 'the Great' greeted as a hero in Rome, while Crassus, to his great chagrin, received neither credit nor glory for saving the Republic from Spartacus. This ingratitude tells us something about the psychology of the slave-owning Roman ruling class.

These wealthy scoundrels and hypocrites could never admit that in Spartacus they had found an enemy that made them tremble. The noble Senators conveniently forgot the terror that the name of Spartacus had struck in their hearts only a few months earlier. How could a war against a slave army merit the honours of a triumph?

Myth and reality

The legend of Spartacus lived on long after his death. For the Romans, the story of the slave revolt was an awful warning: it suggested that a society built on the backs of slaves and subject peoples might one day be overthrown by them. Five centuries later, this is exactly what happened, and Rome fell to the barbarians.

The memory of Spartacus lives on as a symbol of the power of the oppressed masses to confront their oppressors. It retains all its force and is an inspiration for all who today fight for their rights. It is no accident that during the First World War, Rosa Luxemburg and Karl Liebknecht adopted the name of the Roman revolutionary when they launched the Spartacist League.

Karl Marx was also a great admirer of Spartacus. Marx said Spartacus was his hero, citing him as the "finest fellow antiquity had to offer". In a letter to Engels dated 27 February 1861, Marx says that he was reading about Spartacus in Appian's *Civil Wars of Rome*: "Spartacus emerges as the most capital fellow in the whole history of antiquity. A great general [...], of noble character, a *real representative* of the proletariat of ancient times. Pompey a real shit [...]".[22] Anyone

22 Marx, 'Letter to Engels', 27 February 1861, *MECW*, Vol. 41, p. 265.

who has even a superficial knowledge of history would find it hard to disagree with this assessment.

The figure of Spartacus, and his great rebellion, has become an inspiration to many modern literary and political writers. Howard Fast wrote a famous novel about the rising. Stanley Kubrick later adapted Howard Fast's novel to make his outstanding film *Spartacus* (1960).

In his book, *Spartacus*, FA Ridley is dismissive of both Kubrick and Fast, but is unjust in both cases. This is just another sad example of how a narrow and mechanical interpretation of Marxism is always incapable of seeing the wood for the trees.

Fast was not attempting to write a history book but a historical novel, and while he may have taken certain liberties, the novel conveys very well the spirit of its subject. This is not history, but the best kind of historical novel that represents real events in an imaginative way, without seriously departing from the historical record.

Of course, there are some things that are definitely non-historical, especially in the film. Contrary to the celebrated sequence in the film, the survivors of the battle were never asked to identify Spartacus, because he had died on the battlefield. But we must bear in mind that this is a work of art and as such is entitled to a certain latitude in presenting historical events in a dramatic light.

More importantly, a work of art may present a profound truth even when it departs from the strict historical record of events. This dramatic scene, when one by one, the slaves rise to defy their masters, each one declaring "I am Spartacus", does in fact contain a profound truth that is applicable not only to the Spartacus revolt but to every such revolt of oppressed people throughout history.

For the strength of Spartacus was precisely the fact that in his person he embodied the hopes and aspirations of the mass of slaves yearning for freedom. And within each of these rebellious slaves one can say that there was lodged a small particle of Spartacus. As for the subsequent mass crucifixion scene, that is historically accurate.

What little we know about this great man we know from what his enemies wrote about him. We know sufficient to deduce that

Spartacus was a brilliant commander and a skilful battlefield tactician. Probably, he was the greatest general of all antiquity. But he was probably not, as the film and novel presented him, the revolutionary leader of a disciplined fighting force. If he possessed a clearly defined political strategy, we do not know of it. Little united his army except the goal of continued survival and in the end, internal dissent and sheer confusion sealed its fate as surely as Rome's superior forces.

Was Spartacus an early forerunner of communism? In his novel Howard Fast places the following words in the mouth of the slave leader: "Whatever we take, we hold in common, and no man shall own anything but his weapons and his clothes. It will be the way it was in the old times".[23]

Where Fast got the idea for this I do not know, but it is not impossible that some kind of primitive communist and egalitarian ideas existed at the time – in the same way that they later surfaced among the early Christians.

It is possible that utopian or communist currents were present in the great slave revolt of 73-71 BC, based on the dim memories of a remote past when men were equal and property was held in common. But if that were the case, they would have been backward looking, rather than progressive, and would have manifested themselves as a communism of consumption ("equal sharing") and not collective production.

In the given conditions, such an option would not have carried society forward, but backwards. Real communism (a classless society) cannot be built on the basis of backwardness and austerity. It supposes a high development of the productive forces, such that men and women can be freed from the burden of labour and can possess the necessary time to develop their full human potential. These material conditions did not exist at the time of Spartacus.

What would have happened if the slaves had won? Had they succeeded in escaping across the Alps or liberating Sicily this would likely have inspired further slave risings, which would have sapped the

23 Fast, *Spartacus*, p. 166.

economic strength of the slave owners and potentially even threatened Rome itself.

Of course, it is not possible to say exactly what the outcome would have been if the Roman state had been overthrown, but the course of history would surely have been significantly altered. Probably the slaves would have been freed – although even this cannot be taken for granted.

Even if that had occurred, given the level of development of the productive forces, the general tendency could only have been in the direction of some kind of feudalism. Several centuries later, this began to happen under the Empire, when the slave economy reached its limits and entered into crisis.

The slaves were 'freed' but tied to the land as serfs (*coloni*). If this had occurred earlier, it is likely that economic and cultural development would have proceeded more quickly and humanity might have been spared the horrors of the Dark Ages. However, this is just speculation.

The fact is that the rising did not succeed, and could not succeed for a number of reasons. The basic reason why Spartacus failed in the end was the fact that the slaves could not link up with the proletariat in the towns. So long as the latter continued to support the state, the victory of the slaves was impossible.

In the first Sicilian revolt there were cases where the free proletarians joined the insurgent slaves, who came within a hair's breadth of conquering Messana. It is probable that the reason Spartacus tried to lead his army into Sicily was to spark off a new slave revolt there and possibly establish an independent state. But the uprising failed, and after its suppression the slave-owners took their revenge by selling large numbers of proletarian rebels into slavery.

Since the conditions of the free proletarians were not much better than those of the slaves, the logical result should have been the linking up of both classes in a common revolt against the oligarchy. The big question is: why did this not take place?

The conditions of the mass of peasants in the countryside were no better than those of the urban poor in Rome. Yet there is no record of rural uprisings, and only in a few cases did the poor Romans join in the uprisings of the slaves.

The reason for this apparent contradiction is that neither the urban plebs nor the free peasants were the productive base of society. Although they were underprivileged and oppressed, in the last analysis they had more in common with the slave owners than with the slaves who were the real exploited class and the producers of social wealth.

It was their labour that provided the dole of the unemployed citizens of Rome, their sweat, blood and tears that paid for the bread and circuses of the masses as well as the luxurious lifestyle of the slave-owners.

If one wants an historical analogy to the outlook of the free Roman peasants (or the remnant that still survived by the end of the Republic), it can be found in the psychology of the 'poor whites' of the southern states of America at the time of the Civil War.

This social layer had absolutely nothing in common with the wealthy slave-owning aristocracy which treated it with contempt. For the wealthy slave owners they were merely 'white trash'.

Although they lived in conditions of poverty which were not that much better than those of the black families that frequently lived alongside them, they nevertheless always combined with the white slave owners against the blacks, and fought obstinately for the cause of the South in the Civil War.

The poor whites, despite their degrading conditions, always felt themselves to be superior to the blacks. It is an established fact that the lowest and most degraded layers of society like to feel that there are people on a lower level than themselves. A similar psychology must have existed among the poor layers of Roman societies in both town and countryside. At every decisive moment, they united with the Senate to defeat the slaves.

In his article 'The North American Civil War', Marx made this specific comparison:

> Finally, the number of actual slaveholders in the South of the Union does not amount to more than 300,000, a narrow oligarchy that is confronted

> with many millions of so-called poor whites, whose numbers have been constantly growing through concentration of landed property and whose condition is only to be compared with that of the Roman plebeians in the period of Rome's extreme decline.[24]

The Third Servile War proved to be the last opportunity for the slaves and oppressed masses to unite and overthrow the slave owning oligarchy of Rome. Their failure would seal the fate of the republic itself.

Nonetheless, the spectacle of these most downtrodden people rising up with arms in hand and inflicting defeat after defeat on the armies of the world's greatest power is one of the most amazing and moving events in history.

Ultimately, Spartacus failed. It may be that his revolt was always doomed to fail. But this glorious page in history will never be forgotten as long as men and women are motivated by the love of truth and justice. The echoes of this titanic uprising reverberate down the centuries and are still a source of inspiration to all those today who are continuing the fight for a better world.

---

24 Marx, 'The North American Civil War', 20 October 1861, *MECW*, Vol. 19, pp. 40-1.

8. *Julius Caesar*

In the epoch of the decline of the republic and the rise of powerful generals appeared the figure of Julius Caesar, who was destined to play a key role. Caesar (102-44 BC) was a member of the great Julian family – one of the old patrician *gentes* of Rome, which traced its ancestry back to Iulus, son of Aeneas. His name was taken over after his death by the first Roman emperor, Augustus (Octavian), and later used by the emperors as a title. It is the origin of Kaiser in Germany and Tsar in Russia. That is to say, it is synonymous with *absolute power*.

Despite his impeccable patrician origins, Caesar's start was inauspicious. His father had died when he was fifteen years old and he became head of the family. His family was noble, but short of cash. And to make a political career in Rome, one needed a lot of cash.

From the start he was an adventurer. This ambitious young man was preparing for better things. He is reported to have said: "I would rather be the first man in a barbarian village than the second man in Rome."

He was prematurely balding and seems to have suffered from epileptic attacks, but his ambition was accompanied with colossal vanity. We are told he was inordinately preoccupied with his appearance. According to Suetonius he removed body hair with tweezers. Some cast doubt on his sexuality. The story circulated that he was "every wife's husband and every husband's wife", although this was probably propaganda inspired by his enemies to discredit him. He went to Rhodes to study oratory with the best Greek teachers. But despite his smooth skin, impeccable appearance and his acquaintance with rhetoric and Greek literature, Caesar was an utterly ruthless man.

The historian Plutarch informs us that on the way to Rhodes he was captured by pirates who demanded a ransom of twenty talents. The smallness of the sum struck Caesar as amusing. He actually got on very well with these ruffians – probably they reminded him of himself. When he had handed over the money, he promised them he would have them crucified. They may have thought it a joke, but he hunted them down remorselessly, and he kept his word. However, he showed his appreciation of his 'friends': in a gesture of magnanimity, he had their throats cut first.

He married into money – his first smart career move. His choice of partner was not accidental. He married Cornelia, the daughter of the radical leader, Lucius Cornelius Cinna. His aunt Julia was Marius' wife. He therefore had close links with the popular party, which he no doubt hoped would help his advance. Then, as outlined in a previous chapter, came the civil war between the *populares* led by Cinna and the *optimates* led by Sulla. Caesar, however, was on the wrong side. Sulla won and proclaimed himself dictator, not for the traditional six months but for life.

The reign of terror that followed Sulla's victory was more frightful than anything that had gone before. Caesar escaped with his life, but along with many others, had all his wealth confiscated. His first political gamble thus proved to be a failure. But when a gambler loses, he just shrugs his shoulders and gives the dice another throw.

Sulla offered to further Caesar's career, but on the condition that he divorced his wife. This he refused to do, either because he was really in love, or, more likely, because he was already looking beyond Sulla. To cross the man who had murdered thousands was a risky thing to do. His family decided it would be best to get him out of Rome and send him as far away from Sulla as possible. He took up a post in the army and was sent to Asia Minor, where he served with distinction. It was there that he learned of the death of Sulla, and he immediately went back to Rome.

The Senate proved to be too weak to use the power that Sulla had placed in their hands. The popular party was reviving. It was at this time that Italy was convulsed by the great uprising of the slaves led by Spartacus. But when Crassus crushed the revolt, the defeat of the slaves condemned the movement of the masses in the cities to impotence. It led to a kind of stalemate between the classes, in which neither side could inflict a decisive defeat on the other.

As we have seen, this explains the rise of ambitious generals like Pompey, who rose to prominence at this time. The rapid rise of Pompey was both unprecedented and highly irregular. During the civil war, when he was only twenty-three years of age, he had raised three legions to fight for Sulla.

He defeated the Marians in Sicily and Africa, for which he was awarded a triumph. Later he fought against Sertorius in Spain for four years, and was awarded another triumph. By such means, he was preparing his road to power. But he was destined to meet with a formidable obstacle in a man who was every bit as greedy for power and far more cunning and audacious than he was.

The politics of the slums

There was plenty of combustible material in Rome for unscrupulous adventurers to take advantage of. The lower classes were filled with seething resentment after the bloody proscriptions, murders and confiscations by which Sulla had destroyed the popular party. Caesar saw his chance.

His first wife had died, and his second wife, like the first one, was rich (he was always after money). But money alone was insufficient to obtain an admission ticket to the world of Roman high society. Rome's wealthy aristocratic elite regarded him as an upstart. Rejected by the establishment, he looked for a base among the poor of the slum districts.

Many years later, according to the Roman historian, Suetonius, when the Emperor Vespasian's fastidious son, Titus, expressed his feelings of revulsion about a tax that had been levied on the collection of urine (used for laundering clothes and even whitening teeth), his father held up a gold coin and said simply, "*Non olet*!" ("This doesn't stink!").

This celebrated phrase could well serve as an epitaph to the political career of Julius Caesar. He was quite prepared to wade up to his knees in blood and excrement in order to secure his aims.

The slum districts where Caesar looked for a political base were appalling places where people threw shit from the windows of multi-story tenements that were always falling down. But the declassed lumpenproletarians who inhabited these dangerous and unsanitary districts had the vote, and, while Caesar doubtless held his nose when canvassing their support, he needed them as a battering ram to shatter the political power of his enemies.

When his aunt Julia died, Caesar took a bold initiative. Julia's husband, Marius, had been the darling of the populists in his lifetime. But ever since Sulla came to power, his name was utterly prohibited. At Julia's funeral, Julius Caesar not only delivered her obituary speech, in which he praised her and her husband, but had portraits and statues of Marius paraded through the streets. Shortly after, his own wife Cornelia died, and he did exactly the same, publicly praising her late father, Cinna. By these means he attached himself firmly to the populists.

In order to obtain this support, he did not mind currying favour with the urban poor and flattering them, as Dio Cassius informs us. In order to get support, he financed big games for the enjoyment of the populace. He brought in vast numbers of wild beasts and 320 pairs of gladiators who fought to the death, dressed in silver, for the crowd's amusement.

He even had the arena flooded to create a mock naval battle. According to Plutarch, "He was unsparing in his outlays of money, and was thought to be purchasing a transient and short-lived fame at a great price, though in reality he was buying things of the highest value at a small price."[1] In other words, *he bought votes*. However, his extravagance got him into trouble. He was soon in debt again and was forced to go into exile or face death. But then he had a brilliant idea.

At thirty-seven years of age this man, who is not known for his piety, suddenly developed an urgent interest in religion. He stood for the post of *pontifex maximus* – the supreme priest of Rome. This post would give him not only prestige but a huge patronage and therefore lots of money.

In order to secure his election, he probably prayed to the Gods. More importantly, he borrowed huge sums of money to bribe his electors. If he won, he could repay all his creditors with interest. If he failed, he would be in deep trouble. In the event, he won.

The Catiline conspiracy

Events now took a dramatic and unexpected turn. It seems that about this time a plot was hatched by desperate men from many different classes: bankrupt aristocrats, destitute unemployed, speculators in search of extra profits and political adventurers of all kinds.

At the centre of the conspiracy was Lucius Sergius Catilina (108-62 BC), better known as Catiline. He was a man similar to Caesar in many ways. He was yet another of that breed of impoverished upper-class adventurers that were common at that time. He is one of the most enigmatic figures of Roman history.

His memory has been obscured by the insults of Roman historians, particularly his arch-enemy, Cicero. It is practically impossible to disentangle the truth from the calumnies. What we do know is that, like Caesar, he came from an aristocratic but impoverished family and had a distinguished military career, serving in the Social Wars under Pompey's father.

We know that he served under Sulla in the civil war against the Marians, but later took up the interests of the poor and dispossessed, which earned him the hatred of the Roman aristocracy. Whatever else he was, he was certainly not a coward, as he proved in the end.

1 Plutarch, *Lives: In Eleven Volumes*, Vol. 7, 'Caesar', p. 453.

He was put on trial several times, but was acquitted repeatedly, some said through the influence of Caesar, who was suspected of having connections with him. This is quite possible, since Caesar was always prepared to fish in troubled waters, to see what he could catch.

Catiline stood as a candidate in the consular election in 64 BC, when he seems to have had the backing of Crassus. He must therefore have had a lot of money for his campaign, but was not elected. One of the successful candidates was Cicero, a 'new man'.

Catiline stood again the following year, but by this time he had probably lost the backing of Crassus, as he was already making vague threats against the establishment and he had announced a policy of the general cancellation of debts. This would have been popular with Sulla's veterans, but it provoked the hostility of the rich. Predictably, he was defeated once more. Seeing that the road to power by legitimate means was blocked, he decided to adopt other methods.

The ranks of the conspirators included a variety of other patricians and plebeians whose advance had been blocked for different reasons. They were all desperate and displaced people, individuals who had a grudge against the establishment.

But Catiline's main base of support was among the poor, who flocked to his banner as a result of his policy of debt relief. The problem of debt had existed from early times, but had never been greater than in 63 BC. Decades of war had led to a severe economic depression in the Italian countryside.

As we have seen, many poor farmers had lost their farms and were forced to move to the city, where they swelled the numbers of the lumpenproletariat. Prominent among Catiline's supporters were a large number of veterans from Sulla's armies, hungry for land.

They were prepared to march to war under the banner of the 'new Sulla'. One of these, Gaius Manlius, a centurion from Sulla's army, was sent to Etruria where he assembled an army ready for revolt, as Sallust reports:

> Meanwhile, in Etruria, Manlius was agitating among a populace whose poverty, added to the resentment which they felt at their wrongs, made

> them eager for revolution; for during Sulla's tyranny they had lost their lands and all the rest of their possessions. He also approached some of the many types of brigands who infested that part of the country, as well as some veteran soldiers from Sulla's colonies, whose lavish indulgence of their appetites had exhausted the enormous booty they had brought home.[2]

Other men were sent to different locations throughout Italy. The mood of society was explosive. There was even a small slave revolt in Capua, the same place where Spartacus had begun his uprising. Manlius made an appeal that begins with the words:

> We call gods and men to witness, sir, that our object in taking up arms was not to attack our country, or to endanger others, but to protect ourselves from wrong. We are poor needy wretches; the cruel harshness of moneylenders has robbed most of us of our homes, and all of us have lost reputation and fortune. Not one was allowed the benefit of the law established by our ancestors, which should have enabled us, by sacrificing our possessions, to save our persons from bondage; such was the inhumanity of the moneylenders and the praetor.[3]

While civil unrest spread throughout the countryside, Catiline was making the preparations for the conspiracy in Rome, where, as Sallust confirms, he enjoyed the enthusiastic support of the poor:

> Yet there were Roman citizens obstinately determined to destroy both themselves and their country. In spite of two senatorial decrees, not one man among the conspirators was induced by the promise of reward to betray their plans, and not one deserted from Catiline's camp. A deadly moral contagion had infected all their minds. And this madness was not confined to those actually implicated in the plot. The whole of the lower orders, impatient for a new regime, looked with favour on Catiline's enterprise. In this they only did what might have been expected of them. In every country paupers envy respectable citizens and make heroes of unprincipled characters, hating the established order of things and

2 Sallust, *The Conspiracy of Catiline*, p. 196.

3 Quoted ibid., pp. 199-200.

> hankering after innovation; discontented with their own lot, they are bent on general upheaval. Turmoil and rebellion bring them carefree profit, since poverty has nothing to lose.
>
> The city populace were especially eager to fling themselves into a revolutionary adventure.[4]

Here is the authentic voice of the frightened ruling class, faced with the rebellion of the masses in all historical periods. The signal for the commencement would be the assassination of Cicero. It seems Catiline's plans included arson and the murder of a large number of senators. He would then link up with Manlius' army in Etruria, and return to Rome and take control of the government.

But the conspirators were betrayed when Quintus Curius, a senator they had approached, turned informant, warning Cicero of the plot. Cicero escaped death that morning by placing guards at the entrance of his house.

The next day, Cicero convened the Senate and surrounded it with armed guards. To his astonishment, Catiline was present, which shows remarkable coolness of mind. Cicero denounced him before the Senate in his celebrated *Catiline Orations*. But Catiline did not retreat. He took the floor, recalling to the Senate the history of his family, reminding it how it had served the Republic, and advised them not to believe false rumours and to trust the name of his family.

Finally, he played his ace card, rebuking them for taking the word of a 'new man' (*homo novus*), Cicero, in preference to a '*nobilis*' like himself. This might have had some effect, but then he began to threaten the senators, saying that he would "check the fire that threatens to consume me by pulling everything down about your ears".[5]

Before they could react, he dashed out of the Senate, and left Rome under the pretext that he was going into voluntary exile. Instead, however, he joined Manlius' camp in Etruria to continue the fight. But meanwhile, events at Rome took a fatal turn.

---

4 Ibid., p. 203.

5 Quoted ibid., p. 199.

The conspirators discovered that a delegation from the Allobroges, a Gallic tribe, were in Rome to complain about debt and the oppressive conduct of their governor. The conspirators established contact with them and told them of their plans. It seems that the Allobroges wanted nothing to do with the conspirators and informed Cicero. This was the kiss of death to the conspiracy.

The Romans could not bear the thought of foreigners interfering in their political life, and least of all their traditional enemies, the Gauls. Cicero got hold of incriminating letters, which he read before the Senate the following day, and the death sentence was demanded for those implicated.

Caesar made an eloquent protest against such a step, which initially got an echo. But a savage speech by Cato, the thirty-two-year-old great grandson of Cato the Elder, cut across this. He was an implacable defender of the aristocracy. He hated Caesar and Caesar hated him. The fate of the five named conspirators was sealed.

They were condemned to death without even the pretence of a trial and Cicero had them strangled immediately. He even personally escorted some of the condemned men to their execution. Afterwards, he announced to a crowd gathering in the Forum what had occurred. The conspiracy in Rome had collapsed.

When the news reached the rebels in Etruria, many men deserted, reducing the size of the rebel force from about 10,000 to a mere 3,000. In the end, Catiline was forced to fight the legions of Antonius Hybrida's army near Pistoria (now Pistoia).

Despite overwhelming odds, Catiline fought bravely in the front line of battle. Seeing that there was no hope of victory, he threw himself into the thick of the fight. When it was all over, the victors found that all Catiline's soldiers had frontal wounds as none had turned their back to the enemy, and the lifeless corpse of their leader was found far in front of his own lines.

The First Triumvirate

The Catiline conspiracy must have come as a shock to the wealthy classes in Rome. Living in close contact with a mass of impoverished people must at times have felt like living on the side of a volcano. There was no police force to keep order in such circumstances, and so the army was the only resort.

Among the army officers the idea was growing that Rome now needed a monarchy, although nobody was bold enough to pronounce that dreaded word. Rather they spoke in terms of a strong government, stability and order. This meant the rule of a 'strongman' – a general. The only question was which one.

Pompey, who had made his name crushing the revolt in Spain and massacring the last remnants of Spartacus' forces, was in a strong position as the supreme arbiter of Rome's destiny. He had recently returned from a victorious campaign in the East with an army of 40,000 veterans at his back. Cicero's rash conduct in the Catiline affair was probably due more to his fear of Pompey than his fear of Catiline, whose conspiracy seems to have been badly planned and executed.

Cicero wanted to avoid giving Pompey any excuse to intervene. He needed to act quickly to suffocate the conspiracy before Pompey arrived at the gates of Rome with his soldiers, ready to make himself master of the city.

For the Senate, Cicero was, at least for a time, the hero of the hour, considered as "the saviour of the Fatherland." This was not going to last. Later on, Cicero was made to pay a heavy price for his part in the execution of the rebel senators. On the other hand, the Catiline affair had damaged Caesar's position.

Caesar's enemies had triumphed, and he now found himself compromised by his past links with Catiline and his opposition to the executions. He needed to consolidate alliances with powerful men who could protect him. This determined his line of action.

Pompey had returned from the wars not only with a greatly enhanced prestige but also with a considerable fortune. Some said he was now even richer than Crassus, who was considered the richest man in Rome. His campaign in the East had been successful, and had finally crushed Rome's most dangerous enemy, Mithridates.

Before he left for Rome, Pompey made the whole of the Near East secure, with a number of new client kingdoms. Fifty cities were founded or restored, and Rome's revenues from Asia were increased by 70 per cent.

Caesar drew the conclusion that the quickest way to make money was by fighting wars. In addition, the suspicions that he was somehow involved in the Catiline affair made it sensible to make himself absent from the capital for a while. He therefore got appointed governor of Spain, where he once more distinguished himself by his abilities as a military commander.

Like almost every other Roman governor, he plundered the natives (this was regarded as quite acceptable). But as governors went, he was by no means the worst. Like everybody else, the Spaniards were subject to the ruthless laws on debt, by which creditors were allowed to take all the possessions from a debtor. Caesar amended the law to restrict the amount of possessions that a creditor could seize to two-thirds. This may still seem quite a lot to us, but in those days it was a very generous concession indeed.

Caesar returned to Rome, where he resumed his intrigues, an art at which he was extremely skilful. In the streets of Rome rival gangs loyal to one politician or other fought it out, while their masters manoeuvred to strengthen their positions. Bribery and intimidation were the normal tools of the trade.

Chief of the city lumpenproletariat was another aristocrat turned tribune, Publius Clodius. This demagogue, now in his mid-thirties, made a profitable political career out of his influence with the city mob and the gangsters whose headquarters were the slum districts. Caesar had already established his popularity with the plebs at the same time as he made use of the existing machinery to get possession of one office after another. He had close connections with Clodius and the populists. But in his present delicate situation, Caesar needed more – he needed to reach agreement with elements from the establishment.

While posing as the people's champion, Caesar also attempted to get contacts with the rich and build an alliance with the 'respectable classes'. Therefore, after the death of Cornelia he married Pompeia, who was the granddaughter of Sulla, the former dictator and leader of the aristocratic party.

During Pompey's absence, Crassus was trying to increase his own political power and influence in Rome. He was aided in this by Caesar, who in return borrowed large amounts of money to advance his own career.

Crassus was a firm defender of the rights of the *equites*, of which he was one. He proposed the annexation of Egypt, probably with the idea of sending Caesar there to organise the plunder of that wealthy province on his behalf.

But this was defeated by Cicero, with Pompey and the aristocracy behind him. One of the main sources of wealth for the *equites* was the plunder of the provinces by the practice of tax-farming. Most governors did not interfere with the activities of the tax-farmers as they usually got a share of the loot.

However, Pompey, in search of popularity, annoyed the *equites* by relieving the debts of people in Asia. All this did nothing to improve Crassus' opinion of Pompey. But Pompey had his own differences with the Senate, which had refused his request for a grant of land for his veterans.

Although Pompey was supposed to be on their side, the senators obviously were afraid that he might be tempted to use his military muscle to take power. Now Crassus had another clash with the Senate on the issue of tax-farming. Sometimes the tax-farmers would overestimate their profits and lose money. He had asked the Senate to grant a rebate to those who had done this. This was clearly unreasonable and the Senate refused. Crassus was furious at what he saw as this new insult from the Senate.

This was Caesar's chance. Both Pompey and Crassus now had grievances against the Senate. This gave him the possibility of acting as a mediator between them. Cicero understood the danger and, although he knew Crassus' demand to be outrageous, he was bitterly critical of the Senate's decision. He now began to see in Caesar an even more dangerous enemy than Pompey, saying he feared him "as one might fear the smiling surface of the sea".[6]

6 Plutarch, *Lives: In Eleven Volumes*, Vol. 7, 'Caesar', p. 449.

Cicero's fears were well grounded. Caesar now entered into contact with Pompey. He arranged a marriage between Pompey and his only daughter Julia, which was one of the usual ways of establishing a political alliance. Caesar also wanted to include Crassus in the alliance. But there was a problem. The relations between Pompey and Crassus were chilly.

Crassus had not forgotten that Pompey had stolen the credit for defeating Spartacus, which was really his work. Nor had he forgotten the fact that the Senate had awarded his rival a triumph, but refused one to him. In addition, Pompey had stepped on the toes of the tax-farmers, Crassus' friends.

In order to win Pompey's support, it appears that Caesar used his agents to spread rumours that prominent members of the ruling faction were planning to assassinate Pompey. Cicero for one was in no doubt that Caesar was behind this intrigue, the purpose of which was to frighten Pompey and push him into the arms of Caesar in 59 BC.

These were preliminary steps towards a definite goal. Although Caesar did not have the money or influence of his two colleagues, he was able to play a pivotal role in bringing Pompey and Crassus together in an alliance, which is known as the first Triumvirate – Caesar, Pompey and Crassus – as a rival power centre to the Senate. The formation of this formidable alliance was a warning sign that the end of the Republic was in sight.

The consulship of 'Julius and Caesar'

Caesar planned his rise to power with typical single-mindedness and ruthlessness. In 59 BC he became consul, along with the conservative, Bibulus.

There always had to be two consuls at Rome. This was an irritation for Caesar, but he soon hit on an effective solution. With the help of Clodius, he paid ruffians from the slum districts to insult and assault the unfortunate Bibulus every time he appeared in public. A clash with the conservatives was inevitable, and it soon came.

One of the first acts of Caesar as consul was to introduce legislation to distribute to Pompey's veterans whatever public lands remained in

Italy. This was obviously part of a deal that Caesar had struck with Pompey as a condition for his support for his election.

But Caesar was also following his own interests when he added a clause giving part of the land to the poor people of Rome. This action provoked the hostility of the conservatives, for whom it recalled unpleasant memories of the Gracchi.

Cato, Caesar's bitter enemy, opposed the measure violently, and Caesar had him arrested. He was later released, but the two sides were now on a collision course. The conservatives prepared to block the law in the Senate, whereupon Caesar decided to bypass the Senate and take the law directly to the popular assembly, the *comitia centuriata.*

This again brought back frightening memories of the times of the Gracchi. The assembly met in chaotic conditions. To general surprise both Pompey and Crassus spoke in favour of the reform, thus revealing the existence of their alliance with Caesar.

Bibulus, the conservative, opposed the law, but when he spoke against it, he got a very rough reception, during which a bucket of excrement was poured over his head. After this, Bibulus decided to withdraw from public life, alleging that he had read unfavourable omens in the sky (although it seems nobody else saw them).

As a result, he spent most of his time indoors, avoiding both the unfavourable omens and the buckets of foul-smelling organic matter. The local comedians joked that this was the "consulship of Julius and Caesar".

All the time the heightened tension between the classes was becoming ever more violent. In January 52 BC Clodius was murdered on the Appian Way by the supporters of his conservative rival Milon.

Clodius had been a popular figure, who had passed a law authorising the distribution of grain to the people of Rome free of charge. The body of the murdered tribune was put on public display – a sight that, together with the lamentations of his widow, excited the passions of the populace.

This led to a riot that turned into a virtual insurrection. The Curia was set ablaze and mobs of enraged citizens rampaged through the streets smashing property and assaulting anyone who looked wealthy.

This reaction was not surprising when one considers the abysm that separated the conditions of the masses from those of the rich.

The Gallic campaign

Caesar approached politics (and everything else) as a kind of shady business deal. As we know, in order to continue his upwards progress he needed to secure a constant flow of cash. He had spent colossal amounts on buying votes and bribing high officials – and the money was constantly running out.

Now Caesar had a problem. In order to succeed in his political intrigues, he needed more money. The only way he could get this was by borrowing and incurring huge debts. The problem with debts is that they have to be repaid, and the only way to pay these debts off was by securing an appointment to a profitable position in the provinces or by a military command that would enable him to obtain a large amount of booty.

Caesar's enemies in the Senate were well aware of his predicament and therefore offered him a minor position in rural Italy – a position that held out no prospects of enrichment whatsoever. By means of intrigues and bribery he succeeded in getting this decision overturned and instead was given control of the northern part of Italy, then known as Cisalpine Gaul, and Illyria, now Albania.

This was a much better proposition for enrichment. But Caesar had an even greater stroke of luck when the man who had been assigned control of Transalpine Gaul (modern-day southern France) died unexpectedly.

The rebellious state of that province caused panic in the Senate and therefore compelled them, against their wishes, to grant control of this province to Caesar. This was just what he required. What he really needed, he decided, was a nice little war.

As we have seen, Pompey made his fortune through conquests in Asia. In order to defeat his rivals, Caesar had to win even more spectacular victories. If he could kill a few thousand foreigners he would qualify for a triumph at Rome, and the money would start flowing again. Then, in 58 BC, he had another sudden stroke of luck.

A confederation of Gallic tribes, called the Helvetii, began a mass migration from their homes in what is now Switzerland to Western Gaul. In reality, the Helvetian migration posed no great threat to Rome. When their request to move through the Roman province of Transalpine Gaul was rejected, they simply changed their route in order to avoid it.

But the Romans were undoubtedly very sensitive on the issue of invading Gauls. They still shuddered at the memory of the time when, in 387 BC, a Gallic army sacked Rome. This dreadful event was deeply rooted in the collective consciousness, and any suggestion that history might be repeated was certain to provoke a powerful response. Caesar therefore got what he so ardently desired: the command of a Roman army.

Caesar's famous account of his Gallic campaign (*Commentaries on the Gallic War*) has acquired the status of a literary classic and an important historical document. In reality, however, it is not a work of history at all but a brilliant example of self-promotion. The celebrated *Commentaries*, written in the third person singular, are documents of immense value to historians, but they are not strictly historical. Written in a clear, concise Latin style, they are not devoid of literary merits, but they are not strictly literature.

Above all they are masterpieces of *political propaganda*, which one might say Caesar invented. They are designed to glorify Caesar's achievements and magnify his victories. In *De Bello Gallico* the word "Caesar" is repeated no fewer than 775 times.

There are many exaggerations and some downright lies in Caesar's accounts of the war. In the campaign against the Helvetii, Caesar claims to have confronted an army of 368,000. But modern historians like Furger-Gunti consider the actual numbers to have been around 40,000 warriors out of a total of 160,000 emigrants.

Delbrück suggests an even lower number of 100,000 people, out of which only 16,000 were fighters, which would make the Celtic force about half the size of the Roman body of about 30,000 men. Many of them were old people, women and children.

The defeat of the Helvetii was just the beginning. Seizing on whatever pretext lay at his disposal, Caesar then campaigned against the Belgae and the Nervii in the East, and against the Veneti in the Northwest, while his subordinates invaded Normandy and the South West. By 55 BC, most of Gaul was under Roman occupation, although far from pacified.

Caesar claimed to have killed huge numbers of people, including women and children. There is no way of verifying the figures he gives, of course. But there can be no doubt that these wars were accompanied by slaughter on a massive scale.

According to Plutarch's *Lives*, out of 3 million Gallic soldiers engaged in the wars, 1 million were killed and another million captured. It is possible that these figures are exaggerated (the Romans did not react to war casualties in the same way people do today. Their slogan was: the more deaths, the better!)

But it is clear that vast numbers were killed and enslaved. This was seen in Rome as a strong point in Caesar's favour. This was an age when imperialist aggression saw no need to disguise its true nature under the hypocritical cloak of 'humanitarian missions'.

Caesar's campaigns in Gaul were characterised by extreme brutality. Caesar himself confirms Plutarch's estimate of over a million enemy soldiers killed on the battlefields of Gaul, without including the civilian victims.

Here was the real ugly face of Roman imperialist expansionism. If a tribe in Gaul rebelled against Roman rule, every man, woman and child would be slaughtered without mercy. The intention was to terrorise the rest into submission.

The final aim was to obtain a huge number of slaves to feed the insatiable appetite of the Roman economy for slave labour. As in previous wars, in essence these were gigantic slave hunts. Caesar himself reports that after the Veneti surrendered to him in 55 BC, he executed their elders and then had the rest of the people sold into slavery.

Despite the sheer savagery of these campaigns, it cannot be denied that Caesar was a brilliant commander and diplomat. Like most adventurers, Caesar was not short of personal bravery. He had a gambler's instincts and was prepared to risk everything on a desperate throw. We see this tendency continually throughout his life.

From Caesar's point of view, his campaigns in Gaul were a spectacular success. In a few years he had conquered a vast expanse of territory in what is now called France, Switzerland and Belgium. Not satisfied with this, in the year 55 BC he crossed the Channel and led the first invasion of Britain, an island shrouded in mystery, and situated at the very edge of the known world.

Although the conquest of Britain did not succeed, his reputation as a successful general was now made. When the Gauls rose up under the command of Vercingetorix in 52 BC, Caesar defeated the rebellion at the famous (or notorious) siege of Alesia with the most extreme brutality and then went on to crush all further resistance. It was time to return to Rome and capitalise on his success.

Threatened by Caesar's growing power, the upper classes once again saw Pompey as their deliverer. They fawned upon the man whose consulship Cicero called "immortal".[7] But while the 'immortal' Pompey, the darling of the upper classes, rested on his laurels in Rome, Caesar was always on the offensive, followed by a troop of loyal soldiers in search of loot and officers in search of glory, promotion and a promising political career in the future. And there were plenty of ambitious young men prepared to follow Caesar abroad to win fame and wealth in the wars. These provided the shock troops of the Caesarist party.

The formation of the Triumvirate (Caesar, Pompey and Crassus) was already a step in the direction of undermining and overthrowing the republic and replacing it with the rule of one man. But relations within the Triumvirate were now beginning to crack. The question was really very simple. Who would be the future ruler of Rome?

---

7 Cicero, *Letters*, Vol. 2, p. 204.

9. Civil War

The conquest of Gaul enabled Caesar to amass an even more fabulous fortune than that of Pompey. He succeeded in strengthening his political base in Rome, and at the same time he directed the attention of the people towards new horizons. Hitherto the conquest of the world had reached only to the circle of the Alps.

Although his two expeditions to Britain did not leave any tangible results, they enormously enhanced his prestige. Caesar opened a new scene of achievement, extending even to the foggy shores of Britain – at the very boundary of the known world.

He returned to Rome to celebrate his triumph with an astonishing display of gold, silver, slaves and other loot. With this plunder he was able to pay off his debts and then bribe the mob and create a mass of political clients.

Always the astute politician, Caesar played upon the seething discontent of the lumpenproletariat in order to build up the Caesarist party in Rome. Together with a powerful army of soldiers hardened by years of war in Gaul, he had a strong base from which to launch his bid for power. Caesar's main base was always the army.

At this point the Triumvirate suffered a mortal blow. Crassus, the man who defeated Spartacus, was desperate to win military glory that could compare with that of Pompey and Caesar (a victory over an army of slaves was somehow not sufficient). He therefore set out for the East, where he participated in a campaign against the Parthians. But things did not turn out as he anticipated.

In 53 BC his legions were defeated at Carrhae (now Harran in Turkey) by a smaller Parthian force made up of armoured heavy cavalry and horse archers. Later the Parthians lured him into their camp, where he was seized and murdered. It was said that the Parthians poured molten gold into his mouth as a symbol of his thirst for riches. If true, it was a fitting end for the man who killed Spartacus and had thousands of slaves crucified.

With this blow, the Triumvirate was dead. Now a struggle opened up between Caesar and Pompey for control of the Republic. In the persons of Pompey and Caesar the two rival focal points in the state came into hostile opposition. Pompey had at one time been a supporter of Sulla and the aristocracy, but subsequently flirted with the populists and became a close ally of Caesar. Now he joined the Senate, and appeared as the defender of the Republic and the aristocratic party. On the other side stood Caesar with his legions.

This contest between the two most powerful individuals in the Republic could not be decided by peaceful debates in the Senate. Caesar was the supreme political opportunist, a man who knew how to subordinate means to ends. Hegel described him as "a paragon of Roman adaptation of means to ends – who formed his resolves with the most unerring perspicuity, and executed them with the greatest vigour and practical skill".[1]

For Hegel, Caesar was right because "he furnished a mediating element, and that kind of political bond which men's condition required."[2] In other words, Caesar *balanced* between the two opposing forces. But in the process, he concentrated all power into his hands. This is the real meaning of 'Caesarism'.

1 Hegel, *Lectures on the Philosophy of History*, p. 312.

2 Ibid.

The class basis of Caesarism

Caesar the adventurer attracted to his banner all kinds of discontented elements. These were the shock troops that he used as a battering ram to shatter the Senate's hold over state power. But the real class basis of Caesarism was not the lumpenproletarian rabble in Rome. Rather it was the *equites*, the 'new men', the bankers and financiers, especially in the provinces, who felt excluded from power and recognition, and were greedy to lay their hands on the fruits of state power.

These rich men imagined that they were using Caesar and the mob to advance their own interests, whereas in reality Caesar was using them (and their money) to grab power for himself. This relation has been repeated many times in later history, and has a close parallel with the relationship between the French bourgeoisie and Louis Bonaparte, and that between the German capitalist class and Hitler.

In spite of everything, Caesar was in difficulties. The murder of Clodius had weakened the leadership of the *populares*. Cicero was using his very considerable oratorical and literary skills to attack Caesar. The *optimates* had now succeeded in detaching Pompey from Caesar and were using Pompey's considerable authority to oppose Caesar. His enemies still controlled the Senate and Pompey's army was still intact.

Moreover, Caesar's conquests in Gaul were not as sure as they seemed. At any time, one or other of the tribes might rise up in revolt against the Roman oppressors. Under these circumstances, it was essential for Caesar to keep hold of his office – and his army. If he lost his position even for a short time, he would be open to prosecution by his enemies at Rome:

> If he gave way now, it was the end. Returning to Rome a private citizen, Caesar would at once be prosecuted by his enemies for extortion or treason. They would secure lawyers reputed for eloquence, high principle and patriotism. Cato was waiting for him, rancorous and incorruptible. A jury carefully selected, with moral support from soldiers of Pompeius stationed around the court, would bring in the

> inevitable verdict. After that, nothing for Caesar but to join the exiled Milo at Massilia and enjoy the red mullet and Hellenic culture of that university city.
>
> Caesar was constrained to appeal to his army for protection.[3]

Syme's analysis is obviously correct. But it is open to serious doubt whether Caesar would be allowed to go into a comfortable exile where he could enjoy the fish cuisine for the rest of his days. It was far more likely that his enemies in Rome would hand him over to the public executioner. The question therefore arose as to what would happen when the period of his office was over. Would he voluntarily give up control of his legions? Here the question of state power as armed bodies of men emerges with full force.

In June 51 BC the question of Caesar's military leadership in Gaul was raised in the Senate. In the meantime, Pompey let it be known that he also had his differences with Caesar. It was now clear that the destiny of Rome would be settled in an open struggle between the two generals. Although the Senate was theoretically in command, in reality it was already a spent force. It could issue decrees and make eloquent speeches, but ultimately everything boiled down to a show of naked force. Not speeches and resolutions, but swords and spears would decide matters.

Despite this evident fact, the senators continued to play out the constitutional farce. The strange and incurable disease which Marx described as parliamentary cretinism, is by no means a modern invention. In December 50 BC the senators solemnly voted (by 370 votes to twenty-two) that both Pompey and Caesar should dissolve their armies.

Since neither man had the slightest intention of doing such a thing, this was a pointless exercise. In any case, it was clear that the Senate needed Pompey's legions to use against Caesar. This is shown by the fact that the consul elected that year took the step of leaving Rome and placing a sword in Pompey's hands.

3 Syme, *The Roman Revolution*, p. 48.

For his part, Caesar showed that he understood how to play the game of constitutionalism as well as the Senate. He sent letters to Rome laying out all the legal arguments that would justify his retaining control of his legions. The consul Lentulus, who belonged to the aristocratic party, proposed a motion in the Senate that Caesar must lay down his military command by a specific date.

This proposal was vetoed subsequently by the tribunes, one of them a young supporter of Caesar called Marcus Antonius, known to us as Mark Antony. The time for constitutional ballet dancing was now clearly over. On 7 January Lentulus proposed the application of the so-called ultimate decree against those tribunes who had vetoed his proposal. Mark Antony and his comrades understood the meaning of this and fled from Rome to join Caesar.

As a commander, Caesar made use of the same psychological skills he had used in getting a mass base in Rome. He won popularity with his troops who thus became loyal to his person. He cemented this by promising them land. The Senate in Rome guessed his intentions and moved to prosecute him for his conduct as consul.

A test of wills followed. The Senate ordered Caesar to return to Rome. He refused. This was tantamount to a declaration of war. Cicero, who hated Caesar, raged, "Madman! Miserable wretch, that has never seen even a shadow of virtue!"[4] Finally, the Senate sent Pompey to oppose the rebel, arms in hand. Caesar responded by a characteristically daring gesture. He was now in Cisalpine Gaul, with a relatively small number of troops. It would seem that he stood no chance against Pompey's legions. Yet he did not hesitate for a second.

On 10 January he reached the little Rubicon River, which traditionally constituted the northern frontier of Italy. To cross it at the head of an army would be an act of open rebellion. With a theatrical gesture and the famous words, "the die is cast", he crossed the river. Typically, even the words he used come from the gambler's vocabulary. That immortal phrase meant simply: *there is no turning back.* The civil war had started.

---

4 Cicero, *Letters*, p. 241.

Caesar balances between the classes

Cicero, who stood for the Republic – that is to say, the interests of the old aristocracy – as usual, was playing a double game. He had sided with Pompey because he hoped to use his old enemy to crush Caesar, after which the Senate could dispose of Pompey and return to business as usual. The spectacle of civil war between the two erstwhile allies filled him with ill-concealed glee.

Cicero and the Senate thought that Caesar could be easily defeated. They thought they could count on the cities of Northern Italy to resist Caesar's advance. They were mistaken. Despite their numerical disadvantage, Caesar's forces advanced rapidly, meeting with little resistance. Part of the reason for this was that Italy had been plundered and exploited for too long, and the provincials were now utterly indifferent to the fate of Rome and its Senate. The other reason was that Caesar's agents had already bribed the Latin cities to stay out of the conflict.

Cicero complained bitterly that many wealthy Latin families were only too pleased to accept this offer to remain neutral in the civil war. As often happens in history, the men of wealth were not anxious to place their lands and fortunes at stake even in a conflict in which their class interests were involved. Even in Rome, many wealthy families that had supported the Senate tried to remain neutral once the fighting began in earnest. They tried to remain on good terms with both sides, until it became clear which side was more likely to win.

Always a smart politician, Caesar encouraged these wavering enemies in the belief that he was not so bad after all. He spread the idea that he was a defender of liberty and that the name of Caesar was synonymous with 'clemency'. To back up this impression, he sent letters to Pompey offering peace on the most generous terms. Even his most implacable enemy Cicero was fooled by this and agreed to act as mediator between the two generals. But this was all a farce designed to win time for Caesar and disarm the enemy.

Unlike Cicero, Pompey was not fooled. Alarmed at Caesar's rapid advance (he had expected more help from the Latins), Pompey hastily left the city and went south to the port of Brundisium, where he set sail for Greece. He sent messages to the Senate that this was just a tactical move to gather the necessary forces in the provinces with which to defend Rome.

As a matter of fact, this was probably true, as thinking in purely military terms Pompey realised that it was pointless to try to make a stand against Caesar in Italy. His idea was to regroup his armies in Greece, from which he could command the riches of the East and slowly strangle Rome by cutting off its supplies of corn from Egypt. This was not a bad idea. After all, how long could Caesar retain his support of the Roman populace once they had no bread to eat?

Pompey's military reasoning may have been sound, but politically his decision to abandon Rome was a disaster, and in a civil war, factors relating to politics and morale play an even more decisive role than in other wars. To the Senate and the people of Rome it looked like panic and an act of cowardly betrayal. Caesar's veteran army, hardened by years of warfare in Gaul, sliced through the opposition like a hot knife through butter.

The Senate's resistance collapsed. Towns and villages opened their gates along the way and Caesar stood before the gates of Rome, his enemies having fled. The city was now at the mercy of Caesar. The Senate awaited its fate like a condemned man waiting for the morning of his execution, while the populace awaited its liberator with suppressed elation. Both were in for a surprise.

Caesar's tactic from the beginning was to manoeuvre between the classes to concentrate the state power into his hands. When in April 49 BC he finally appeared before Rome, he did not order his army to enter and sack the city but, observing the laws and customs, halted respectfully at the gates. The aristocratic party must have been astonished.

All of a sudden, the noose that had been tightening around their plump necks, slackened. Yes, Caesar seemed to say to them, I respect the rule of law and the sacred constitutional rights of the Roman Senate. But like so much of the politics of the period this was just play-acting. Caesar was prepared to let the Senate retain the shadow of power, and encouraged them in the belief that they were still in charge, as long as he held the real power firmly in his hands.

The real state of affairs was quickly revealed. Caesar was now in complete command of the situation. He entered Rome in triumph at the head of his army. As the crowds roared their adulation, a slave stood behind him on the chariot whispering in his ear: "Remember, you are only a man". All this was done in the name of the Senate and the Roman people. But the Senate was powerless in the face of his military might. It meekly named him dictator.

As always, Caesar's actions were determined by two fundamental considerations: money and force, and the two were closely linked. His real power base was the legions, but soldiers have to be paid. Ever since he had left Gaul, he had been promising to reward his troops handsomely for their services. Unfortunately, although he had huge quantities of loot in Gaul, he lacked ready cash to make good his promises. This had already led to one mutiny and he could not afford discontent among the troops to spread any further.

They now held Rome and its treasure within their grasp and there was no time to be lost. Caesar demanded the keys to the treasury as a matter of urgency. But one of the tribunes, acting in the name of the laws and the constitution, refused, whereupon Caesar showed the precise limits of laws and constitutions by threatening to kill him. Needless to say, the gates of the treasury were opened rather quickly.

Pharsalus

Having established his base in Rome, Caesar now took the initiative on the military front. He first went to Spain where, with some difficulties, he smashed Pompey's most important base of support. The truth is that at this stage in the conflict, the result was still in the balance and at one point it looked as if Caesar would be defeated. But in the end his adventurer's luck did not desert him. The stage was now set for the decisive battle against Pompey in Greece, where the latter was attempting to assemble a powerful army.

Caesar had the support of the plebeian masses in Rome, although he himself was an aristocrat. He was supposed to be fighting for the rights and freedom of the people, whereas Pompey was supposed to be fighting for the rights and freedom of the Senate and to defend the Republic. The problem was that these rights and freedoms were mutually exclusive.

The Republic and its institutions had been long monopolised by a privileged aristocracy of slave-holders, and behind the banner of the Republic it was the rights and freedoms of these wealthy exploiters that were really being defended.

In reality, Caesar and Pompey represented different factions of the same class. In the words of Ronald Syme:

> The ambition of generals like Pompeius and Caesar provoked civil war without intending or achieving a revolution. Caesar, being in close contact with powerful financial interests and representatives of the landed gentry, was averse from any radical redistribution of property in Italy. He maintained the grants of Sulla. Further, many of his colonies were established on provincial soil, sparing Italy. A party prevailed when Caesar defeated Pompeius – yet the following of Caesar was by no means homogeneous, and the Dictator stood above parties. He did not champion one class against another. If he had begun a revolution, his next act was to stem its advance, to consolidate the existing order.[5]

If Pompey had succeeded in defeating Caesar, the outcome would have not been substantially different. Instead of one gang of marauding Mafiosi, there would have been a different gang in charge. That is all. Almost certainly the dictatorship of Pompey would have been more open and bloody, like that of Sulla, whereas the dictatorship of Caesar was more discrete and hypocritical, and one-man rule was disguised by the fig-leaf of 'respect' for the Republic and its laws and constitution.

But whoever won, in reality the old Republic was dead. All that was left was a name and an empty husk that was ready to be blown away by the slightest breeze.

5 Syme, *The Roman Revolution*, p. 194.

> This important change must not be regarded as a thing of chance; it was *necessary* – postulated by the circumstances. The democratic constitution could no longer be really maintained in Rome, but only kept up in appearance.[6]

Cicero and the other leaders of the republican faction attributed the corrupt state of the Republic to individuals and their passions. Cato said of Caesar: "His virtues be damned, for they have ruined my country!" They therefore considered that to preserve the Roman Republic was to eliminate its chief adversary. This showed a complete failure to understand the nature of the state and of the Roman state in particular. As Hegel points out:

> But it was not the mere accident of Caesar's existence that destroyed the Republic – it was *Necessity*. All the tendencies of the Roman principle were to sovereignty and military force: it contained in it no spiritual centre which it could make the object, occupation, and enjoyment of its Spirit. The aim of patriotism – that of preserving the State – ceases when the lust of personal dominion becomes the impelling passion. The citizens were alienated from the state, for they found in it no objective satisfaction…[7]

The Republic died because it could no longer exist. In Cicero's writings we see how all public affairs were decided by the private authority of the more eminent citizens – by their power, their wealth. All political transactions were accompanied by riots, murders and tumult.

There was no longer any security for the rich, or satisfaction for the poor. Such conditions, if they are prolonged without any perspective of a lasting solution, inevitably give rise to a yearning for stability, for 'Order', which must be expressed by subordination of all to a single will: the rule of a 'strongman'.

In this civil war many interests were at stake. In most cases on both sides it was a case of naked self-interest, a desire either to defend existing fortunes (frequently the result of the looting and confiscations carried out by previous regimes, notably that of the

6 Hegel, *Lectures on the Philosophy of History*, p. 311.

7 Ibid., pp. 311-2.

dictator, Sulla) or, on the contrary, to seize the estates and offices of those who held them.

But there were some, like Cicero and Brutus, who seemed to be genuinely attached to the cause of republicanism. If one is inclined to believe their public statements, they had convinced themselves that they were fighting for 'freedom'. In the opposing camp there must have been others who believed exactly the same thing.

Among those who had joined Pompey's force was Cicero, the most outspoken opponent of Caesar, who, however, was shocked by what he saw and heard in Pompey's camp. Here he soon grasped the reality of the situation as he listened, horrified, to the bragging speeches of Pompey and his officers, which were so bloodthirsty that he "trembled to think of his victory".

These gangsters were already sharing out the plunder and offices that they would obtain, even before they had won the war. But one little detail had escaped them: the war was not yet won. Pompey also made a serious political blunder: he had called upon the kings of Eastern lands to come to his aid.

This was a gift to Caesar, who, as we have already noted, was a very skilled propagandist. When it became known in Rome that Pompey was enlisting the aid of barbarian kings to conquer Rome, Pompey's support, already weakened by his desertion of Rome, plummeted, while that of Caesar's party increased in the same measure.

Revolutions and counter-revolutions are always a struggle of living forces. Pompey was taken by surprise by the rapid reaction of Caesar's forces, which, against all accepted practice, crossed the sea in the dangerous winter season and entered Greece with a relatively small force, which was later reinforced by Mark Antony.

On at least two occasions after he landed in Greece it looked as if Caesar had lost. The second of these occasions was the famous battle at Pharsalus in Thessaly, Greece, where, on 9 August 48 BC, the two armies met.

Pompey's forces enjoyed a considerable advantage in numbers. Despite this, the ever-cautious Pompey did not want to engage in combat with Caesar's veteran army. The fact was that Caesar was in serious difficulties at this point. His supplies were running out, whereas Pompey, who controlled all the main cities, had plenty of food.

Therefore, despite the unfavourable balance of forces, Caesar was desperate to provoke a battle there and then, or else withdraw his army. His initial efforts failed to provoke Pompey, who only agreed to go into battle reluctantly under the pressure of the other leaders. These men were arrogant and overconfident, and, unlike Pompey, they underestimated Caesar's army. They paid a heavy price for this excessive confidence.

The result of this battle was by no means preordained. Pompey commanded 45,000 infantry and 10,000 cavalry, against Caesar's total force of 22,000. His troops were well fed and rested, whereas those of Caesar were undernourished, tired after many exertions, and had already suffered one serious defeat at the hands of the Pompeians. On the other hand, Caesar's troops were seasoned veterans of the Gallic wars, whereas many of the opposite side were inexperienced.

Above all, the result of the battle was determined by superior leadership – the over-cautious and defensive Pompey versus the bold and energetic adventurer, Caesar. Here, once again, we see the correctness of Danton's famous advice to revolutionaries: "Audacity, audacity, and yet more audacity!"

Before the battle, as was usual, Caesar delivered a speech to his troops to boost their morale. The man who rebelled against the legal authority of the Senate now attempted to justify his rebellion to his soldiers. According to Lucan, who wrote the most famous account of the battle, he used a most striking phrase: "What, after all, is an illegal act? The answer depends upon who judges it after the battle is over."[8]

He reassured them that, in spite of the disparity in numbers, the quality of Pompey's forces was infinitely inferior to their own, appealing to Roman national pride and contempt for foreigners, Greeks and barbarians:

---

8 Lucan, *Pharsalia*, p. 157.

> Do not think that you have a serious task ahead of you. Pompey's army consists largely of levies from the Greek gymnasia, trained in wrestling and athletics but hardly able to carry a full weight of arms and equipment, let alone use them; and of undisciplined barbarians, shouting gibberish to each other, who hate fighting and even marching.[9]

He also warned them of the consequences of a defeat:

> Today will decide whether we are to be rewarded or punished for going to war. Picture to yourselves what will happen if Pompey beats us: Caesar dragged off in chains, Caesar crucified, Caesar's head cut off and displayed on the Rostrum, Caesar's body left unburied! And do not forget how Sulla behaved, the Sulla against whose pupil Pompey we are fighting the second civil war. He promised to spare 6,000 Marian prisoners, yet butchered them in the voting pens of the Campus Martius.[10]

So defeat would mean certain death, whereas victory would mean an end to all their suffering: "You need not pause to think where you will sleep tonight; Pompey's troops have comfortable quarters, which you will take over from them."[11]

In this battle, Mark Antony distinguished himself as the leader of Caesar's army on the left wing. To the astonishment of Pompey, his army gave way and was routed. He never recovered from the blow. After the battle, Pompey complained bitterly that he had been betrayed by the cavalry, who outnumbered Caesar's mounted troops almost two-to-one.

The bulk of this elite corps was composed of pampered young aristocrats. Caesar understood only too well the psychology of these spoilt brats of the rich. He carefully prepared an ambush, concealing a band of infantrymen, who emerged suddenly to confront the enemy cavalry, taking them by surprise.

Caesar advised his soldiers to strike at the faces of the young patricians, because they would be more afraid of good looks spoiled

9 Ibid.

10 Ibid., p. 158.

11 Ibid., p. 159.

than of being wounded in any other part of their anatomy. This proved to be very sound advice: the Pompeian cavalry panicked and fled, which was a key factor that decided Caesar's victory.

Thus, a bloody civil war in which the battle lines shifted from North Africa, to Spain, to Greece, came to an abrupt end on the battlefield at Pharsalus. There, though outnumbered two-to-one, Caesar defeated Pompey, killing 15,000 of his best troops.

Soon afterwards, the life of Pompey the Great came to a suitably miserable end. Realising that the battle was lost, he fled to Egypt, where he probably dreamed of regrouping with new forces. Instead, he was treacherously murdered.

Although it was in theory an independent state, Egypt was in fact at the mercy of Rome. Its rulers, therefore, anxious to win the favours of the victors – and keep the Roman army out of Egypt – deemed it expedient to send him on a one-way voyage to the underworld.

It is said that when his rival's head was presented to him, Caesar protested with the words: "I am not king but Caesar." Whether his words were sincere or feigned, it is impossible to say. What is indisputable is that at Pharsalus, by a single audacious throw of the dice, the gambler had won the highest prize. The path leading Caesar to power was suddenly thrown wide open before him.

10. The Death of the Republic

News of Caesar's victory reached Rome in October, but he did not return for nine months. This period was spent in the East, mainly in Egypt where, as is well known, Caesar entered into an amorous relationship with Cleopatra.

In addition to fathering a son with the Egyptian queen and putting down a dangerous rebellion, Caesar also led a short and successful military expedition against Pontus. It was at this time that he was supposed to have uttered the celebrated words: "I came, I saw, I conquered" – *veni, vidi, vici.*

Naturally, in all this time he did not neglect business. His conquests in the East provided him with a new supply of booty, with which to replenish his depleted coffers in Rome. The cash was much needed, since unpaid soldiers are likely to mutiny. Eventually, this actually happened, forcing Caesar to return to Italy in haste. Mark Antony did not show his master's skill in dealing with this situation, probably because his attentions appear to have been fully occupied by a beautiful mistress.

Having secured the East, Caesar returned to Rome with a spectacular triumph, which further strengthened his position and weakened that of his enemies. In the course of four days in August 46 BC huge processions wound their way through the streets of Rome, including a statue of Cleopatra together with Venus (who was supposed to be Caesar's ancestor).

After the processions came the games, a lavish spectacle featuring wild beast hunts, in which for the first time giraffes were seen in Rome. The whole extravaganza ended with a feast. In Caesar's absence there had been a shortage of grain, and now the populace looked to their saviour to provide all their needs. This extravagant show must have cost him a fortune.

He continued to use his wealth to bribe his opponents. His legions were never far away in the background to intimidate them if that became necessary. However, having installed himself as master of Rome, Caesar took care not to push the aristocracy too far. His measures were surprisingly moderate – and therefore disappointing to the populists.

Unlike his forerunner, Sulla, and against all expectations, Caesar did not launch a reign of terror, with proscriptions and executions of his enemies and the confiscation of their property. In those cases where estates were taken from his rivals and ended up in the hands of his supporters, they were auctioned or sold.

All this was intended to win over the rich and powerful to Caesar's cause and to neutralise the extreme republicans. This explains why he so quickly 'forgave' many of his enemies and tried to attach them to his cause.

Although he posed as 'the People's Friend', and had leaned on the masses to strike blows against the Senate and the aristocratic party, Caesar had absolutely no intention of handing power to the plebs. That is why, once he was installed at Rome, he made strenuous attempts to conciliate the aristocratic party. This must have come as a disagreeable surprise to his partisans on the streets, who expected to be allowed to loot and burn the houses of the rich as soon as Caesar returned. Instead, he kept strict order on the streets.

In fact, as soon as he was in power Caesar took measures to clip the wings of the popular party by banning all clubs and associations unless they had a licence, which very few did. The dictator was not willing to share power either with the conservatives or with the populists. Why should he? The new ruler of Rome had to appear as a force above all classes, representing 'the State'. This is a common feature in all Caesarist or Bonapartist regimes.

He severely restricted the number of people eligible to receive dole in the form of free grain. But the army was another matter. The bill for the army was by now colossal, since every soldier was due to receive the equivalent of a lifetime's wages, as well as a plot of land. The delay in meeting these expectations was causing unrest in the army.

When some of his soldiers protested about the lavish spectacle put on by Caesar on his return from Egypt, he had them immediately executed and their heads displayed in the forum "to encourage the others", to use Voltaire's expression. But he had to take care to preserve and strengthen his real power base, which was the army. He therefore used the money looted from the East to pay the soldiers and created new colonies to give to his soldiers land on retirement (a very important objective for a Roman soldier).

To some extent this measure was used to resettle part of the poor population in Rome. This was doubtless a popular measure, which was intended to remind the masses that 'Caesar was on the people's side' and to arouse echoes of the tradition of the Gracchi and the *populares* of the past.

However, these schemes had nothing in common with the revolutionary agrarian policies of the Gracchi. There must have been disappointment that these new lands were not in Italy but in the provinces. But it was by these means that Caesar could go some way to satisfying the masses' hunger for land without expropriating the big *latifundia* of the slave-owners in Italy.

The convulsions, revolutions and civil wars of the previous half century meant that many Romans and Italians had fallen seriously into debt. The harsh laws governing such situations placed them completely at the mercy of voracious money lenders, casting many into utter destitution. Caesar was aware of this, and the dangers that it posed to social stability. But what was to be done? He faced a dilemma that was well expressed by the historian, Michael Grant:

> On the one hand, something must obviously be done to rescue the ruined debtors. On the other hand, however, the rehabilitation of these unfortunate men must not be allowed to turn into a general cancellation of debts, which would destroy private property, the basis of the entire social system, and thus plunge Rome into a state of revolution: and that was what even moderate conservatives greatly feared.
>
> During the months that had elapsed since the beginning of the civil war, the debt crisis had become much greater. This was partly because of a shortage of currency. Money had been withdrawn from circulation to be hoarded until times became better, and such cash as could still be found had gone to pay the rival armies. This meant that whereas debtors were now receiving pressing claims for repayment, they were unable to respond to them and had to forfeit their land and other possessions instead, at wretched prices.[1]

To placate the poor, he introduced some restrictions on the laws relating to debt and bankruptcy, and suspended rents for twelve months. However, he failed to cancel all debts, which was one of the most pressing demands of his supporters. One of the reasons for this was that Caesar himself was owed huge sums of money by many people who he had 'helped' (and turned into clients) by lending them money in the past.

It was now time to call in these debts, or at least to remind the debtors of where their loyalties lay. To Caesar, cancelling debts would be like cutting off an arm – or probably some other, even more painful, extremity. None of his measures came close to touching the property of the slave owners. As Grant remarks:

> Creditors, of course, complained bitterly. But some of them were prepared to admit that they had expected even worse. At least Caesar had not proved the totally revolutionary destroyer of private property that he had

1 Grant, *Caesar*, pp. 121-4.

> been widely feared to be. Indeed, it was reassuring for property owners to note that, even if the senior senators were against him on political grounds, the able financiers were mostly on his side. So confidence began to come back, and men started to lend money once again.[2]

Caesar balanced between the classes, now appealing to the poor against the rich, now leaning on the rich to suppress the poor. But all the time he was concentrating power into his own hands. Caesar kept up the appearance of maintaining the Republic, and the Senate thanked him for it by licking his boots.

When he had first entered Rome after crossing the Rubicon, the Senate granted Caesar dictatorial powers but only for eleven days – just enough time to rig the consular elections. Later it made him dictator for four months, one year, ten years and finally for life. His triumphant return from Egypt gave this august body an excellent opportunity to display its utter servility before the military jackboot. It heaped honours upon him. It even voted to erect in the heart of Rome a statue of Caesar on a chariot with a globe in his hand and an inscription designating him a demi-god.

A rebellion in Spain led by Pompey's sons was quickly put down and when the news of Caesar's victory reached Rome the Senate once again lost no time in grovelling before their new master. They bestowed upon Caesar the title of 'Liberator', replete with unconscious irony, and even consecrated a temple to Liberty in his honour.

Later he was granted unprecedented honours: sacrifices on his birthday (something reserved for kings in Greek mythology), annual prayers for his health and well-being, and so the list goes on and on. And while the Senate heaped honours and praises on Caesar, with every passing day he was strengthening his power and forging new chains for the Republic.

The Caesarist party now had its boot placed firmly on the neck of the Senate and the people of Rome. It was also the *war party*. Partly, this was to add to Caesar's greatness. But war had a more immediate and practical aim – it was the only way to fill the state's coffers.

---

2 Ibid., p. 124.

The economic crisis in Rome was unprecedented. After years of revolutions, upheavals and civil war, the treasury was bankrupt. Yet Caesar distributed land to his veterans and ordered the construction of lavish public works, of libraries, canals, even a harbour. To pay for all this, there had to be new wars every year, like the war Caesar planned against Parthia.

Pursuing his internal revolution, Caesar increased the number of senators from 600 to 900 to reward his own party and undermine the old aristocracy. But far from increasing the Senate's weight and power, this was merely another way of expressing its irrelevance.

All the real decisions were now taken by Caesar and his entourage. From his point of view, it made sense to pack the talking-shop of the Senate with loyal supporters and thus weaken still further the specific gravity of the old aristocratic party.

Ronald Syme writes on the composition of Caesar's party and the character of those adherents with whom he stuffed the Senate:

> Many of Caesar's partisans were frank adventurers, avid for gain and advancement, some for revolution. […]
>
> Caesar's following was heterogeneous in composition – at its kernel a small group of men paramount in social distinction, not merely *nobiles* but patrician; on the outer fringe, many excellent Roman knights, 'the flower of Italy'.[3]

These 'excellent knights' were a collection of bankers, speculators and tax-farmers, who provided a reliable support for the Caesarist party. The huge increase in the numbers of senators was therefore not just a means of diluting the senatorial power and increasing that of Caesar: it was also very good for business.

Naturally, those promoted to senatorial rank – many of whom were provincials from Gaul and Spain with no connection with the old senatorial aristocracy – would not only be grateful to their benefactor but would also be anxious to express their gratitude by paying important sums of money into his coffers.

---

3 Syme, *The Roman Revolution*, p. 51.

And if he arranged, as he did, that the senators should be the men he wanted, he also found ways to mould the leading offices of state to his own pattern. Under his direction as dictator, the annual elections to the consulships and other offices still continued. But he secured the passage of a law allowing him to 'recommend' quite openly to a large proportion of the more important posts – and indeed to fix who their holders should be, for a number of years ahead. In the old days the consuls had been rulers of the state. Now, they were convenient henchmen for Caesar: and their posts were appropriate ones to hand to loyal supporters as a recompense for their services.[4]

The assassination of Caesar

Caesar announced a reform of the calendar with 365 days – the basis of our modern calendar. Behind this was a definite idea. The old calendar was in a mess, and he wished to introduce order out of chaos at all levels. The dictator decided even what day of the week it was! Naturally, one of the months was named after him (July).

He had himself declared dictator for life, although it was supposed to be a temporary office. He appeared in a purple toga, this being the colour traditionally associated with royalty. Finally, he consorted with the Egyptian queen Cleopatra, though still married to Calpurnia, his third wife. In other words, he was behaving like an oriental despot.

Inevitably, the question was raised of making Caesar king. It is likely that these rumours were spread by his enemies as a provocation. The title of king was hated in Rome ever since the distant days when the Tarquins were expelled from the city.

Caesar, who in practice enjoyed almost all of the attributes of a monarch, understood very well the risks entailed in accepting such a title. On one occasion, his faithful supporter and friend Mark Antony publicly offered him a golden crown, which he made a great show of rejecting, hurling it away from his person with great force.

It is obvious that the whole thing was a prearranged show designed to prove to the people that he had no ambitions to wear a crown.

---

4 Grant, *Caesar*, p. 185.

And why should he? A man who holds real power in his hands is not interested in possessing the outward signs and insignia of power.

On the contrary, Caesar was quite content that an impotent Senate should carry such meaningless insignia, as long as it was he, and not they, who actually ruled. Caesar did not overthrow the Republic, but only the empty shadow of a thing that already lacked all real substance. Hegel understood the situation very well:

> His position was indeed hostile to the republic, but, properly speaking, only to its shadow; for all that remained of that republic was entirely powerless. Pompey, and all those who were on the side of the senate, exalted their *dignitas auctoritas* – their individual rule – as the power of the republic; and the mediocrity which needed protection took refuge under this title. Caesar put an end to the empty formalism of this title, made himself master, and held together the Roman world by force, in opposition to isolated factions.[5]

The diehard republicans could only curse under their breath as they witnessed the inexorable decline of the senatorial power. Conservative republicans like Cicero had to be content with whispering in corners or writing sarcastic letters like the following:

> Caesar who had taken the auspices as for a *comitia tributa*, held a *comitia centuriata*, and between twelve and one o'clock announced the election of a consul to hold office till 1 January, which was the next day. Thus I may inform you that no one breakfasted in the consulship of Caninius. However, no mischief was done while he was consul, for he was of such astonishing vigilance that throughout his consulship he never had a wink of sleep.
>
> You think this a joke, for you are not here. If you had been you would not have refrained from tears. There is a great deal else that I might tell you; for there are countless transactions of the same kind.[6]

In this way, Rome and all its world-wide sovereignty became the property of a single man. The extreme republican wing of the

5 Hegel, *Lectures on the Philosophy of History*, p. 313.

6 Cicero, *Letters*, Vol. 3, p. 358.

aristocratic party was implacable in its opposition to Caesar, whose connections with Cleopatra and the kings and despots of the East made his intentions even more suspect.

The aristocrats stifled their indignation when Caesar sent a Gaul into the Senate but could do nothing about it except complain furtively for fear of Caesar's spies, who were everywhere. The enemies of Caesar were now on the defensive.

While the majority of the old senatorial aristocracy acted in a cowardly fashion in surrendering power to a man they hated and despised as much as they feared, the extreme republican faction, feeling the last vestiges of power slipping inexorably from their hands, resorted to desperate measures: they decided to get rid of Caesar.

A decisive step was taken in February 44 BC, when the Senate finally voted to make Caesar dictator for life. This was the final act of self-abasement of this miserable and spineless group of men. But for some it was the last straw.

A conspiracy was organised by a small group of senators headed by Brutus and Cassius, who hit on a plan childish in its simplicity: the problem was Caesar, and therefore his removal was the solution. Once Caesar was assassinated the republic would be restored and everything would be as it was before. Cicero, Brutus and Cassius imagined that Caesar's rule was a mere accident, and the entire position of affairs to be dependent on his individuality.

The chief organiser of the conspiracy was Gaius Cassius Longinus, a man with great practical energy who had come over to Caesar's side after the battle of Pharsalus, but who evidently thought he had not been sufficiently rewarded for his services. He won over his brother-in-law, Marcus Brutus, who had a special place in Caesar's affections (some thought he was Caesar's natural son).

Brutus is generally held to be a man of noble character ("This was the noblest Roman of them all", wrote Shakespeare).[7] But he

7 Shakespeare, *Julius Caesar*, Act 5, Scene 5, line 74.

defended the same class interests as the others – the interests of the old aristocratic, senatorial class.

The conspirators believed that if this one individual were out of the way, the republic would be *ipso facto* restored. Possessed by this delusion, they plotted the assassination of the individual who, in their mind, was responsible for all their ills. The outcome of all this is well known. On the Ides of March (15 March) 44 BC, only days before he was due to leave for a military campaign in the East, Caesar was murdered on his way to the Senate.

One of the great mysteries is why he had no real protection. He had even dismissed his personal bodyguard of Spaniards. Was this an excess of confidence? Or was it the result of his fatalistic Stoic philosophy, as Shakespeare implies:

> Cowards die many times before their deaths;
> The valiant never taste of death but once.
> Of all the wonders that I yet have heard,
> It seems to me most strange that men should fear,
> Seeing that death, a necessary end,
> Will come when it will come.[8]

Whatever the reason, the conspirators had it easy. They surrounded Caesar, who, having been stabbed twenty-three times, finally covered his face in his cloak and collapsed in a pool of blood under the statue of Pompey, it was said. According to Suetonius, some said that when Brutus struck his blow, Caesar said: "You too, my son."[9]

The conspiracy succeeded in its immediate objective. But his murder could not save the Republic. It immediately became clear that the Roman state had been transformed, and it was impossible to put the clock back.

The conspirators imagined that by eliminating one man they could save the system. But the results of their actions were

8 Ibid., Act 2, Scene 2, lines 34-9.

9 Ziogas, 'Famous Last Words: Caesar's Prophecy on the Ides of March', *Antichthon*, Vol. 50, pp. 134-153.

diametrically opposed to their intentions. Instead of restoring the Republic, they only succeeded in ushering in the Empire. The problem of this analysis is that its basic assumption was false. All attempts to revive a corpse that is already beginning to smell bad are doomed to failure.

The Republic was dead because the old economic and class relations that created it had disappeared long since. Caesar only gave it a shove and it collapsed. All that was left was an empty husk, which was blown away by the first puff of wind.

Even the tactics adopted by the conspirators revealed a fatal weakness. Individual terrorism is always an expression of weakness. The assassins believed that one bold stroke for 'liberty' would galvanise the old aristocratic party to fight in its own defence. But that party was already in ruins, split and demoralised. It was not even prepared to fight in its own defence. As Michael Grant says:

> Curiously blinkered by their own traditions, the Roman nobility just did not realise that they could not simply pick up the threads where it had dropped them at the beginning of the Civil War. For the power was no longer theirs to recapture: it had passed for ever into the hands of the general who could marshal the most formidable armed forces.[10]

Augustus

In the moment of truth Brutus and the other conspirators found themselves isolated and rapidly crushed. By their actions, far from saving the Republic, they accelerated its destruction.

The leader of the Caesarist party was at first Mark Antony, who took advantage of the outrage of the mob at Caesar's murder to consolidate his position. In the confused and turbulent situation that followed, he was forced to manoeuvre and arrive at an uneasy compromise with Brutus and Cassius, who were allowed to leave Rome and establish a base in the East.

Antony was greedy for power and lost no opportunity to fill his pockets, as Syme points out:

---

10 Grant, *Caesar*, p. 198.

> Invective asserts, and history repeats, that the consul Antonius embezzled the sum of 700 million sesterces deposited in Rome at the Temple of Ops.[11]

But Antony's position was still insecure, and he had an important rival for the leadership of the Caesarist party: a clever, cold and calculating young man called Gaius Octavius (Octavian), who was Caesar's great-nephew. Since Caesar had no children by Calpurnia, and they had adopted Octavian, he was also Caesar's legal heir.

At first, they were on a direct collision course. Amidst rumours that Octavian was plotting his assassination, Antony left Rome with an army to take over the province of Cisalpine Gaul, which was governed by one of Caesar's killers, Decimus Brutus. The Senate declared in favour of Brutus and appealed to Octavian, who had assembled his own private army, recruited from some of Caesar's old veterans. With this army Octavian defeated Antony during the siege of Mutina (new Modena) in April 43 BC. But in November that year they patched up their differences and formed the Second Triumvirate together with the general, Marcus Aemilius Lepidus.

They then went onto the offensive, defeating Brutus and Cassius at Philippi in October 42 BC. In September 40 BC, Octavian and Antony agreed to divide the provinces of the Republic into three spheres of influence. Octavian took control of Spain and Gaul, while Antony took over the East, and Lepidus was left with only the province of Africa (roughly present-day Tunisia, Northeastern Algeria and Western Libya). This pact was known as the Brundisium Agreement. It could not last.

Octavian, who had boundless ambition, started calling himself '*Divi filius*' ('son of the God'). This was a direct imitation of Caesar, who had been deified as *Divus Iulius* ('Divine Julius'). Later he simply styled himself 'Imperator Caesar'. Imperator, a military term for a victorious general, is the origin of our word Emperor.

The triumvirs immediately embarked on a ferocious campaign of proscriptions against anyone perceived as having sympathies for the

11 Syme, *The Roman Revolution*, p. 131.

assassins of Julius Caesar. The methods of the Caesarists are described by Ronald Syme:

> The consequences of compelling a general to appeal to his army in defence of life or honour were now apparent – the generals themselves were helpless in the hands of the legions. The proletariat of Italy, long exploited and thwarted, seized what they regarded as their just portion. A social revolution was now carried out, in two stages, the first to provide money for the war, the second to reward the Caesarian legions after victory.
>
> War and the threat of taxation or confiscation drives money underground. It must be lured out again. Capital could only be tempted by a good investment. The Caesarian leaders therefore seized houses and estates and put them on the market. Their own partisans, astute neutrals and freedmen of the commercial class got value for their money in the solid form of landed property. Freedmen, as usual, battened upon the blood of citizens.
>
> The proscriptions may not unfairly be regarded as in purpose and essence a peculiar levy upon capital. As in Sulla's proscription, *nobiles* and political adversaries might head the list: the bulk is made up by the names of obscure senators or Roman knights. The *nobiles* were not necessarily the wealthiest of the citizens: men of property, whatever their station, were the real enemies of the Triumvirs. In concord, senators and business men upheld the existing order and prevented a reconstitution of the old Roman People through a more equitable division of landed property in Italy; now they were companions in adversity. The beneficiaries of Sulla suffered at last. The Triumvirs declared a regular vendetta against the rich, whether dim, inactive senators or pacific knights, anxiously abstaining from Roman politics. That was no defence.[12]

Octavian not only had the opportunity of robbing the state treasury. He also had behind him the richest men in Rome:

> The diversion of public funds was not enough. Octavianus also won the support of private investors, among them some of the wealthiest

---

12 Ibid., pp. 194-5.

> bankers of Rome. Atticus, who refused to finance the war-chest of the Liberators, would not have looked at this venture. No matter: Caesar's heir secured almost at once the financial secretaries and political agents of the Dictator.[13]

Sooner or later Octavian was bound to come into a head-on collision with Mark Antony for possession of the immense wealth of Egypt and the East. First Octavian got rid of Lepidus, the weakest link in the Triumvirate, and sent him into exile.

Then he manoeuvred to turn public opinion in Rome against Mark Antony, using his relations with Queen Cleopatra to discredit him. He illegally obtained Antony's will in July 32 BC, and exposed it to the Roman public. It promised substantial legacies to Antony's children by Cleopatra, and instructed that his body should be shipped to Alexandria for burial. These shocking revelations caused outrage in Rome, and the ground was psychologically prepared for war.

At the naval battle of Actium in Greece (2 September 31 BC), Octavian's forces decisively defeated those of Antony and Cleopatra, although by all accounts the battle itself was a bit of a farce, ending in Octavian's fleet chasing the enemy back to Egypt, where Antony and Cleopatra committed suicide. All power was now concentrated in the hands of one man – Octavian, who is known to history as Augustus, the first Emperor of Rome.

The natural result of Caesarism was the Empire, where all traces of the old republic vanished without trace. The hypocritical Augustus kept up the pretence of respect for the Senate and the republican forms, making a great show of handing back his triumviral powers to the Senate after his triumphal return from Egypt.

Instead of the title of 'king' or 'dictator', the absolute ruler of Rome humbly took the informal title of *princeps civitatis*, or 'First Citizen', but everybody knew that it was just pretence. Octavian retained the *imperium*, or command, of the bulk of the Roman legions throughout his life, and over time he was formally granted the powers of legislative initiative and veto by the servile Senate.

---

13 Ibid., p. 131.

On 16 January 27 BC, he was 'granted' the title of Augustus, which would become an imperial title for centuries to come. The great Roman historian, Tacitus, summarised the new order founded by Augustus masterfully in the first book of his *Annals*:

> When the killing of Brutus and Cassius had disarmed the Republic; when Pompey had been crushed in Sicily, and, with Lepidus thrown aside and Antony slain, even the Julian party was leaderless but for the Caesar; after laying down his triumviral title and proclaiming himself a simple consul content with tribunician authority to safeguard the commons, he first conciliated the army by gratuities, the populace by cheapened corn, the world by the amenities of peace, then step by step began to make his ascent and to unite in his own person the functions of the senate, the magistracy, and the legislature. Opposition there was none: the boldest spirits had succumbed on stricken fields or by proscription-lists; while the rest of the nobility found a cheerful acceptance of slavery the smoothest road to wealth and office, and, as they had thriven on revolution, stood now for the new order and safety in preference to the old order and adventure.[14]

For over a century the Roman ruling class had desperately strived for order. At last, their wish was granted, by the common submission and plunder of all classes by the mailed fist of military despotism.

The state is transformed

The rise of autocratic rule had been prefigured in the latter period of the Republic. The intense class struggles of the period had already produced a series of strongmen including Marius and Sulla, and later Pompey and Caesar. An explanation for the transformation of the Roman state under Caesar and Augustus must therefore be sought beyond the subjective will of any 'Great Man', or the many battles that made up the various civil wars of the period.

Marx famously explained, "Men make their own history, but they do not make it as they please; they do not make it under

14 Tacitus, *In Three Volumes*, Vol. 2, *Annals*, Book 1, p. 245.

circumstances chosen by themselves, but under circumstances already existing, given and transmitted from the past."[15] And the individuals whose actions make up the history of the downfall of the Republic lived in a society that had already been fundamentally and irrevocably changed.

The rise of slavery had destroyed the free Roman peasantry that had been the backbone of the Republic. In the absence of a free peasantry, the state was obliged to rely on a mercenary army to fight its wars. This was the soil upon which the phenomenon of Caesarism took root and flourished.

The formation of a mass lumpenproletariat in the cities introduced a powerful destabilising factor into Roman politics. The rival parties alternated in power, and took advantage of the opportunity to slaughter their opponents. The internal cohesion of the state was fatally undermined, as nobody recognized the authority of the other side, or the validity of its laws and statutes, as Hegel affirms:

> The sovereignty was made dependent on the people – that people which was now a mere mob, and was obliged to be supported by corn from the Roman provinces. We should refer to Cicero to see how all affairs of state were decided in riotous fashion, and with arms in hand, by the wealth and power of the grandees on the one side, and by a troop of rabble on the other. The Roman citizens attach themselves to individuals who flatter them, and who then become prominent in factions, in order to make themselves masters of Rome.[16]

Eventually, the class struggle at Rome reached a complete deadlock. The real cause of this situation was the inability of the poor plebeians to unite with the slaves in their struggle against the ruling oligarchy. In the last analysis, the Roman lumpenproletariat shared in the fruits of the exploitation of the slaves and the plunder of the provinces. This doomed the Roman revolution, which had begun with the Gracchi, to failure.

---

15 Marx, *The Eighteenth Brumaire of Louis Bonaparte*, p. 2.

16 Hegel, *Lectures on the Philosophy of History*, p. 311.

The contending classes fought each other to a standstill, but neither could prevail. Under such circumstances, the state itself becomes the master of society, imposing its absolute rule to prevent society from devouring itself in internecine conflicts. It is in this fact that we can find the real cause of the Republic's downfall.

In *The Communist Manifesto*, Marx and Engels pointed out that the class struggle eventually ends either in the total victory of one of the classes, or else in the common ruin of the contending classes. The fate of Roman society is the clearest example of the latter case.

Wars, civil wars, slave uprisings and constant factional strife between different layers of the ruling class for possession of the state, led to a state of utter prostration and exhaustion of the contending classes. This fact was already understood by the idealist, Hegel, when he wrote:

> We see the internal contradiction of Rome now beginning to manifest itself in another form; and the epoch which concludes the second period is also the second mediation of that contradiction. We observed that contradiction previously in the struggle of the patricians against the plebeians: now it assumes the form of private interest, contravening patriotic sentiment; and respect for the state no longer holds these opposites in the necessary equipoise. Rather, we observe now side by side with wars for conquest, plunder and glory, the fearful spectacle of civil discords in Rome, and intestine [civil] wars.[17]

History knows many revolutions and it is customary to refer to the changes made by Caesar and his followers as 'the Roman Revolution'. But in fact it was a revolution that affected only the political superstructure. It did not alter in any way the existing property relations in society. Rather, it saved them.

Caesar and his successors plundered the slave-owning oligarchs and stole their estates. But in the last analysis, they stood for the defence of the slave system and allied themselves with the wealthy oligarchs and bankers to save private property from 'anarchy' and the mob. In fact,

17 Ibid., p. 307.

it was only by abandoning the rule of the Senate and the Republic that the slave system, and with it the wealth of the slave owners, could be preserved.

The fruits of plunder

Under Augustus, the wealth of the rich flourished to a scale unheard of even in the most decadent years of the Republic. They lived lives of extravagant luxury, a world of palaces of marble imported from far distant lands, of Greek statues and fabulously beautiful mosaics. Augustus boasted that he had found Rome "built of brick and left it in marble".[18]

Deprived of political power, the Roman ruling class could enjoy all the more thoroughly the fruits of its economic power, dissipating the wealth of society in endless feasting. And what feasts! A dining room typically held three broad couches, each of which seated three individuals, thus allowing for a total of nine guests. But the feasts of the super-rich had many more guests to entertain. Their couches were not made of wood, but of costly materials, such as ivory and bronze.

Armies of slaves toiled in the kitchens to prepare the most extravagant dishes. The food and wine were naturally served by slaves in silver utensils. The *Cena Trimalchionis* (Trimalchio's Dinner), written by Petronius Arbiter, provides a vivid account of wealthy Romans during the first century AD.

The character of Trimalchio was a freedman (an ex-slave) who had made his fortune speculating on the shipping trade: a typical example of the *nouveaux riches* of the period. His guests are treated with numerous dishes, including a roasted pig stuffed with sausages, a hare decorated with wings to resemble Pegasus, and various foods arranged in the shape of the twelve signs of the zodiac. But there was even more exotic fare, such as sow's udders, stuffed snails, peacock tongues, fried dormice, stuffed larks' tongues and so on and so forth. All was to be washed down with great quantities of wine poured by naked waiters.

---

18 Suetonius, *The Lives Of The Twelve Caesars*, p. 70.

In addition to the temples and statues of marble, the Roman elite also patronised the literary arts, always of course for their own glorification and that of the emperor. Ovid's *Metamorphoses* concludes with the metamorphosis of Julius Caesar into a god, and thereby the metamorphosis of the Republic into the Empire. Another of Rome's most famous poets, the freedman, Horace, was supported in his poetic career by Augustus' right-hand man, Gaius Maecenas.

Virgil, the greatest of all Latin poets, was commissioned to write *The Aeneid* by none other than the emperor himself. The poet repaid his benefactor in verse, placing the following words in the mouth of Jupiter:

> From this glorious source a Trojan Caesar will be born,
> who will bound the empire with Ocean, his fame with the stars,
> Augustus, a Julius, his name descended from the great Iulus.
> You, no longer anxious, will receive him one day in heaven,
> burdened with Eastern spoils: he'll be called to in prayer.

By such means, the humble first citizen of Rome traced his heritage to the foundation of Rome itself, and placed his destiny in the heavens for the rest of eternity. Past, present and future, there was no escape from the Emperor.

But beneath its thick coating of marble and propaganda, the imperial state was nothing more than a vast machine for the holding down of millions of slaves and the extraction of plunder from the provinces. In time, it would devour Roman society itself.

Epilogue: Decline and Fall

What are we waiting for here in the square?
    The barbarians will arrive today.

Why is there such paralysis in the Senate?
Why do the Senators just sit there and pass no laws?
    Because the barbarians will arrive today.
    What laws will the Senators vote for now?
    The barbarians when they come will pass their own laws.

Why does our Emperor rise from his slumbers so early,
and sit by the widest gate in the city upon the throne,
in splendour, wearing the imperial crown?
    Because the barbarians will arrive today.
    And the Emperor is waiting to receive their leader.
    He is ready to give him a parchment.
    On which he has written so many titles and honours.

Why did our two consuls and praetors go out today
dressed in their red, embroidered togas;
why did they wear bracelets with so many amethysts,
and rings with richly sparkling emeralds?

Why today do they clutch precious staffs
so exquisitely carved with silver and gold?
Because the barbarians will arrive today;
and such things impress the barbarians.

Why do the worthy orators not come as before
to deliver their speeches, to pronounce their speeches?
Because the barbarians will arrive today;
and speeches and rhetoric bore them.

Why this sudden concern and unease.
(Look how serious the faces have become!).
Why are the streets and the squares emptying so fast,
and everyone goes to their homes with such thoughtful faces?
Because night came and the barbarians did not arrive.
And some arrived from the border,
and told us barbarians no longer exist.

And now what will happen without the barbarians?
Even they were some kind of a solution.

– Konstantinos Kavafis, *Waiting for the Barbarians*

A regime of social decay

The haunting verses of *Waiting for the Barbarians* by the modern Greek writer Konstantinos Kavafis effectively capture the tortured soul and angst of a society that feels itself to be standing on the edge of an abyss. That feeling must have gripped the minds of many people in the final years of the Roman Empire. A similar feeling is now growing stronger by the day.

The question of the causes of the decline and fall of the Roman Empire falls outside the scope of the present work. The decline lasted centuries and was not an uninterrupted process. There were periods of recovery and even brilliance, but the general line was downwards.

A more detailed treatment will have to wait for another day, but without attempting to plumb the depths of this important subject, it will be worthwhile drawing a few threads together in the form of a brief epilogue, for two reasons.

First, the social and economic decay that fatally undermined the Empire was clearly rooted in the previous period, which forms the subject of the present work. Second, and more important, it holds very important lessons for the world in which we live today.

It often happens in history that outworn institutions can survive long after their reason to exist has disappeared. They drag out a miserable existence, like a decrepit old man who clings onto life, until they are swept away by a revolution.

The forms of the old Republic survived for a long time after its final ignominious collapse. But they were just that – hollow forms with no real content, empty husks that in the end could be blown away by the wind. The Senate was devoid of all real power and authority.

Augustus took care to observe the forms and 'consult' the Senate, and even contrived not to laugh out loud when doing so. Naturally, none of the senators ever dared to contradict his friendly advice. For some time later, the emperors continued this farce, but they soon got tired of it and openly regarded the Senate with contempt – if they regarded it at all. Caesar scandalised people by sending a Gaul into the Senate, but when the emperor Caligula planned to make his favourite horse a consul, everybody knew that this action expressed very well the real situation.

In the last period of the Empire, when, as a result of the decline of production, corruption and looting, the finances were in a lamentable state, wealthy Romans were regularly 'promoted' to the rank of senator in order to extract extra taxes from them. One such reluctant legislator was said by some Roman humorist to have been 'banished into the Senate'.

The emperors

From the reign of Augustus onwards, control of the state was effectively handed over to a powerful clique of banditti. The rule of the emperors most closely resembles that of a mafia gang. Only instead of controlling, looting and terrorising a city or a local district, these gangsters dressed in imperial purple had an entire empire to plunder.

And what an empire! Rome was now the undisputed master of much of the known world. Its dominions stretched from the Pillars of Hercules on the shores of the Atlantic to the Persian border in the East.

History informs us that many of the emperors were either insane or very close to that condition. This should surprise no-one. In the celebrated phrase of Lord Acton, power tends to corrupt and absolute power corrupts absolutely. This remark is perfectly applicable to the Rome of the emperors.

What is madness, except the total inability to distinguish between reality and fantasy? And when every rational boundary of thought and conduct is removed, the inevitable result is insanity. That was undoubtedly the case with both Hitler and Stalin in the end. And it was certainly the case with Roman emperors from a very early period.

When a human mortal is given absolute power, and is surrounded by a gang of servile courtiers who constantly repeat that the emperor is all-wise, all-knowing and all-powerful, those boundaries are indeed abolished.

Since there was no external power over the imperial family – with the exception of the army, which always held a sharp sword suspended over the throne – the political life of the Empire was reduced to constant intrigue, divorce, murder and banishment within the royal family.

According to Tacitus, Augustus' successor, Tiberius, "plunged into every wickedness and disgrace" before he was smothered in his own bed clothes at the behest of his heir, Caligula.[1] Caligula himself was clearly insane. We have already mentioned that he planned to make his favourite horse consul, which accurately exposed the real state of affairs. Other exploits are too gruesome to relate. In the end he went too far and the Praetorian Guard decided to get rid of him. After just four years of chaos and mayhem, he was assassinated.

1 Tacitus, *Annals*, Book 6, p. 180.

This established an effective mechanism for effecting a change of ruler in the later Roman Empire. It was the only one possible. His infamous nephew Nero was proclaimed emperor when he was only sixteen years old. Nero saw himself as a patron of taste, high culture and art. But at heart he was a pure lumpenproletarian, a mafioso and a sadist.

He commenced his career by murdering his half-brother, Britannicus. Then, with breathless speed, one by one, he killed all his relations. The culmination of his career came when, at the age of only twenty-two, he murdered his mother, Agrippina.

In order to justify this abominable crime, he accused Agrippina of plotting his assassination, and he held a public thanksgiving to celebrate the matricide. He went on to banish his wife Octavia on an island where he had her murdered. He then married the depraved Poppaeia, presenting her with Octavia's head as a gift.

In 68 AD, after a turbulent thirteen-year reign, his luck finally ran out. Even the servile Roman Senate concluded that he had gone too far. Abandoned by the praetorians and declared a public enemy, Nero was forced to commit suicide, thus ending the Julio-Claudian dynasty.

It would be a tedious and quite pointless task to make a list of every one of the emperors who came to power, and lost it in just the same way. The army was the sole power in society, especially the Praetorian Guard, a privileged elite that was supposed to protect the ruling emperor and his family, but in reality was the supreme arbiter of power.

It was sufficient for the praetorians to get tired of the man in charge, for them to murder him and then raise some successor on their shields and proclaim him emperor. In 193 AD they went as far as to publicly auction the Empire to the highest bidder, having murdered the previous emperor days before. Even after the Praetorian Guard was dissolved by Constantine, this procedure was repeated many times by the legions in the final centuries of the Empire.

Over a period, the wealth of Rome was steadily exhausted by the corrupt rule of one mafioso after another. The treasury was emptied by the rising cost of purchasing the loyalty of the troops and maintaining a vast and unwieldy bureaucratic administration.

One layer upon another of parasites satisfied their gluttony, like a legion of fat and voracious leeches, on the body of the Empire. One ruinous foreign war followed another, to the point where the amounts extracted in loot no longer exceeded the costs of war. One ambitious emperor after another spent extravagant sums on monuments to their own glorification.

And the unemployed army of lumpenproletarians that swelled the population of Rome, had to be kept fed and amused for fear of serious disturbances. This was no easy task. It was the poet Juvenal who coined the notorious phrase, 'Bread and Circuses'. But quite often, there was not enough bread to feed a city with a population of one million people, and there are at least nineteen food riots recorded in Rome – and many more that were not recorded.

Impasse

Uncontrolled inflation acted like a dreadful syphilis that corroded economic life at every level in the later stages of the Roman Empire, with the same devastating effects as the inflationary crisis today. Only, the inflation experienced under the Roman Empire was a thousand times worse.

Although it is impossible to offer definitive figures, a couple of examples from surviving records can illustrate the process. Papyri surviving from Roman Egypt tell us that the price of one artaba of grain had remained fairly stable at seven to eight drachma until the crisis at the end of the second century AD, at which point it more than doubled to between seventeen and eighteen drachma. By the end of the third century, an artaba of grain reached the astonishing price of 120,000 drachma: an increase of more than 666,000 per cent.[2] In Italy, one Roman pound of gold was valued at 72,000 denarii in 301 AD. Nowadays, this is what one would call hyperinflation.

2 Rostovtzeff, *The Social and Economic History of the Roman Empire*, p. 54.

This, in turn, was directly related to the debasement of the currency. By such simple means, the state conjured vast amounts of money from thin air, as if by magic. But history shows that the end result of these black arts is to 'magically' raise prices and cause galloping inflation.

In the early years of the Empire, the most basic coin, the denarius, contained 4.5 grams of pure silver, that is to say, it was worth its weight in silver. But by the reign of Marcus Aurelius (161-180 AD), the silver content had dropped to about 75 per cent.

His son and heir, Commodus (180-192 AD) debased the denarius to about 70 per cent silver. And the next emperor, Septimius Severus (193-211 AD) debased the Roman denarius to about 50 per cent silver.

That seemed to work wonders. In twenty-four hours, the emperor had twice as much money as before and with the added currency, the government could pay for more soldiers and pay existing soldiers more. One might say that it was the Roman equivalent of quantitative easing. And the end result was more or less the same.

By the time the emperor Gallienus was able to reign as the sole emperor from 260-268 AD, the silver content was a mere 5 per cent. The coins were made of bronze with a thin layer of silver that soon wore off to reveal the inner debasement of the currency. That was a perfect analogy to the real state of the Empire itself.

Gallienus thought he could even pay the barbarian hordes not to cross the borders of the Empire. Unfortunately for him, the barbarians understood the principles of political economy better than the emperors. They demanded payment in real money – solid gold.

But in fact, this was just the surface manifestation of a far more fundamental problem. The ultimate cause of the decline of Rome is to be found, not in constitutional changes, religious revolutions, or the eccentricities of this or that emperor, but in the inability to develop the productive forces as a result of the impasse and internal contradictions of the slave economy. There were, of course, many other factors, but in the final analysis, they will be seen to derive from this first cause.

The Roman Empire was hugely dependent on forced labour. This was the real foundation on which Rome's power, wealth and influence was built. A vast number of slaves were necessary to maintain the key elements of the Roman economy: including agriculture, mining and construction. In many cases, such as the mines, this signified a drawn-out death sentence.

But forced labour, by its very nature, is unproductive. We have already seen that slave labour is only profitable if it is employed in great numbers. Slaves could be literally worked to death and then simply replaced with new slaves.

But when five centuries of expansion finally came to an end in the reign of Hadrian, whose famous wall marked the northernmost boundary of the Empire, the supply of cheap slaves began to dwindle. The problem was only intensified by the Antonine plague, which is estimated to have killed 10 per cent of the population of the Empire between 165-180 AD.

By the third century AD, there was a severe labour shortage, which compelled large landowners increasingly to base themselves on the labour of tenant farmers instead of slaves. These *coloni* were technically free, but in practice, remained wholly dependent on their master. They were merely sharecroppers, paying landowners with a portion of their crops in exchange for use of their farmlands.

Reforms to the system of taxation introduced by Diocletian (284-305 AD) made it administratively more difficult for peasants to leave the land where they were counted in the census, because taxes were assessed on both the land and its inhabitants.

The *coloni* were bound to the soil by debts that were heritable. Eventually their freedom of movement was limited by law. Although the *colonus* could not lose his land as long as he paid the rent, he was forbidden to leave or change his occupation.

In 332 AD, the Christian emperor Constantine enacted a law that abolished whatever minor rights the *coloni* had, and tied them permanently to the land. Here we already see the embryo of mediaeval serfdom in Europe. Landlords were permitted to chain *coloni* suspected of planning to escape. *Coloni* were forbidden to transfer their property without the permission of the landlord.

Another significant factor in the decline of Rome was the monstrously oppressive nature of the state itself, with its bloated bureaucracy and army of predatory tax collectors who battened on the wealthy provinces like a swarm of bloated leeches and sucked them dry. This was slowly but surely undermining the whole system.

Corrupt officials treated the provinces as gold mines. The unfortunate provincials were the helpless victims of every sort of robbery and extortion. Roman governors dedicated themselves systematically to the task of enriching themselves and the swarms of greedy hangers-on that had accompanied them.

They acted with complete impunity. In the late Republic the poet Catullus expressed outrage at the selfishness of Memmius, who prevented his staff from plundering a poor province. Under the Empire any remaining scruples were abandoned. The Emperor Caracalla, who reigned from 198-217 AD, made all the inhabitants of the Empire Roman citizens, not to alleviate but to *increase* the taxes he could impose on them. Bankruptcy became chronic.

Poor Romans voluntarily became *coloni* on the estates of the great landowners, signing away their own freedom and that of their wives and children in perpetuity, in order to escape the clutches of the grasping tax collectors.

Zosimus, a late fifth century writer, moaned that "as a result of this exaction of taxes, city and countryside were full of laments and complaints, and all… sought the help of the barbarians."[3] And the burden fell with greatest force on the poorest layers of society. The position of the *coloni* steadily eroded. Marx wrote:

> In the last years of the Roman Empire, the provincial decurions – not peasants but landowners – fled from their houses, abandoning their lands, even selling themselves into slavery, all in order to get rid of a property

3 Zosimus, *New History*, Quoted in Mazzarino, *The End of the Ancient World*, p. 65.

which was no longer anything more than an official pretext for extorting money from them, mercilessly and pitilessly.[4]

Religion

A generalised sensation of angst is something we have in common with the period of the decline of the Roman Empire. For the great majority, life was, to cite the famous words of Hobbes, "poor, nasty, brutish and short".[5]

There was no longer any hope of salvation in this life. The only hope was for a better life after death. Death, indeed, might seem the better option, particularly if there was a prospect of paradise, which Christianity held out before them.

In periods like this, there is a general sense of malaise. The predominant mood is one of scepticism, and pessimism about the future. The old traditions, morality and religion, things that act as a powerful cement holding society together, lose their credibility.

The rich attempted to dispel their nihilistic moods by constant feasting and amusement at the Colosseum. But the dark foreboding that hung in the air of those times found its expression in the upper classes in philosophical trends. The general angst was reflected in philosophy in Scepticism and Stoicism.

But philosophy could only affect a layer of the educated classes. For the rest of society, the general mood found its expression in religion. The old gods did not seem to offer any hope or consolation to people who were increasingly losing all faith in the existing order.

In place of the old religion, people seek out new gods. In its period of decline, Rome was inundated with a plague of religious sects from the East. Christianity was only one of these, and although ultimately successful, it had to contend with numerous rivals, such as the cult of Mithras.

When people feel that the world in which they live is tottering, that they have lost all control over their existence and that their lives

4 Marx, 'Drafts of the Letter to Vera Zasulich', *MECW*, Vol. 24, p. 354.

5 Hobbes, *Leviathan*, p. xix.

and destinies are determined by unseen forces, then mystical and irrational tendencies get the upper hand. People believe that the end of the world is nigh.

Nowhere was this feeling so clearly expressed than in the religion of Christianity, which loudly proclaimed the imminence of the end of the world and the Second Coming of Christ. The early Christians believed this fervently, but many others suspected it.

The world, the Christians said, was evil and sinful; it was necessary to turn one's back on the world and all its works and look forward to another life after death. For very many people, crushed by the weight of a monstrously oppressive state, there was probably not much to choose from between the two.

Perhaps the best way to penetrate the mindset of those early Christians is to read what is undoubtedly the most authentic of their texts, the Book of Revelation, which predicts the end of the world as an immediate perspective.

In point of fact, what was coming to an end was not the world but only a particular form of society – slave society. The success of Christianity was rooted in the fact that it connected with this general mood.

The barbarians

The end of their world was approaching faster than anyone could have imagined. In 376 AD, there was a large-scale migration of a Germanic people known as the Goths across the Danube frontier into the territory of the Empire.

The initial contacts between the Romans and Goths were not necessarily of a violent character. There was considerable trade along the eastern frontier for centuries, which led to a progressive romanisation of those tribes living in close proximity to the Empire.

Many became mercenaries and served in the Roman legions. Alaric, the Gothic leader who was the first to enter Rome, was not only a former soldier of Rome but a Christian (albeit of the Arian kind).

But the Goths had been forcibly driven from their lands by a terrifying explosion. The cause was an even greater movement of the peoples far to the East, where the nomadic steppe dwellers known to us as the Huns and other tribes had been pushed back from the Great Wall of China.

They moved westward in an irresistible tide, sweeping all before them. When a mass of terrified refugees from two Gothic tribes, the Tervingi and the Greuthungi, sought to escape from the marauding Huns within the boundaries of the Roman Empire, the emperor Honorius, after some hesitation, allowed them to settle on the Balkan frontier.

That proved to be a costly mistake, although it is not clear that he could have stopped them in any case. A number of agreements were made, and promptly broken, leading to a war that cruelly exposed the inner rottenness of the Empire. First Greece, then Italy, were plundered and ravaged.

Finally, for the first time in six centuries, on 24 August 410 AD Rome was sacked by the Visigoths led by their king, Alaric. This was only the beginning. After the Visigoths, and Ostrogoths, came the Vandals, Alans, Lombards, Suevi, Alemanni, Burgundians, Franks, Thuringians, Frisians, Heruli, Gepidae, Angles, Saxons, Jutes, Huns and Magyars. They crashed their way across the frontiers in successive waves. When the Vandals conquered the African provinces in the fifth century AD, Rome's food supply was suddenly interrupted, dealing a mortal blow to the Western Empire.

Whole populations were massacred or enslaved. The cities were destroyed or abandoned. Priceless works of art were destroyed and melted down for their precious metals. The ruin of agriculture brought in its train the inevitable horrors of famine and epidemics.

St. Jerome graphically describes the results of this devastation when he writes:

> … that, in those desert countries, nothing was left except the sky and the earth; that, after the destruction of the cities and the extirpation of the human race, the land was overgrown with thick forests and inextricable brambles; and that universal desolation, announced by the prophet

Zephaniah, was accomplished in the scarcity of the beasts, the birds, and even of the fish.[6]

These lines were written twenty years after the death of the emperor Valens, when the barbarian invasions started. They describe the state of affairs in Jerome's native province, in present day Slovenia, where successive waves of invaders caused death and destruction on an unimaginable scale.

The vicious cycle of massacre, rape and pillage that continued, with greater or lesser intensity for several centuries, left behind a trail of devastation that inflicted upon Europe a terrible heritage of backwardness.

The immediate effect of the barbarian onslaught was to wipe out civilisation and throw European society into a dark night of economic and cultural backwardness. The development of the productive forces suffered a violent interruption. The cities were destroyed or abandoned as people fled to the land in search of food.

The barbarians sacked and destroyed many cities. But why did they do this? Why did they not simply occupy them? The answer is related to the backward stage of economic development of the invaders. The barbarians in general were hostile to the towns and their inhabitants (a psychology that is quite common among peasants in all periods). They were nomads and herders of cattle and sheep and saw no use for towns and cities, except for the purpose of plunder.

However, the decline of the cities was not caused by the depredations of the barbarians. Long before the violent eruption of the Goths and Huns there was a steady drift to the countryside where the basis was already being laid for the development of a different mode of production – feudalism. But it was a long time before anything like a restoration of equilibrium was restored.

The fall of the Roman Empire was accompanied by a long period of cultural stagnation in all Europe. With the exception of the water

6 Quoted in Gibbon, *The History of the Decline and Fall of the Roman Empire*, Vol. 3, p. 122.

wheel and windmills, there were no real inventions for about over a thousand years. *In other words, there was a complete eclipse of culture.*

In this, the most appalling role was performed not by the barbarians, but by the Christians, who systematically destroyed every element of civilisation that did not coincide with their own religious fanaticism and prejudices. A particularly pernicious role was played by the Christian emperor, Theodosius I (ruled 379-395 AD), who deliberately mobilised mobs of fanatical monks and lumpenproletarians in an orgy of destruction directed against pagan temples, statues and other works of art.

The sad ruins of Greece and Rome, which now bear mute witness to the wholesale destruction of what was once a glorious culture, testify to a crime far greater than anything the barbarian hordes ever perpetrated against the culture of humanity.

A descending line of civilisation

There are two possibilities before the human race today: socialism or barbarism. The fate of Rome stands as a stark warning in that respect. Under the Empire Rome entered into a prolonged period of decline that eventually led to a complete collapse and a regression to barbarism.

Recently, there has been a tendency on the part of some academics to rewrite history so as to present the barbarians in a more favourable light. This is not 'more scientific' or 'more objective' but simply childish.

It is the result of the pernicious influence of so-called postmodernism, which claims that history knows no laws, that one society is just as good as another, and that, since there is no such thing as progress, there can be no such thing as backwardness either.

These ladies and gentlemen, following the 'Sacred Gospel of Political Correctness', attempt to falsify the historical record by airbrushing out all unpleasantness.

This is roughly the equivalent of those popes who, while indulging themselves in all manner of drunken sexual orgies, ordered the paintings of Michelangelo to be altered, so that the private parts of the Almighty should be covered by a fig-leaf.

We are now asked to believe that the barbarians were really quite nice fellows who lacked any interest in warfare or rapine, that the Vikings were merely peace-loving traders who came to our shores like the Mormons who knock on our doors to offer us friendly advice on the subject of religion.

The fact that all the contemporary witnesses tell a very different story is of no interest to our postmodernist friends. After all, why let the facts spoil a good story?

Despite the ridiculous fairy stories of postmodernism, it is absolutely clear that there are definite periods in human history when society and culture has experienced great advances, and others characterised by stagnation and regression.

This was the case in Europe after the fall of the Roman Empire, in the period known (at least in the English language) as the Dark Ages. A single example will suffice to underline this point. A thousand years after the fall of the Empire, the only serviceable roads in Europe were Roman roads.

Does history repeat itself?

In many ways, the present state of capitalist society reminds one of the decline and fall of the Roman Empire that was so graphically depicted in the great work of Edward Gibbon. The same picture of degeneration with which he fills the pages of that book reminds us forcibly of our own times.

The yawning abyss that separates rich and poor – between obscene wealth in the hands of a few parasites and poverty, destitution and despair for the great majority of the human race – has never been greater. The level of alienation and degradation of human beings, the indifference to human suffering and obscene egotism and greed are elevated to supreme virtues.

The Roman state developed into a real monster – a power standing above society and alienating itself from it. But that state was only a child's toy compared to the modern state that has been perfected by imperialism.

The Roman Empire was administered by a bureaucracy that numbered no more than 10,000 men, although beneath them was an army of tax collectors and other sub-exploiters. Today, in Britain alone the numbers involved in the state bureaucracy are at least half a million.

This is a far greater monster consisting of vast armies of bureaucrats, soldiers, police, secret police, prison wardens and judges who lord it over society and absorb unheard-of quantities of the wealth created by the working class.

The wars of Julius Caesar were bloody and destructive affairs. In his campaign in Gaul alone, he claimed to have killed a million people. Yet Caesar could have never imagined the destructive power of our modern armies, which killed at least 65 million men, women and children in the Second World War alone. Now, everywhere we look we see wars, crisis, death and destruction.

Have we advanced no further, then? Have the last 2,000 years of history served no purpose but to repeat the crimes of the past, but on a vastly greater scale? That is one possible interpretation of history, which was graphically expressed by the author of *The Decline and Fall of the Roman Empire*.

But no, we Marxists do not share this pessimistic view. Despite all the crimes, violence, wars and cruelties inflicted on humanity, history nevertheless expresses itself as progress, in the deepest and most scientific sense of the word. The development of the productive forces, under slavery, under feudalism and finally under capitalism, has laid the material foundation for a new and qualitatively higher stage of human society – socialism.

The modern working class has nothing in common with the Roman proletariat. The latter produced nothing and, in effect, lived off the labour of the slaves. The modern working class creates all the wealth of society. Without their labour, not a wheel turns, not a telephone rings and not a light bulb shines.

The worker who has been educated in the Marxist method looks back on history and sees, not just a catalogue of crimes and errors, but the actual development of industry, agriculture, science and technique – the real material base upon which the reconstruction of society can at last be achieved.

The revolutionary workers and youth of today will derive fresh inspiration from the heroic struggle of the Gracchi and above all by that greatest of all the fighters of antiquity, Spartacus. And from a scientific understanding of the class struggles of the past, we draw the necessary lessons to prepare the ground for future victory.

Appendix: Caesarism, Bonapartism and the State

Historical materialism explains that, in the last analysis, the movement of history is determined by the development of the productive forces and the changes in class relations that result from it. These constitute the solid ground upon which rises the superstructure of legal forms, constitutions, governments and the state, morality and religion, philosophical schools and so on.

However, the relation between all these elements is complex and contradictory, and not at all easy to determine. Under Caesar and Augustus, the Roman Republic had been transformed into the rule of one man, far more powerful than any of the ancient kings. To understand this dramatic metamorphosis, it is essential to analyse the nature of the state itself. And in order to understand this, it will be necessary to examine the Marxist theory of the state in greater detail.

Marxism explains that the state is an instrument for the oppression of one class by another. In the last analysis, it consists of special bodies of armed men: the army, police and the bureaucracy that sustains them. However, this general definition by no means exhausts the question.

Engels explains:

> The central link in civilised society is the state, which *in all typical periods* is without exception the state of the ruling class, and in all cases continues to be essentially a machine for holding down the oppressed, exploited class.[1]

Note that Engels uses very careful and precise language. *In typical periods*, the state is normally the state of the ruling class. But there can be periods that are abnormal and atypical, in which this does not apply.

Engels points out that the state arose to prevent the contending classes from consuming society in "fruitless struggle". The state 'regulates' the struggle between the classes, and, once having arisen, and *within limits*, it develops a *certain* independence and a logic of its own. Elsewhere, he writes:

> Exceptional periods, however, occur when the warring classes are so nearly equal in forces that the state power, as apparent mediator, acquires for the moment a certain independence in relation to both.[2]

The period that we have been describing here, the last period of the Roman Republic, was just such a period. The struggle between the classes had exceeded all normal bounds and the contending classes had fought each other to a standstill. At the head of this power there arises the 'strongman', or dictator.

Trotsky, writing in 1932, put it as follows:

> Two mighty camps are locked in irreconcilable conflict. Neither side can win by parliamentary means. Neither would willingly accept a decision unfavourable to it. Such a split in society foreshadows a civil war. The threat of civil war creates a need in the ruling class for an arbiter and commander, for a Caesar. That precisely is the function of Bonapartism.[3]

---

1 Engels, *The Origin of the Family, Private Property and the State*, p. 162, emphasis added.

2 Ibid., pp. 157-8.

3 Trotsky, 'The German Puzzle', August 1932, *The Struggle Against Fascism in Germany*, p. 349.

Relative independence

In essence, Caesarism (and its modern equivalent Bonapartism) is rule by the sword. It emerges in certain periods, when the class struggle reaches a point of deadlock, and the state power (in particular, the army) raises itself above society and acquires a relative independence from all classes, *including the ruling class*. We are therefore faced with a seeming paradox.

An analogy can be drawn with the enormous variety of political forms that have been observed over the history of capitalism. What, for instance, was the ruling class under the Second French Empire of Louis Bonaparte, or Napoleon III as he styled himself? The answer is: the bourgeoisie. Yet in *The Eighteenth Brumaire of Louis Bonaparte* Marx described how Bonaparte's drunken soldiery *shot down the bourgeoisie.*

This would appear to be a contradiction, and so it is: not an absurd contradiction but a dialectical contradiction. The state of Napoleon III, like that of Caesar, was composed of gangsters and adventurers who were defending their own interests, plundering the nation and also the very class they represented – the bourgeoisie.

This complex question was dealt with masterfully by Ted Grant in his reply to Tony Cliff on the question of so-called state capitalism:

> Let us take as a case extremely rich in examples the history of France. The bourgeois revolution took place in 1789. In 1793 the Jacobins seized complete power. As Marx and Engels pointed out, they went beyond the framework of bourgeois relations and performed a salutary historical task because of that, accomplishing in a few months what would have taken the bourgeoisie decades or generations to accomplish; the complete cleansing from France of all traces of feudalism. Yet this regime remained rooted in the basis of bourgeois forms of property. It was followed by the French Thermidor and the rule of the Directory, to be followed by the classic dictatorship of Napoleon Bonaparte. Napoleon re-introduced many feudal forms, had himself crowned Emperor and concentrated the supreme power in his hands. But we still call this regime bourgeois. With the restoration of Louis XVIII the regime still

> remained capitalist… and then we had not one but *two revolutions* – 1830 and 1848. These revolutions had important social consequences. They resulted in significant changes even in the personnel of the state itself. Yet we characterise them both as bourgeois revolutions in which there was no change in the class which held power. […]
>
> Take, similarly, the diversity of regimes in more modern times to see the extreme differences in super-structures which are on the same economic base. For instance, compare the regime of Nazi Germany with that of British social democracy. They are so fundamentally different in super-structure that many theorists of the non-Marxist or ex-Marxist school have found new class structure and a new system of society entirely. Why do we say that they represent the same class and the same regime? Despite the difference in super-structure, *the economic base of the given societies remained the same.*[4]

The state balances between the classes

There are many other cases in history in which one section of the ruling class has attacked other sections and the state has risen above society. In the Wars of the Roses of the fifteenth century, the two most powerful factions of the English barons (the Houses of Lancaster and York) virtually exterminated one another.

At one time or another a big section of the ruling class were either in prison or were executed, and the throne occupied by adventurers of one gang or another. Finally, a new dynasty emerged, the Tudors, which balanced between the bourgeoisie in the City of London and different factions of the barons to establish an absolutist regime, which would persist for more than a hundred years. Similar processes occurred in other countries.

These absolute monarchs, in an attempt to consolidate themselves as a power standing above society, and increasingly alienating themselves from it, leaned on the nascent bourgeoisie to strike blows against the feudal nobility. Yet the class nature of the regime remained

4 Grant, 'Against the Theory of State Capitalism', 1949, *The Unbroken Thread*, pp. 323-3, emphasis in original.

feudal. It was determined by existing property relations, not by the political configuration of the government.

Engels wrote the following on the Bismarck regime in Germany, which he regarded as a variant of Bonapartism:

> Bonapartism is the necessary form of state in a country where the working class, at a high level of its development in the towns but numerically inferior to the small peasants in rural areas, has been defeated in a great revolutionary struggle by the capitalist class, the petty bourgeoisie and the army. When the Parisian workers were defeated in the titanic struggle of June 1848 in France, the bourgeoisie had at the same time totally exhausted itself in this victory. It was aware it could not afford a second such victory. It continued to rule in name, but it was too weak to govern. Control was assumed by the army, the real victor, basing itself on the class from which it preferred to draw its recruits, the small peasants, who wanted peace from the rioters in the towns. The form this rule took was of course military despotism, its natural leader the hereditary heir to the latter, Louis Bonaparte.
>
> As far as both workers and capitalists are concerned, Bonapartism is characterised by the fact that it prevents them coming to blows with each other. In other words, it protects the bourgeoisie from any violent attacks by the workers, encourages a little gentle skirmishing between the two classes and furthermore deprives both alike of the faintest trace of political power. No freedom of association, no freedom of assembly, no freedom of the press; universal suffrage under such bureaucratic pressure that election of the opposition is almost impossible; police-control of a kind that had previously been unknown even in police-ridden France. Besides which, sections of the bourgeoisie and of the workers are simply *bought*; the former by colossal credit-swindles, by which the money of the small capitalists is attracted into the pockets of the big ones; the latter by colossal state construction-schemes which concentrate an artificial, imperial proletariat dependent on the government in the big towns alongside the natural, independent proletariat. Finally, national pride is flattered by apparently heroic wars, which are however always conducted with the approval of the high authorities of Europe against the general

scapegoat of the day and only on such conditions as ensure victory from the outset.[5]

Caesarism and Bonapartism

Leon Trotsky drew an explicit parallel between Caesarism and Bonapartism, explaining:

> Caesarism, or its bourgeois form, Bonapartism, enters the scene in those moments of history when the sharp struggle of two camps raises the state power, so to speak, above the nation, and guarantees it, in appearance, a complete independence of classes – in reality, only the freedom necessary for a defence of the privileged.[6]

But this is not to say that all Caesarist and Bonapartist regimes are identical. Far from it. The term Bonapartism itself is very elastic and covers many different variants. In 1932, Trotsky explained:

> Such terms as *liberalism*, *Bonapartism*, *fascism* have the character of generalisations. Historical phenomena never repeat themselves completely. It would not have been difficult to prove that even the government of Napoleon III, compared with the regime of Napoleon I, was not 'Bonapartist' – not only because Napoleon himself was a doubtful Bonaparte by blood, but also because his relations to the classes, especially to the peasantry and to the lumpenproletariat, were not at all the same as those of Napoleon I. Moreover, classical Bonapartism grew out of the epoch of gigantic war victories, which the Second Empire did not know at all. But if we should look for the repetition of *all* the traits of Bonapartism, we will find that Bonapartism is a one-time, unique occurrence, i.e., that Bonapartism in general does not exist but that there once was a general named Bonaparte born in Corsica. The case is no different with liberalism and with all other generalised terms of history. When one speaks by analogy of Bonapartism, it is necessary

---

5 Engels, *The Prussian Military Question and the German Workers' Party*, *MECW*, Vol. 20, pp. 72-3, emphasis in original.

6 Trotsky, *The Revolution Betrayed*, p. 199.

to state precisely which of its traits found their fullest expression under present historical conditions.[7]

What distinguishes these phenomena of Caesarism, Absolutism and Bonapartism is their class basis, which is fundamentally different in each case. What unites all three is the process by which the state, and in particular the individual ruler, raises itself further and further above the rest of society as a result of the mutual exhaustion of the contending classes.

The Roman emperors rose above society and viciously oppressed the ruling class, the slave-owners, who found themselves looted by taxation, arrested, tortured and even murdered by the state. Yet this fact did not change one iota the class nature of the Roman state as a slave state. As Trotsky explained:

> The sabre by itself has no independent program. It is the instrument of 'order'. It is summoned to safeguard what exists. Raising itself *politically* above the classes, Bonapartism, like its predecessor Caesarism, for that matter, represents *in the social sense,* always and at all epochs, the government of the strongest and firmest part of the exploiters…[8]

Learn from history!

After the overthrow of the Republic, the same slave-owning aristocracy remained the ruling class and continued to hold economic power just as before. But it lost control of the state apparatus, and was compelled reluctantly to hand power to a military strong man.

Trotsky compared Bonapartist and fascist regimes to the legend of the Old Man of the Sea, who sits on the shoulders of the ruling class and guides it to safety, but at the same time digs his heels into its side and spits on its bald patch. But such a regime creates new dangers for the ruling class.

---

7 Trotsky, 'German Bonapartism', 30 October 1932, *The Struggle Against Fascism in Germany*, p. 432, emphasis in original.

8 Trotsky, 'Bonapartism and Fascism', 15 July 1934, *The Struggle Against Fascism in Germany*, p. 577, emphasis in original.

When the German bourgeoisie handed power to Hitler, as a means of preventing revolution, it lost control of the state, and was unable to regain it, even though this meant the total defeat and destruction of Germany by the end of the Second World War.

This lesson has not been lost on the bourgeoisie today, which will only resort to such a desperate measure in the very last moment, when all other avenues are closed to it. To hand the power to unstable adventurers who they cannot control is a very risky option. Apart from this, the class balance of forces today is infinitely less favourable for a Bonapartist solution.

Today, at least in the advanced capitalist countries, their preferred method of rule remains bourgeois democracy. It is far less risky and more cost-effective than the alternative. But this is a very fragile system and will be tested to the limits in the stormy period of class struggle that lies ahead.

Therefore, the lessons of the class struggles in the Roman Republic still hold great importance for the revolutionary workers and youth of today. In the words of the American philosopher George Santayana: "Those who cannot remember the past are condemned to repeat it."[9]

9 Santayana, *The Life of Reason*, p. 82.

Maps

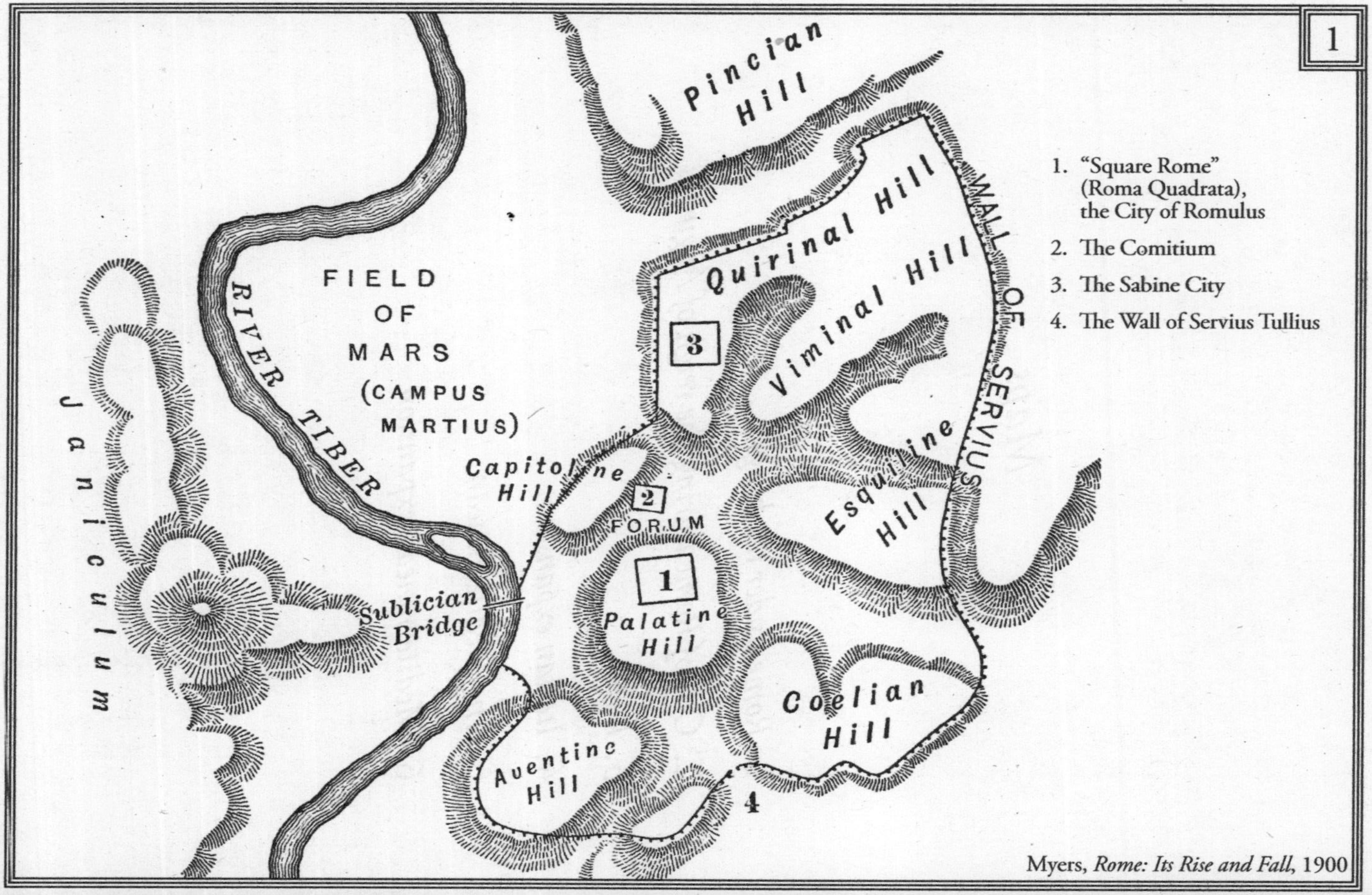
1
Pincian Hill
Quirinal Hill
Viminal Hill
Esquiline Hill
WALL OF SERVIUS
FIELD OF MARS (CAMPUS MARTIUS)
RIVER TIBER
Capitoline Hill
FORUM
Palatine Hill
Coelian Hill
Aventine Hill
Sublician Bridge
Janiculum
1
2
3
4
1. "Square Rome" (Roma Quadrata), the City of Romulus
2. The Comitium
3. The Sabine City
4. The Wall of Servius Tullius

Myers, *Rome: Its Rise and Fall*, 1900

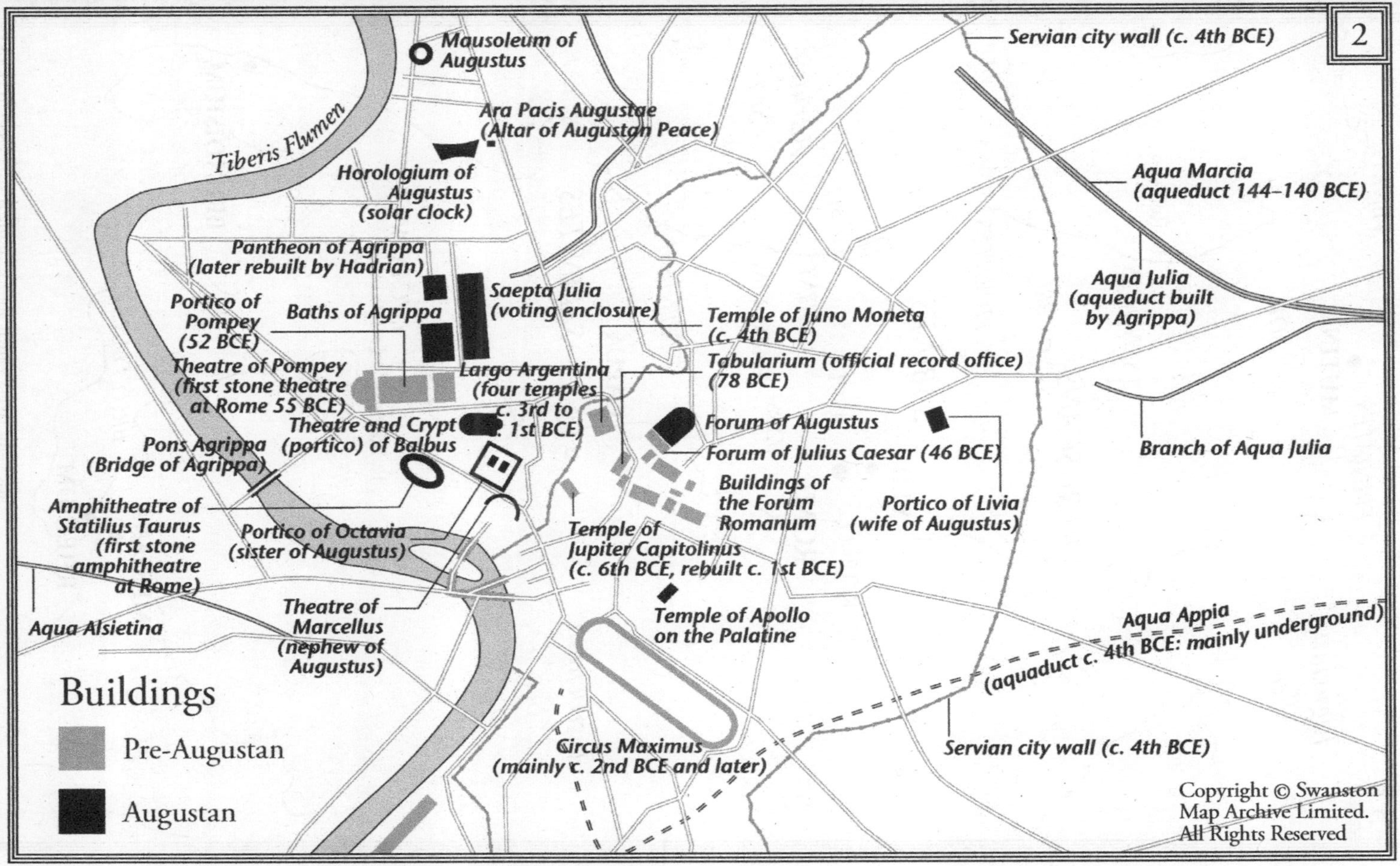
2
Mausoleum of Augustus
Ara Pacis Augustae (Altar of Augustan Peace)
Tiberis Flumen
Horologium of Augustus (solar clock)
Pantheon of Agrippa (later rebuilt by Hadrian)
Saepta Julia (voting enclosure)
Portico of Pompey (52 BCE)
Baths of Agrippa
Theatre of Pompey (first stone theatre at Rome 55 BCE)
Largo Argentina (four temples c. 3rd to c. 1st BCE)
Theatre and Crypt (portico) of Balbus
Pons Agrippa (Bridge of Agrippa)
Amphitheatre of Statilius Taurus (first stone amphitheatre at Rome)
Portico of Octavia (sister of Augustus)
Aqua Alsietina
Theatre of Marcellus (nephew of Augustus)
Servian city wall (c. 4th BCE)
Aqua Marcia (aqueduct 144–140 BCE)
Aqua Julia (aqueduct built by Agrippa)
Branch of Aqua Julia
Temple of Juno Moneta (c. 4th BCE)
Tabularium (official record office) (78 BCE)
Forum of Augustus
Forum of Julius Caesar (46 BCE)
Buildings of the Forum Romanum
Portico of Livia (wife of Augustus)
Temple of Jupiter Capitolinus (c. 6th BCE, rebuilt c. 1st BCE)
Temple of Apollo on the Palatine
Aqua Appia (aquaduct c. 4th BCE: mainly underground)
Circus Maximus (mainly c. 2nd BCE and later)
Servian city wall (c. 4th BCE)
Buildings
Pre-Augustan
Augustan
Copyright © Swanston Map Archive Limited. All Rights Reserved

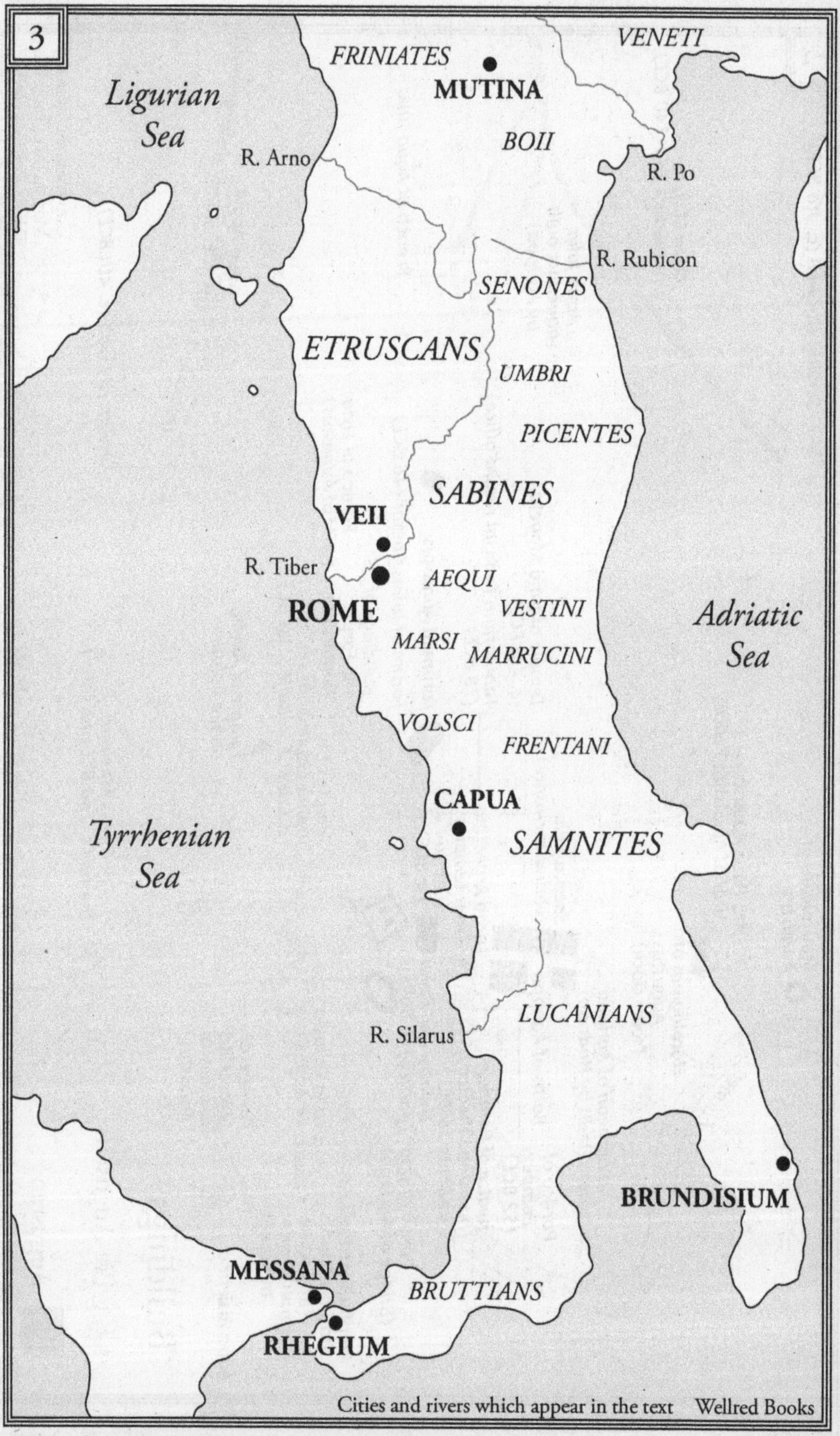
3
Ligurian Sea
FRINIATES
MUTINA
VENETI
BOII
R. Arno
R. Po
R. Rubicon
SENONES
ETRUSCANS
UMBRI
PICENTES
SABINES
VEII
R. Tiber
AEQUI
ROME
VESTINI
Adriatic Sea
MARSI
MARRUCINI
VOLSCI
FRENTANI
CAPUA
Tyrrhenian Sea
SAMNITES
LUCANIANS
R. Silarus
BRUNDISIUM
MESSANA
BRUTTIANS
RHEGIUM
Cities and rivers which appear in the text
Wellred Books

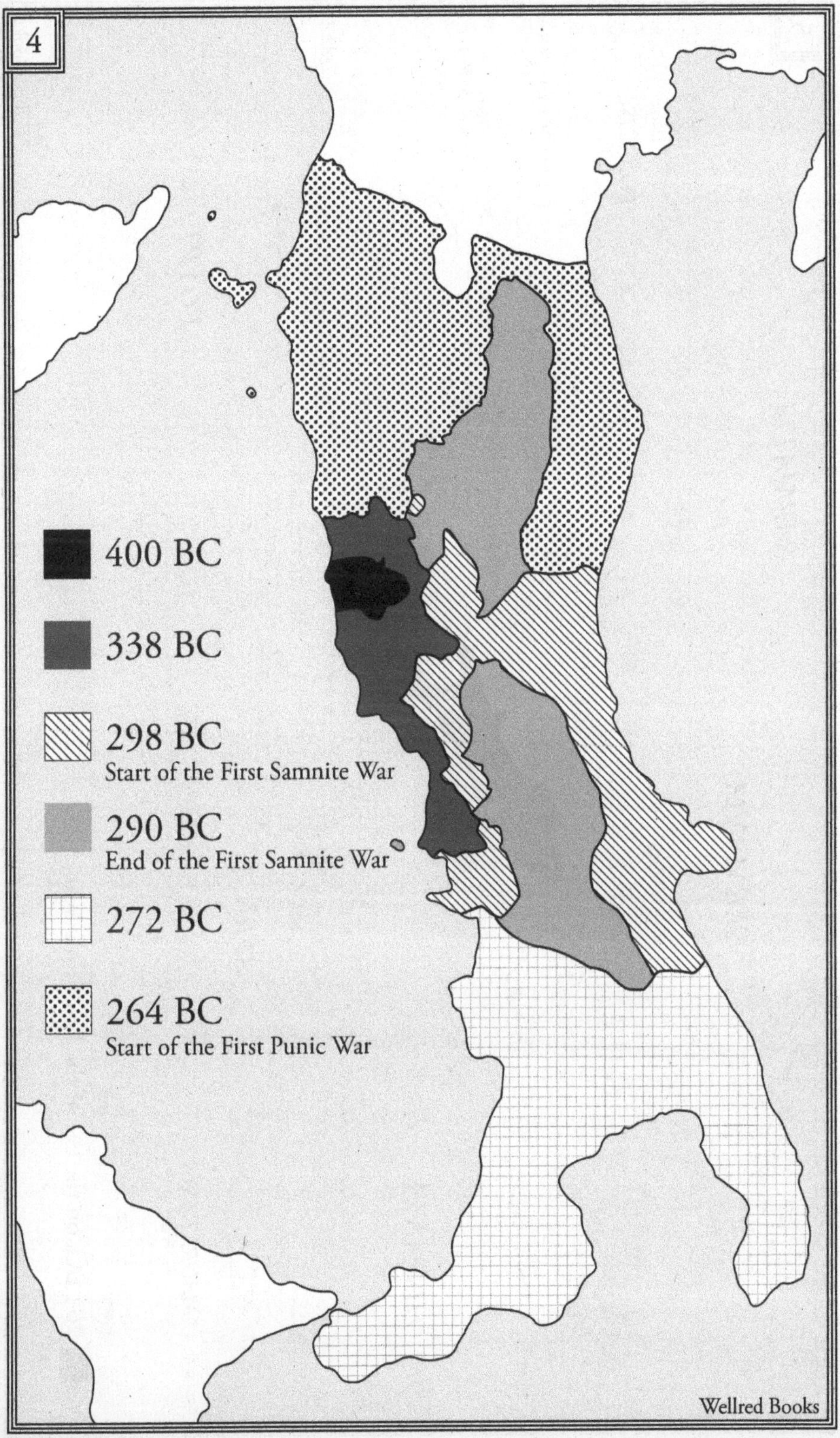
4
400 BC
338 BC
298 BC
Start of the First Samnite War
290 BC
End of the First Samnite War
272 BC
264 BC
Start of the First Punic War
Wellred Books

5
SARMATIA
GERMANIA
Black Sea
ALPS
PONTUS
GAUL
Atlantic Ocean
THRACE
BITHYNIA
ILLYRIA
MACEDONIA
CAPPADOCIA
MASSALIA
EPIRUS
PERGAMON
ASIA
ROME
SYRIA
ATHENS
ACTIUM
CORINTH
HISPANIA
SYRACUSE
CARTHAGE
JUDAEA
Mediterranean Sea
ALEXANDRIA
AFRICA
MAURETANIA
EGYPT
264 BC, on the eve of the first Punic War
Wellred Books

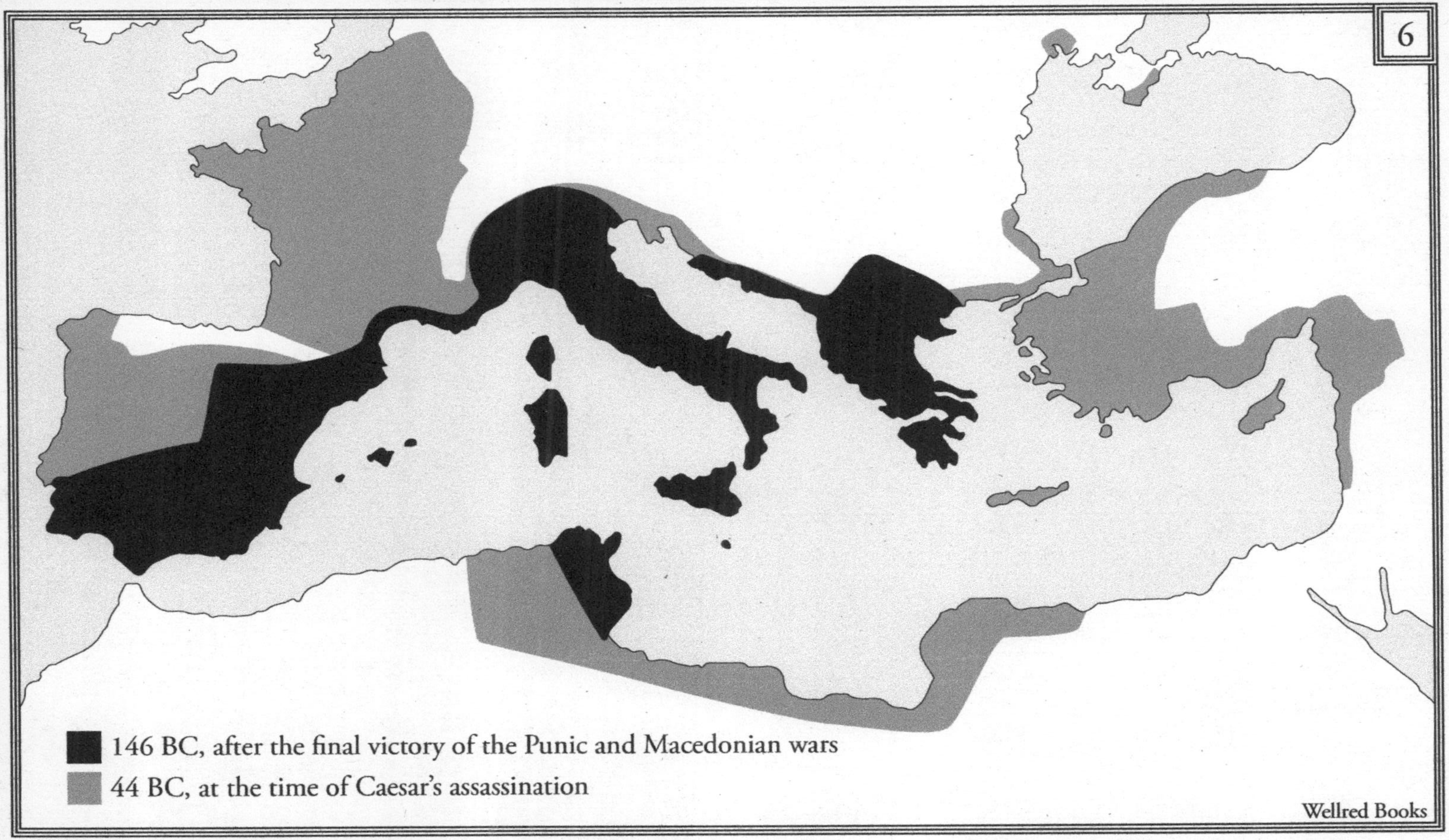
6
146 BC, after the final victory of the Punic and Macedonian wars
44 BC, at the time of Caesar's assassination
Wellred Books

Glossary

ager publicus – State-owned land that had been seized from conquered enemies.

censor – Roman magistrate, originally tasked with carrying out the census of citizens and their property. The responsibilities of the censor would eventually be expanded to include the maintenance of the senatorial rolls and supervision of public morality.

clientes ('clients') – Free individuals who were tied to a customary relationship of dependence to a *patronus*, or 'patron', usually someone of a higher status. In return for protection and favours, clients would be expected to perform services for their patrons.

coloni – Tenant farmers of the Late Roman Empire who paid a share of their produce to a landlord.

comitia centuriata ('Centuriate Assembly') – Assembly of all citizens, excluding women and slaves, organised by property class into voting units of one hundred each called 'centuries'. The Centuriate Assembly had the power to pass laws, elect consuls and other officials, including censors, and to declare war.

comitia curiata ('Curiate Assembly') – Early assembly of the Roman people, assembled into thirty voting units, called *curiae*. This assembly elected the early kings and was eventually superseded by the *comitia centuriata*.

comitia tributa ('Tribal Assembly') – Assembly of all Roman citizens, divided into tribes based on geographical districts. This assembly had the power to pass laws, elect civil officials and acted as the highest court to decide on serious public offences.

concilium plebis ('Plebeian Council') – Assembly of the common people of Rome, the plebs, which excluded patricians. This assembly elected the tribunes and passed laws (*plebiscita*) which initially only applied to the plebs. A series of laws in the third century BC made laws passed by the Plebeian Assembly binding on all citizens and on the Senate.

consul – Highest elected office of the Roman Republic. Two consuls were elected every year, each with the power of veto over the other. Inside the city they formed the head of the government, presiding over the Senate, the Centuriate Assembly and the Tribal Assembly. The consuls were given the responsibility for executing the laws passed by the voting assemblies, with the power to arrest and punish citizens, short of having them executed for capital offences. Outside of the city of Rome, the consuls served as the commanders-in-chief of the Roman legions with unlimited powers during a military campaign.

contiones – Informal popular assemblies, often attended by poorer citizens, in which magistrates would report directly to the people. These assemblies had no legislative power and did not vote.

curia (plural, *curiae*) – Subdivisions of the original three tribes that made up the *Populus Romanus* ('Roman People'). Each tribe was divided into ten curiae, which contained all of the original *gentes* or 'clans' of Rome.

decemviri ('Decemvirate') – A ten-man commission appointed with consular powers to draft a code of laws for the Roman Republic.

denarius (plural, *denarii*) – Small silver coin introduced in the late third century BC.

dictator – Individual given extraordinary powers by the Senate to resolve a specific issue for a prescribed period of time. During the period of his dictatorship, all other officials, including consuls, would be subject to his authority, but he could not act outside the bounds of his assigned task without permission from the Senate.

equites ('knights') – Originally those citizens who could afford to maintain horses and therefore served in the cavalry. Later, the *equites* became the second highest property class in the Republic, below the senatorial order.

fasces – Symbol of official authority in the Roman Republic, thought to have been inherited from the Etruscan civilisation. It was made up of a bundle of wooden rods, to which an axehead was added outside the city.

gens (plural, *gentes*) – Group of families sharing a name and common male ancestors, often translated as 'clan'.

imperator – Originally a title for a military commander, in the Late Republic it became an honorific title conferred upon a victorious general by his troops, which then entitled him to a triumph. It became an imperial title under Augustus, from which our word, 'emperor' is derived.

imperium – Military command, which could be over a legion, an army, a province, or a region.

latifundia – Large rural estates, usually producing agricultural products for exchange using slave labour.

lumpenproletariat – A term coined by Karl Marx to denote the layer of the population who own no property but, unlike the modern proletariat, or working class, do not sell their labour power and are not a productive class, such as the unemployed, homeless, criminal gangs etc.

nexus – A free man who becomes a slave in order to pay off his debts.

nobiles ('well known') – The class of wealthy citizens, both patrician and plebeian, whose families had held high office, from which our word 'noble' is derived.

optimates ('the best') – Supporters of the authority and interests of the Senate and the Roman nobility, in opposition to the *populares*.

paterfamilias – Male head of the family.

patrician – A member of the original Roman ruling class, made up of the descendants of the first hundred senators who, according to legend, were appointed by Romulus.

patroni ('patrons') – See entry for *clientes*.

plebeians (singular collective noun, plebs) – The majority of free Romans, who did not belong to the ancient patrician families of Rome. Some plebeians became wealthy and won entry into all of the important offices of state and the Senate. Under the Late Republic the plebs did not therefore constitute a single homogeneous class, but was itself divided between wealthy *equites* and *nobiles*, poor peasants who owned property, and the propertyless urban masses (proletarians).

plebiscitum (plural, *plebiscita*) – Law passed by the *concilium plebis*, from which our word 'plebiscite' is derived.

pontifex maximus – Chief high priest of Rome.

populares ('supporters of the people') – Supporters of the popular assemblies, such as the *concilium plebis*, and the interests of the common people, as opposed to the *optimates*.

praetor – Elected official with both civil and military powers, usually instructed to perform certain tasks by the Senate.

Praetorian Guard – An elite unit of the Roman army, which served as an escort for high-ranking officials under the Republic, and as the emperor's personal bodyguard from the reign of Augustus up to Constantine I, who dissolved it.

princeps civitatis ('First Citizen') – Official title for the Roman emperor, created by Augustus, from which our word 'prince' is derived.

proconsul – Roman official acting with consular powers outside the city of Rome, in order to carry out a military campaign, for example.

proletarians ('*proletarii*') – The poorest class of free Romans who owned no property.

publicani – Public contractors, usually tax farmers who would bid for contracts to collect taxes from particular regions.

quaestor – Elected official who would carry out administrative functions, such as managing the public treasury.

rex ('king') – Military, religious and judicial head of the early Romans. The office of *rex* was more like that of a tribal chieftain than later monarchs, as he was elected and had little power over the lives and property of the people.

Senate – Derived from *senex*, meaning 'old man', the Senate was originally formed as a council of elders, made up of the heads (*patres*) of the leading clans. Although legally the Senate was an advisory body, in practice it was the leading authority under the Republic. It issued 'advice' (*senatus consultum*) by majority vote to magistrates on both civil and military matters, which in practice were usually carried out as instructions. The Senate also had the power to appoint a dictator. Originally only patricians could become senators, but wealthy plebeians eventually won the right to be appointed to the Senate, if they had held political office previously and owned enough property.

The Senatorial class, composed of those eligible for the Senate, was made up of the biggest landowners in the Republic.

socii ('allies') – Italian tribes and city-states that were bound to Rome as dependents, paying tribute and contributing soldiers to Rome. Most *socii* did not have Roman citizenship until the Social War (91-87 BC), after which all free inhabitants of Italy south of the Rubicon River became Roman citizens.

Tribune of the Plebs (*tribunus plebis*) – Official elected by the Plebeian Council, with the power to convene both the Plebeian Council and the Senate, to propose legislation, and to veto the acts of consuls. Ten tribunes were elected every year, each with the power of veto over the others.

triumph – A public celebration of a military victory, featuring a procession through the city of Rome, honouring the victorious commander.

Timeline

753 BC	Traditional date of the foundation of Rome by Romulus and the beginning of the Roman calendar (*ab urbe condita*).
c. 600 BC	Construction of the Cloaca Maxima under the Etruscan king, Tarquinius Priscus.
509 BC	Traditional date of the eviction of the last king, Tarquinius Superbus. Foundation of the Republic with two elected consuls as co-rulers.
494 BC	First secession of the plebs. Establishment of the office of Tribunes of the Plebs.
471 BC	Establishment of the Plebeian Council (*concilium plebis*).
451-450 BC	Twelve Tables written by a commission of ten, the Decemvirate.
449 BC	Second secession of the plebs. Abdication of the Decemvirate. Promulgation of the Twelve Tables.
396 BC	Conquest of Veii by Rome.
387 BC	Battle of Allia. Rome sacked by the Senones.

367 BC	Licinio-Sexian laws passed, limiting interest on loans, restricting the amount of public land that could be held by individuals, and stipulating that one of the two consuls elected must be a plebeian.
343-341 BC	First Samnite War. Rome acquires control over most of Campania.
326-304 BC	Second (Great) Samnite War. Rome acquires total control over Campania.
298-290 BC	Third Samnite War. Rome conquers most of Central Italy and becomes the undisputed power on the Italian peninsula.
287 BC	Lex Hortensia passed, making all resolutions of the Plebeian Council binding on the state.
280-275 BC	Pyrrhic War. Rome acquires control over Southern Italy.
265-264 BC	Roman conquest of Etruria (modern-day Tuscany). Rome acquires complete control over Central Italy.
264-241 BC	First Punic War. Annexation of Sicily by Rome.
218-201 BC	Second Punic War. Hannibal's army crosses the Alps and invades Italy. Rome drives Carthage out of Spain and annexes a part of its territory in Africa.
214-205 BC	First Macedonian War. Kingdom of Macedon withdraws from alliance with Carthage.
200-197 BC	Second Macedonian War. Kingdom of Macedon loses control over Southern Greece, Thrace and Asia (Western Anatolia). Rome declares "freedom of the Greeks".
192-188 BC	Third Macedonian War. Kingdom of Macedon broken up.
150-148 BC	Fourth Macedonian War. Macedon annexed by Rome.
149-146 BC	Third Punic War. City of Carthage completely destroyed.
146 BC	Achaean War. Corinth sacked. Mainland Greece annexed by Rome.

135-132 BC	First Servile War. Thousands of slaves in Sicily revolt under the leadership of Eunus.
133 BC	Tiberius Gracchus elected as tribune. Lex Agraria passed, limiting ownership of public lands. Gracchus murdered on the Capitoline Hill by supporters of the senatorial aristocracy.
123 BC	Gaius Gracchus, brother of Tiberius, elected as tribune.
121 BC	Gaius Gracchus fails to be re-elected for a third term as tribune. Gracchus and his supporters killed in conflict with a militia led by consul Lucius Opimius.
107 BC	First consulship of Gaius Marius. Marius begins to reform the Roman military, recruiting from the lowest, propertyless class of citizens for the first time.
104-100 BC	Second Servile War. Slaves in Sicily rise up under the leadership of Salvius and Athenion.
91 BC	Marcus Livius Drusus elected as tribune. Drusus proposes that Roman citizenship be granted to Rome's Italian allies. Drusus assassinated by opponents of his reforms.
91-87 BC	Social War. Rome's Italian allies revolt. Citizenship granted to all Italians who support Rome. Italian rebels defeated.
89-88 BC	Beginning of First Mithridatic War. King Mithridates VI of Pontus defeats the Roman army in Bithynia, then invades Roman provinces of Asia and Greece.
88 BC	Sulla marches on Rome with six legions and enters the city. Marius exiled to Africa. Sulla takes his army east to fight Mithridates after having replaced both consuls at Rome.
87-85 BC	Conclusion of First Mithridatic War. Pontic armies defeated in Greece and Asia Minor. Mithridates signs a peace treaty on Sulla's terms.
87-83 BC	Marian terror. Cinna marches on Rome with his own army supported by Marius and his legions. Supporters of Sulla killed. Marius dies of natural causes, leaving Cinna in power.

83-82 BC	Civil War. Sulla lands at Brundisium with his army. Marian army crushed at Scariportus. Sulla has himself declared dictator.
81-79 BC	Sullan dictatorship. Thousands proscribed and murdered under the terror. Senate expanded from 300 to 600 senators. Law passed restricting power of the tribunes to propose legislation.
80-71 BC	Sertorian War. Quintus Sertorius, a supporter of the Marian side in the Civil War, leads a rebellion against Rome in Hispania (Spain).
73-71 BC	Third Servile War. Slave rebellion begins near Capua, led by the gladiator, Spartacus. After winning many victories the slaves are eventually defeated by the armies of Crassus and Pompey.
73-63 BC	Third Mithridatic War. Kingdom of Pontus destroyed. Pontus and Syria annexed by Rome. Armenia and Judea become Roman client states.
63 BC	Cicero elected as consul. Catiline conspiracy.
59 BC	Formation of the First Triumvirate. First consulship of Julius Caesar.
58-51 BC	Roman conquest of Gaul.
53 BC	Crassus defeated and killed by the Parthians at Carrhae.
52 BC	Pompey elected as sole consul.
49 BC	Caesar declared a public enemy. Caesar crosses the Rubicon with his legions. The Civil War begins.
48 BC	Pompey defeated at Pharsalus and killed in Egypt.
46-44 BC	Dictatorship of Caesar.
February 44 BC	Senate votes to make Caesar dictator for life.
15 March 44 BC	Assassination of Caesar.

27 November 43 BC	Lex Titia passed, granting special powers to Octavian, Antony and Lepidus. Second Triumvirate formally established for a term of five years.
3 October 42 BC	First Battle of Philippi between Octavian and Antony on one side, and the 'Liberators', Brutus and Cassius, on the other. Result inconclusive as Octavian's troops routed by Brutus while Cassius' troops routed by Antony.
23 October 42 BC	Second Battle of Philippi. Victory for Octavian and Antony.
41-40 BC	Perusine War. Brother and wife of Mark Antony lead an uprising against Octavian in Italy. Defeated by Octavian at Perusia (Perugia).
September 40 BC	Brundisium agreement. Octavian and Antony agree to divide Rome's territories between themselves, leaving Lepidus with only the province of Africa.
37 BC	Treaty of Tarentum. Triumvirate renewed for another five-year term.
September 36 BC	Sextus Pompey defeated in Sicily. Lepidus stripped of his triumviral powers and forced into exile by Octavian.
2 September 31 BC	Battle of Actium. Antony and Cleopatra flee to Egypt.
1 August 30 BC	Octavian captures Alexandria. Antony and Cleopatra commit suicide. End of the Civil War.
16 January 27 BC	Senate confers the name and title of 'Augustus' on Octavian.

Bibliography

Appian, *Roman History*, Harvard University Press, 1912

Aristotle, *Metaphysics*, Harvard University Press, 1961
— *Politics*, Harvard, 1959

Bax, Belfort, 'Meeting with Engels', in Institute of Marxism-Leninism (Moscow, Russia), *Reminiscences of Marx and Engels*, Foreign Languages Publishing House, 1955

Cato, Varro, *On Agriculture*, Harvard University Press, 1934

Cicero, *Letters*, Bell and Sons, 1912
— *On Government*, Penguin, 1993

de Leon, Daniel, *Two Pages from Roman History*, New York Labor News Co., 1915

Diodorus Siculus, *In Twelve Volumes*, Harvard University Press, 1967

Engels, Friedrich, *Anti-Dühring*, Wellred Books, 2017
— *The Origin of the Family, Private Property and the State*, Wellred Books, 2020

Fast, Howard, *Spartacus*, North Castle Books, 1996.

Florus, Lucius Annaeus, *Epitome of Roman History*, William Heinemann, 1929

Santayana, George, *The Life of Reason*, Scribner, 1953.

Gibbon, Edward, *The History of the Decline and Fall of the Roman Empire*,

Methuen and Co., 1909

Grant, Michael, *Caesar*, Folett, 1975
— *History of Rome*, Book Club Associates, 1978

Grant, Ted, *The Unbroken Thread*, Fortress, 1989

Hegel, Georg Wilhelm Friedrich, *Lectures on the Philosophy of History*, Prometheus Books, 1991

Hobbes, Thomas, *Leviathan*, JM Dent and Sons, 1914

Hunt, Peter, *Ancient Greek and Roman Slavery*, Wiley Blackwell, 2018

Kautsky, Karl, *The Foundations of Christianity*, Russell and Russell, 1953

Lenin, Vladimir I, *The State and Revolution*, Wellred Books, 2019

Livy, *History of Rome*, JM Dent and Sons, 1937
— *History of Rome: The First Eight Books*, John Childs and Son, 1853
— *In Fourteen Volumes*, Harvard University Press, 1967

Lucan, *Pharsalia*, Penguin, 1957

Madden, John, 'Slavery in the Roman Empire Numbers and Origins', *Classics Ireland*, Vol. 3, Classical Association of Ireland, 1996

Marx, Karl and Engels, Friedrich, *Selected Correspondence, 1846-1895*, Lawrence and Wishart, 1936
— *Marx and Engels Collected Works*, Lawrence and Wishart, 1975
— *The Communist Manifesto*, *The Classics of Marxism: Volume One*, Wellred Books, 2013

Marx, Karl, *The Eighteenth Brumaire of Louis Bonaparte*, Wellred Books, 2022

Mazzarino, Santo, *The End of the Ancient World*, Knopf, 1966

Mommsen, Theodor, *History of Rome*, Scribner and Co., 1970

Pliny, *Natural History*, Harvard University Press, 1938

Plutarch, *Lives*, John D Morris and Co., 1860
— *Lives: In Eleven Volumes*, Harvard University Press, 1914
— *The Lives of Noble Grecians and Romans*, Encyclopaedia Britannica, 1953
— *The Makers of Rome*, Penguin, 1965

Polybius, *The Histories*, Heinemann, 1922

Rostovtzeff, Michael Ivanovich, *The Social and Economic History of the Roman Empire*, Clarendon Press, 1957

Sallust, *The Jugurthine War and The Conspiracy of Catiline*, Penguin, 1963

Suetonius, *The Lives Of The Twelve Caesars*, Modern Library, 1931

Syme, Ronald, *The Roman Revolution*, Clarendon Press, 1939

Tacitus, *Annals*, MacMillan and Co., 1876
— *In Three Volumes*, William Heinemann, 1931

Trotsky, Leon, *History of the Russian Revolution*, Wellred Books, 2022
— *The Revolution Betrayed*, Wellred Books, 2015
— *The Struggle Against Fascism in Germany*, Pathfinder Press, 2019

Ziogas, Ioannis, 'Famous Last Words: Caesar's Prophecy on the Ides of March', *Antichthon*, Vol. 50, Australasian Society for Classical Studies, 2016

Titles by Wellred Books

Wellred Books is a publishing house specialising in works of Marxist theory. Among the titles we publish are:

Anti-Dühring, Friedrich Engels
Bolshevism: The Road to Revolution, Alan Woods
Chartist Revolution, Rob Sewell
China: From Permanent Revolution to Counter-Revolution, John Roberts
The Civil War in France, Karl Marx
Class Struggle in the Roman Republic, Alan Woods
The Class Struggles in France, 1848-1850, Karl Marx
The Classics of Marxism: Volumes One & Two, Various authors
Dialectics of Nature, Friedrich Engels
The Eighteenth Brumaire of Louis Bonaparte, Karl Marx
The First Five Years of the Communist International, Leon Trotsky
The First World War: A Marxist Analysis of the Great Slaughter, Alan Woods
Germany: From Revolution to Counter-Revolution, Rob Sewell
Germany 1918-1933: Socialism or Barbarism, Rob Sewell
History of British Trotskyism, Ted Grant
The History of Philosophy: A Marxist Perspective, Alan Woods
The History of the Russian Revolution: All Volumes, Leon Trotsky
The History of the Russian Revolution to Brest-Litovsk, Leon Trotsky
The Ideas of Karl Marx, Alan Woods

Imperialism: The Highest Stage of Capitalism, VI Lenin
In Defence of Marxism, Leon Trotsky
In the Cause of Labour, Rob Sewell
Ireland: Republicanism and Revolution, Alan Woods
Lenin and Trotsky: What They Really Stood For, Alan Woods & Ted Grant
Lenin, Trotsky & the Theory of the Permanent Revolution, John Roberts
Marxism and Anarchism, Various authors
Marxism and the USA, Alan Woods
Materialism and Empirio-criticism, VI Lenin
My Life, Leon Trotsky
Not Guilty, Dewey Commission Report
The Origin of the Family, Private Property & the State, Friedrich Engels
The Permanent Revolution and Results & Prospects, Leon Trotsky
Permanent Revolution in Latin America, John Roberts & Jorge Martin
Reason in Revolt, Alan Woods & Ted Grant
Reformism or Revolution, Alan Woods
Revolution and Counter-Revolution in Spain, Felix Morrow
The Revolution Betrayed, Leon Trotsky
The Revolutionary Legacy of Rosa Luxemburg, Marie Frederiksen
The Revolutionary Philosophy of Marxism, John Peterson (Ed.)
Russia: From Revolution to Counter-Revolution, Ted Grant
Spain's Revolution Against Franco, Alan Woods
Stalin, Leon Trotsky
The State and Revolution, VI Lenin
Ted Grant: The Permanent Revolutionary, Alan Woods
Ted Grant Writings: Volumes One and Two, Ted Grant
Thawra hatta'l nasr! - Revolution until Victory!, Alan Woods & others
What Is Marxism?, Rob Sewell & Alan Woods
What Is to Be Done?, VI Lenin
Women, Family and the Russian Revolution, John Roberts & Fred Weston
Writings on Britain, Leon Trotsky

To make an order or for more information, visit wellred-books.com, email books@wellred-books.com or write to Wellred Books, 152-160 Kemp House, City Road, London, EC1V 2NX, United Kingdom.

Ingram Content Group UK Ltd.
Milton Keynes UK
UKHW042243090623
423206UK00006B/129

9 781913 026868